Cheating, Dishonesty, and Manipulation

Why Bright Kids Do It

Kate Maupin, M.A.

Great Potential Press, Inc.™

Cheating, Dishonesty, and Manipulation: Why Bright Kids Do It

Edited by: Jessica Atha and Gwendolyn Combs
Interior design: The Printed Page
Cover design: Hutchison-Frey

Published by Great Potential Press, Inc.™
1325 N. Wilmot Road, Suite 300
Tucson, AZ 85712
www.greatpotentialpress.com

© 2014 by Kate Maupin

18 17 16 15 14   5 4 3 2 1

At the time of this book's publication, all facts and figures cited are the most current available. All telephone numbers, addresses, and website URLs are accurate and active; all publications, organizations, websites, and other resources exist as described in this book; and all have been verified as of the time this book went to press. The author(s) and Great Potential Press make no warranty or guarantee concerning the information and materials given out by organizations or content found at websites, and we are not responsible for any changes that occur after this book's publication. If you find an error or believe that a resource listed here is not as described, please contact Great Potential Press.

Library of Congress Cataloging-in-Publication Data
Maupin, Kate.
  Cheating, dishonesty, and manipulation : why bright kids do it / Kate Maupin.
        pages cm
  Includes bibliographical references.
  ISBN 978-1-935067-29-0
1. Gifted children--Education. 2. Cheating (Education) 3. Students--Conduct of life. 4. Parents of gifted children. 5. Teachers of gifted children. I. Title.
  LC3993.M37 2014
  371.95--dc23
                        2014013972

To Bob, who raised a bright cheater
and Rob, who married one.

In loving memory of Janis K. Nelson

Table of Contents

Tables and Figures

Foreword

What is ethical behavior?

In American society, it is unclear. The line between cheating and honesty is one that is often imprecise and easily blurred. Actions that are acceptable in one context might be cheating in another.

For example, it might not be okay for two students to work together on a take-home test, yet it may be all right for two students to work together on a project. It is okay to hire a tutor to help your child master material, but what if the tutor has access to the test the child will be given? You can quote or paraphrase a source when writing a paper, but does too much of a source become plagiarism? You can help your child with a project for the science fair, but at what point does the project become your work and not the child's?

What about the ethics of hiring consultants to get your child into an Ivy League university versus hiring a ghost writer to write the admissions essay? Then there's the dialogue about the sensationalized non-academic cheating that takes place over such things as extra-marital relationships, tax fraud, journalists manufacturing sources, or athlete steroid use.

Yes, we talk a lot publically about cheating, but Kate Maupin's approach and insight is unique. Her passion for high-ability students of all ages and desire to support and nurture their social, emotional, and academic needs is obvious. She has worked with gifted children around the world, and early on she recognized what she herself calls "the good, the bad, and the ugly" of the various gifted education programming she had participated in during her youth. She truly wants to understand what would make a bright person take a less-than-ethical way out.

"Not my child" is going to be a likely reaction from parents about this book. That is probably one reason Maupin begins by debunking the commonly held beliefs: Children don't cheat. Elementary students are too young to cheat. Gifted children have no reason to cheat.

Truth is, she finds that more than 80% of bright students self-reported they have cheated but never been caught. She then breaks down the reasons they are crossing the ethical line. She finds that kids, much like adults, cheat for a variety of reasons including boredom and a lack of challenge, to avoid being stereotyped as smart, to help others, the thrill of risk taking, and perfectionism and fear of making a mistake or failing.

The style of Maupin's writing makes the book highly readable for parents as well as both new and highly-experienced educators. She presents case studies of bright children who cheat or manipulate the system. This well-documented book gives readers the tools to determine if a child is cheating and, if so, what to do about it. Strategies for talking with the child and the child's teacher are presented in detail and in easy to use bullet point or chart form.

Yes, cheating is a moral issue and Maupin's book goes beyond the obvious and points out that it is not likely a one-time problem for the child. It will continue to escalate if the cheating is successful. This can result in long-term negative academic consequences.

As a criminal defense lawyer and an appointed superior court judge in Arizona, on a daily basis I dealt with the repercussions of dishonest behavior that escalated way beyond manipulation and cheating. Court life is often sad, but also it can be funny and poignant at the same time, and I was always interested in its possible intricacies. Even when I watched shows like *Perry Mason*, I always wanted to help the underdog.

I have seen a lot of lying, manipulation, and cheating. My specialty was criminal defense. I handled a lot of child molesting and sexual assault cases, but I worked on everything from DUI to murder. Our boss thought juries might be more sympathetic to men accused of sex crimes if they had women lawyers. I also defended several juveniles charged with murder. Now as a novelist, I mix my experiences into my plots and I have learned truth, of course, can be stranger than fiction.

Our society often rewards the outcome and ignores how you got there. Certainly, as parents, we don't want to believe our children are capable of cheating. But for parents, educators, and anyone with an interest or concern about the ethics of American society, ignore this book at your child's peril.

Barbara Sattler, J.D.
Parent, former Superior Court Judge,
and author of *Dog Days* and *Anne Levy's Last Case.*

Acknowledgments

This book would not have been possible without the support and contribution of many wonderful individuals.

As I remember, I grew up a bright little girl who tried to "creatively adapt" the rules whenever I felt out of place. This book never would have been written without the teachers who supported me and taught me to embrace my individuality: Mrs. Frye, Mrs. Leslie, Mr. Lightle, Mrs. Blachly, Mrs. Hauck, and my friend, Phyllis Brazee. A special thank you goes to those parents, colleagues, and students who have allowed me to use parts of their lives to highlight an aspect previously overlooked in high-achieving students' experiences. Though many of the students profiled in this book are long done with their elementary school experience, I hope they read this and always remember how proud I am of them! Thank you to the professors at the National Research Center on Gifted and Talented who taught me the gifted education ropes. Without their guidance and endless knowledge, this book would not have been possible.

To all the oft-unsung allies: the librarians at the University of Connecticut and Eastern Connecticut State University, the layout editors, designers, printers, cover artist, the entire team at Great Potential Press, and especially Aerin Raymond, whose patient eye and photography skills are both top quality. You are all greatly appreciated.

I cannot acknowledge enough the support of my family and friends. You were the distractions and the cheerleaders that I needed to get through the long days and nights of researching, writing, and editing. Two individuals in particular deserve special credit. My mother has saved everything I've ever written since I was four years old and, to her credit, didn't bat an eye when I told her what the book was about. Her unwavering belief in me has made me a better teacher, author, and person. Finally, my husband, Rob Giokas, took his role of support system very seriously. He, more than anyone, wore dozens of hats during the writing of this text: reader, tech consultant, sounding board, chef, editor, pet-sitter, psychologist, and cheerleader. He is the heart and soul of this book.

Working with Great Potential Press has been a life-changing experience. Their patience, good humor, and expertise helped transform a unique idea into something meaningful. To James Webb, Janet Gore, Jessica Atha, Gwen Combs, and all of the other wonderful editors and individuals whose combined insight and expertise shaped every iteration of this text, thank you for having faith in this first-time author.

Introduction

The cheating culture in the United States has risen to epic proportions. According to the Center for Academic Integrity, up to 86% of students agree that everyone cheats at some point before they leave high school.[1] Another study reports that up to 90% of a certain student population admitted to cheating.[2] It is baffling and a little terrifying when you look at the numbers, but perhaps even more so when the identity of this population is revealed. You might think that these high numbers of high-volume cheaters represent struggling students or those from economically depressed areas, but the shocking truth is that many of these cheaters are our highest ability learners. Like it or not, high-ability learners, including our brightest children, make up a sizable portion of the overwhelming cheating demographic in this country. Eric Anderman, a specialist on cheating behaviors from Ohio State University, suggests that anywhere from 80-90% of high-functioning students have cheated at least once before they leave high school, and that most students begin cheating at the elementary level. The numbers continue to rise as students age, suggesting that cheating behaviors become habitual and that students do not grow out of it.[3]

Authors of almost every comprehensive text on cheating allude or outright admit to high-ability students being a part of the cheating culture. One text, *Cheating in School*, urges parents and teachers not to discount smart children and to admit that cheating behaviors may exist in any or all of their students; it is the "deep, dark secret" of dishonesty.[4] Students who are smart enough to figure out how to cheat without getting caught are engaging in academic dishonesty in increasing numbers from all segments of education from elementary school through graduate school. The idea that high-ability learners cheat is far from a unique concept, yet a recent rash of high-profile cheating scandals at high-performing schools has elevated the focus on dishonesty among bright youth into the national spotlight. In 2012, both the elite Stuyvesant High School and the famed Ivy League Harvard University received media attention revealing broad cheating efforts perpetrated by the best and brightest in their ranks. These incidents sparked a media storm that prompted articles like the *New York Daily News* "Why Smart Kids Cheat," and the *American Institutes for Research Education Sector* "Why Are All the Smart Kids Cheating?"[5] It was clear that the press as well as the educational institutions themselves were baffled, not by the *how* but the *why.* Why would students who ostensibly had everything going for them—natural ability, motivation, creativity, as well as a quality education—feel the need to cheat?

And yet another question emerges, and perhaps one that gets to the heart of this national sense of confusion: If this phenomenon is so well documented, why has no one focused on high-ability cheaters, particularly at the elementary level? Dishonesty among bright students is still underrepresented in the literature, particularly in regard to ways to support our high-ability learners and prevent academic dishonesty. Students at every ability level and grade have been found to cheat; in fact, cheating has become more widespread over the past few decades.[6] The availability of data from cheating studies focusing on upper grades vastly outweighs the amount of data on elementary-age students, and noticeably absent are studies that focus on bright youth in regard to how, why, and under what circumstances they practice deceit. Perhaps the cause for such limited data is that people seldom think of bright children as being involved in cheating. The result of a survey on teachers' perceptions yielded that only 5.7% of elementary school teachers think that their high-achieving students are likely to cheat.[7]

Not all teachers, however, are unaware of this phenomenon in their classrooms. As early as 1939, Leta Hollingworth, an educator and investigator into the lives of the "Self" of the young, gifted child, warned that many high-ability students hide their talents to avoid rejection or ridicule. The deception that they learn and practice is a result of the way they feel about how they are perceived. Hollingworth called for support for these students and for recognition of the so-called "benign chicanery" that they were capable of as a way to cope with their giftedness.[8] The picture of talented individuals who use their abilities for less than honest purposes is not wholly unfamiliar to us: The media is filled with images of the suave, brilliant con artist, such as Frank Abagnale and Kevin Mitnick, for example (who are discussed in Chapter 8). You would be hard pressed to find a portrayal of a con artist that is not highly intelligent, in fact, suggesting that the two are synonymous in our collective consciousness. And yet, the concept of a talented cheater who also happens to be a child is difficult for us to perceive. We do not want to believe that our elementary-aged bright children are capable of dishonesty, so the issue is largely ignored.

It is understandable, however, why individuals who are knowledgeable about high-ability children may resist believing that children are capable of deceit. Bright children often show a deep understanding of moral issues from a young age, are blessed with quick processing time, possess high-volume memory, and are driven and fascinated by learning—none of which suggest either the need or the desire to cheat. In actuality, many high-ability children engage in manipulation and deceit on a daily basis, whether by cheating the system in the form of creating an advantage on a test or paper, plagiarizing, telling lies to teachers or parents, or simply by cheating themselves out of the full use of their abilities and talents. Many of the traits that seem inconsistent with bright cheaters may actually accentuate their ability to cheat well—and prolifically.

Many parents and teachers of bright children point to their students' high moral and ethical understanding as proof that they would not engage in academic dishonesty. However, the link between morality and dishonesty is not as direct as it might seem. Hugh Hartshorne, Mark May, and Frank Shuttleworth tested thousands of children's cheating behaviors and came to the conclusion that those behaviors were inconsistent. A child who cheated on one test may be honest or even altruistic in another cheating opportunity or moral dilemma. Most students' choice to cheat or not comes from situational determinants of morality or the individual circumstances that allow students to feel that their dishonesty is necessary or justified.[9] In addition, high-ability children tend to progress quickly through moral stages from heteronomous to autonomous morality.

Heteronomous morality is imposed on children by others, and wrongdoing is set as something fixed and rigid. Children who are still in the heteronomous stage are highly literal in their interpretation of "good vs. bad" and are unable to take intentions or justifications into account. More than once, I have heard young, clever children propose that in a perfect world everyone who committed any crime, even a small one, should be punished by jail or worse, which is why we should all be glad that we don't live in a world where laws are imagined by young children.

Many bright children develop past this stage quickly and progress into an autonomous understanding of morality in which the rules that govern their actions are the product of a group agreement, meaning that they are willing to set more flexible rules through cooperation and mutual understanding. Students in this stage judge actions more by intention than consequences. Bright children in this stage are more likely to break rules, including the act of cheating in school or at home, if they can justify the behavior as purposeful. Although they understand the rules of the group and conform to those that are meaningful within the context of their lives, the flexibility and creativity that gifted students possess can allow them to justify even the largest loopholes or indiscretions. Not only do our talented children have the capacity to cheat, but they may be far better at it than their peers. Bright students have admitted to cheating and, although they did not think it was necessary for them to cheat, they were prepared to do so if they thought the outcome was important enough. High expectations, intense internal psychological pressures, and the role of grades were also cited as causes for their deceit.[10]

It is vitally important to identify and prevent cheating in order to accurately assess student work. Educators require assessment in order to judge the impact of the curriculum and our teaching, and how to proceed. For this reason alone, it is important to address cheating behavior regardless of the moral implications. The moral outrage of parents and teachers that cheating is unfair can cause us to lose sight of the goal of ensuring appropriate assessment of our students and their abilities. Teachers and parents focus on obtaining accurate information about students' academic achievement, and they rarely broaden the discussion on morals to include the impact it has on society. More often than not, they turn a blind eye to the possibility that their brightest students may be engaging in academic dishonesty.

There are many possible reasons why a bright child's cheating behaviors may not be identified. Cheating is often subtle and ambiguous; it's rare to catch a bright student "in the act," and when they are caught, plausibility of even far-fetched excuses coupled with a teacher's desire to believe their students often wins. The emotion involved with cheating can lead to many dishonest behaviors being ignored. We want to see our students, particularly our high-ability students, as honest. The fact of the matter is that addressing cheating is unpleasant, and most teachers and parents go out of their way to avoid it. Accusations of cheating are difficult to make and often arouse strong emotional responses from all parties involved.

It is important for educators and parents to learn not only about how to separate the emotional aspect of cheating from the underlying problems that caused them, but also about the larger issue of prevention. Emotions certainly have a place in the larger discussion of high-ability cheaters, but too often we use moral outrage to tell students why they should not cheat or why they are being punished: Cheating is wrong, or unfair, or an uncivilized way to behave. Rather than extending the idea that cheating is wrong because it is unfair, it is more important to teach students how to view it from the perspective of their parents and teachers: Cheating is wrong because it does not serve either party. It is not what the teacher intended because it precludes accurate information that would identify academic achievement, and it keeps the student at an artificial plateau. Whenever possible, treat an assessment of any kind like it what was meant to be—an assessment of particular skills and an information-gathering tool. If our bright children deprive themselves of authentic educations through deceit, we are helpless to give them the tools they need to succeed and find challenge in their educational careers.

We can begin to search for the truth through anecdotal evidence— what we see, what we hear, and what we know about them, both from our perspective as the adults in their lives and from their perspective as students. Every intellectually talented child is different; no two are exactly alike. Their reasons for cheating are varied and sometimes complicated, but they all seem to have one thing in common: the ability to create the most beautiful, intricate, and sometimes, seemingly pointless falsehoods and deceptions. They are the best deceivers in the world.

Arthur's story is a perfect example.

Meet Arthur

Arthur is not a boy that a teacher would picture when asked to describe a dishonest student. A Boy Scout and dedicated clarinet and piano player for the school band, Arthur was identified as academically gifted in the third grade. His IQ was tested in the mid-140s, and he had never been referred to the office by his teacher for any negative behaviors. In fact, he had often held positions of leadership on his classroom's "job wall" due to his trustworthiness and respect for rules.

Despite this impressive social and educational profile, Arthur was in fact placed on suspension in sixth grade when the office discovered that he had been forging his mother's signature. Remarkably, Arthur had forged her signature not once, or even twice, but closer to 200 times over a three-year period. His scam finally came to light when he forged his mother's signature on a document that required a check to be attached. When the document was sent "back" to his mother, she noticed the forgery and contacted the school to say that the signature was not hers. Close comparison to saved progress reports, notes, and permission slips, however, showed the signature to match the samples on file in the office, which went back approximately three years.

In the investigation, it came to light that in the three years of Arthur's lying, never once had he actually needed to hide anything—especially his perpetually A grades—from his parents. It was certainly perplexing! When asked by the principal why he had done it, Arthur's reply was so unexpected that it created a stir.

"I wanted to see if I could."

His explanation was free of bravado. He had not gotten a thrill from getting away with it for all those years, and he had not done it to act out or for defiance's sake. He had once heard a teacher say that the office kept samples of parents' handwriting for comparison when a teacher was curious about the origin of a signature. The nature of the system intrigued him, and he was excited to have identified a possible flaw—that comparison was the only measure the office had to determine forgeries. If all signatures were the same, regardless of the appearance of the actual parent signatures, it would brook no suspicion. From that day on, Arthur signed everything that was supposed to go home with a signature he designed to look "adult enough." The first bump in the road Arthur had was his semester report cards. Although he could sign notes for class and permission slips without arousing parental suspicion, they would have noticed if he never brought home a report card. He also could not have his mother sign it, as the office would recognize that her true signature and Arthur's facsimile were not a match. Arthur's solution was to ensure that his father always signed his report cards, freeing him up to continue to use his "mother's" signature on everything else.

Arthur had simply identified a system and tested its limits, seeing which laws and rules could apply to a different set of standards—namely, his. It was less of a lie than a con. The day Arthur looked at the rules of the system and thought, "I could do that. I wonder how I could get everyone to believe it too," he became a third-grade con artist. There was an art to it, a focus completely driven by something internal. The old saying "the end justified the means" did not apply to his case because there was no end, in the traditional sense, to be achieved. He was not seeking to avoid trouble or to improve his grades. If anything, Arthur's *means* justified his end.

That is not to romanticize it. What these children do is seldom desirable, but it is remarkable because the means are so often intricate and the ends so decisively sad. When we are made aware of their falsehoods, we are allowed a brief glimpse into the minds of these amazing children with intellects so underused that they turn their brains into Rube Goldberg machines, prolonging simple activities into detailed machinations with the same basic, if pointless, result. The tests, for which they could have studied merely 10 minutes and aced, morph instead into elaborate hoaxes that require more energy and resolve than the original intention of the assignments.

I was not present for the discovery of Arthur's wrongdoing or for the many conversations that must have followed in the office with him and his parents; in fact, I wasn't aware of the incident until I received a visit from the school's vice principal. Somewhere in the week after the events took place, he came to see me between enrichment meetings. The school where I worked at the time did not have a designated resource room for gifted-education classes, so the students met for classes behind a partition in the teacher's lounge. I don't know how long the vice principal waited there, tucked behind the big, green partition, but as soon as the students filed out he popped his head around the corner and, without greeting, said, "We had a little incident."

He recalled to me the moment of the office's discovery, the scope of the offense, and the aftermath that had followed. What began as a meeting between two professionals—one informing the other of action taken against a student they both had in common—gradually became something more informal and puzzling.

"I wanted to see if I could," the vice principal said. He was quoting Arthur, yet the way he said it diminished the "stern disappointment" tone that all teachers seem born with the ability to muster. Even the man's posture went into a question mark with shoulders bowed, lower back balanced precariously on the edge of the partition, palm on his chin, and he shook his head slowly back and forth as he kept repeating, "He never needed to cheat. He was an A student. He was an A student." The vice principal was amazed at how calm Arthur had sounded, how his actions did not seem to cause him shame *or* pride, and that when he was suspended, he had gone without protest.

Then, finally, it came out. The real reason he had come to see me.

"Ms. Maupin, why do you think a child so smart would feel the need to cheat?" It was unfathomable to him, something isolated and strange, and, from the look on his face, frightening.

For me, it was a moment I'll never forget. I thought of all the innocent, noncommittal answers that I could have given to that question. It would have been so easy to glibly tell him that it was a puzzle—a mystery. Who knew why kids did what they did? I could have superficially said that Arthur had been trying to pull the wool over our eyes, or that he relished the idea of subverting authority. The vice principal could have even been thrown a kernel of the truth—that the child was bored and acting out, although even that would be a sham, like presenting a cooked, hollow pie crust and trying to pass it off as a full dessert.

The truth was so much more complicated. The thought of explaining why Arthur had lied would lead to the truth that *all* of my students probably did. I had proof of some and suspicions about others. Some of the cons were far more elaborate than Arthur's, some more amusing, and others more tragic. The conversation of what I knew of their lies would inevitably lead to *how*, and I felt weak at what that truth would entail—namely, that I knew because I had been one of those students. Even 20 years after it all happened, I wasn't prepared to explain *myself*. I never had to—because, unlike Arthur, I was never caught.

Then, just like that, I was gone, taken back to the last time I sat in front of a vice principal and talked about a cheater. I was in eighth grade, sent to the vice principal's office for an "I know what you were doing" scare and mortification technique. I was incensed. The source of my outrage—which I was not going to tell the stone-faced woman as she glared at me—was that I had been cheating on almost a daily basis for the entire history of my school career and that it hardly seemed fair to be busted for what she accused me of, as it was a rare case in which I had not cheated in any way. I had a solid hunch that my explanation would only get me in further, albeit more interesting, trouble. It probably also would not have helped to note that my pride had been hurt; the cheat I'd been accused of was rather uninteresting—looking at a friend's paper, something I would never, and have never, done. It brooked no challenge, but moreover I cannot remember ever having any faith in my neighbors' abilities to have any answers I did not.

Using cheating as a coping mechanism is a strategy I recognize in the talented students that I teach. Cheating, to use a broad definition, may include note passing, getting out of school "sick," skipping a class, avoiding the need to take a test altogether, and many other actions that lean on the side of derelict. Cheating, of course, can also be the more traditional during-class ploys to get answers in any other way than authentic learning, and cheats can be used during tests or quizzes or to know an answer during a classroom game or assignment. For bright students, however, cheating is rarely about getting the right answers above all else. Most of my students are not perfectionists, terrified of failure and driven to cheating to fill the gaps in their performance left by their humanity, nor are they lazy students looking to profit off of their neighbor at their expense. When bright children cheat, it more often is a coping mechanism to help them deal with their differences and how society fails either to recognize or to celebrate those differences. Getting a better grade is sometimes the furthest thing from their minds.

Personally, I remember only once that I came to school and realized I had forgotten about an upcoming test. It instilled pure panic, as in no-recollection, what-are-you-talking-about, oh-no-it's-happening-in-20-minutes-and-it's-a-monster-chunk-of-my-grade sort of panic. I hastily hashed together cheats: writing answers on the bottom of my sneaker in the grooves so they wouldn't wipe off when I walked on them, leaving my book in the bathroom just in case I needed to go check—everything from Cheating 101. I remember taking that entire test feeling nauseated. I felt I would be caught any moment, and I kept rehearsing, not a bevy of excuses but something I could do or say to keep myself from crying if I were caught. That kind of cheating made me feel like a fraud—truly sick to my stomach. And I only ever did it once.

When confronted so many years later, not by an angry vice principal but by a frightened one, I felt as if I should explain my own actions and not just Arthur's. Since I had never actually been caught, I had never been asked why. I imagine that, if I had been discovered and made to defend my actions, I could not just say that it was about a struggle towards perfection or a bout of laziness. It was not even an issue of avoiding hard work. In fact, the exact opposite was true. The crooked street was more challenging than the straight-and-narrow alley, which is true for many bright children who act out because they are bored out of their mind.

That phrase, by the way, "bored out of their minds," is apt. The human mind reaches a point when it becomes so flooded with redundancy that choke points begin to develop; heavy pools of repetition and simplicity make passage through impossible. The consciousness retreats into other places—staring into space, daydreaming, doodling, messing around, not paying attention—all common teacher phrases for what is essentially a young mind choked and looking for a way out.

Although cheating among high-ability students is not a subject that is adequately documented, studies have revealed that bright children are known to create ways to increase stimulation in ways that are unidentifiable or hidden from researchers. When an environment does not provide sufficient challenge for growth, high-ability children are usually equipped to create their own.[11] Cheating can be a natural consequence of this phenomenon.

Traditionally, a very simple reason has been cited for *why* students cheat; as *Detecting and Preventing Classroom Cheating* notes: "... the reason students give for cheating is simple and straightforward: They want a higher grade than they might have earned without cheating."[12] But Arthur wasn't cheating to improve his grades; they were already stellar. Although some bright students do cheat to maintain—or for fear of not being able to maintain—the illusion of perfection, Arthur was not one of those students. Arthur was accustomed to exerting little effort for a substantial result. There was little to connect that cause-and-effect relationship; the means were not associated in his mind as being real, so the end had lost value to him. Arthur had not forged his mother's signature to get ahead; he had no need for what seemed like "the means." He was not trying to avoid his parents or trouble; he was avoiding boredom, and he had done it in a creative and memorable way.

What Bright Students Need Us to Recognize

Most bright children live with the mistaken belief that their cheating is not only for their own good but also for the good of those around them—their classmates and their teachers. In my time as an educator of high-ability students, I have been astounded not only by the extensive nature of this underground culture of cheating but also by the complexities and camaraderie associated with it when bright kids—normally stranded alone in their classroom settings—come together in my room to share their lies. What's more, they don't do it with pride or bravado, but in a matter-of-fact way, as if they were sharing vital survival information. They have a common core of feeling lost in a system that was not designed with them in mind. When caught, they expect punishment, and they accept it, but unless the underlying cause for the behavior is addressed, the behavior returns. Bright children who are deprived of the normal consequences of the cause-and-effect relationship between hard work and success risk becoming trapped in a cycle where they can understand that what they are doing is wrong, and may even hate themselves for it, but still continue the behavior.

For those bristling at the generalization that "all bright children are cheaters," consider the children that you know who are exceptionally bright and talented, and ask yourself if they have ever seemed uncomfortable with who they were or with how others saw them or related to them. They may have never cheated on a test, forged a signature, or skipped class, but it is almost certain that there has been a time that they have misrepresented themselves in something they have said or done to fit in or to try to be like everyone else. Sometimes the most tragic way these students lie is not to others but to themselves. Some cheat the system, but others cheat their own abilities by not living up to their potential, or by letting themselves be ruled by the fear of not being good enough. The stories in this book have been chosen to illustrate just this point: that the *why* and *how* of cheating are as varied as the *who*.

Furthermore, failing to acknowledge that cheating exists among the ranks of bright children risks damaging both their educational and social development. In the process of cheating, a child creates a tests bias that negates the fairness—and certainly the validity—of a test instrument by affording an unequal advantage to one student over others. Cheating is like adding a pollutant to the air, clouding a teacher's vision of not only the educational needs of their students but also the true social and emotional dynamics that drive students to cheat.[13] When bright students are being open and honest, they can still be "tough nuts to crack" due to their extremely individual educational profiles, asynchronous development, and other unique characteristics that are common to high-ability individuals, such as high intensity and emotional sensitivity. The extra "noise" created by cheating only further derails an educator's ability to accurately assess and guide the bright children under their care. In addition, the keen sense of moral sensitivity, which is a typical trait of high-ability students, is more likely to be underused or lost through exposure to a negative environment.[14] Even more concerning is the realization that cheating is habit-forming; punishment alone will not address the issue of recidivism if the underlying causes persist or if cheating is perceived to be a nonissue.

Who They Are: Their Stories

Slowly but surely, the phenomenon of cheating among bright students is revealed by students like Arthur. Many talented adults who were once high-ability children can speak of their childhoods and describe incidents of deceit that were connected to how they coped with being a gifted youth. It suggests that this same battle of using intellect as a salve for boredom and loneliness may be occurring on the battlegrounds of all gifted children, not only those in my classroom or in the memories of our talented adults. After Arthur, I found myself on a journey to discover my students' battles and share them with their parents and teachers in a way they did not feel equipped to do themselves.

Please understand that the goal of this book is not to reveal these students or their methods in order to punish or reproach them. The goal is to try to help gifted and talented students, and the parents and teachers who care about them, by highlighting the cheating and manipulation that is rarely explored but often executed by high-ability students in crisis. The stories that follow offer a look at real students who cheat for far more varied reasons than perfectionism or an increased pressure to get good grades, which are two commonly believed reasons for high-ability students to use deception in school. Because very bright children are unique in so many ways—their development, creativity, problem solving, emotions, even the way they think—it stands to reason that the ways and motives for their cheating are more complicated, as well.

Here are some of the apparent causes for cheating. Bright children cheat due to boredom or because the difficulty of cheating affords more challenge and stimulation than a basic assignment. They cheat for fear of taking risks and failing at something when they believe that their identity and worth are derived from their abilities. They cheat the system to ensure a façade of perfection to others, as well as having an excuse that, if they do fail, it wasn't their fault. Bright students cheat because they feel misunderstood or trapped in their own minds. They cheat to set themselves free, or to prove to themselves that they can fit in, or to prove the opposite—that they don't need anyone else. Cheating can also help them to prove to themselves and others that it is okay to be so smart and that there is no such thing as "too smart"; it becomes a protection when they feel like someone wants to see them brought down to make themselves feel better. Bright kids cheat because they can. Because they like to find out how things work. Because they are trying to find out who they are.

The stories told in this book should serve as a message for teachers and parents, not just as a list of behaviors to simply watch for and prevent, but also to convey that there are liars and cheaters among them who need something greater if they are to successfully manage their greatest coping mechanism—their mental abilities. [15] The liars and cheaters in your house or in your classroom need challenge and depth to quench their thirst not only for knowledge but also, even more importantly, for understanding the need to fill the deep well of loss that they feel. Most bright students don't know why they cheat, but when asked to explain it, they fish in that well and surface with stories of how they are terribly sad or scared or bored. They are not proud of their lies; they are protective of them, clutching them like security blankets or invisible friends. And just as with an invisible friend, they grow up and grow out of their lies and forget—for the most part—that they ever existed. Until one day, something reminds them of that past life—like my experience with Arthur—and they feel a little lost, and reminiscent, because even if the friend wasn't real, the loneliness that brought it into existence was.

In the end, I did not tell the vice principal why Arthur cheated. I was not brave enough to tell the depth of the whole truth and to expose the enormity of the struggle these students deal with inside themselves. I wish I had; we need to understand our bright children before they grow out of their lies because the only things that time and maturity eliminate are the symptoms of the lies—the means. The underlying cause of the cheating, dishonesty, and manipulation will remain unless we identify how we can serve this unique population.

This book tells the story of Arthur and nine other beloved, brilliant little cheaters, manipulators, and liars. Their stories are real, though details have been changed to protect their identities, and in some cases, descriptions of students with similar experiences have been combined to create a more cohesive example of an underlying cause.

One

Martin

As Martin dropped the half-crumpled essay on my desk, I couldn't understand the expression on his long, freckled face. He had seemed so angry during class that day, yet as he stood at my desk after the rest of the students had left, the expression on the fifth grader's face was something between annoyance and indifference. His body posture was stooped and forlorn.

Martin didn't meet my eyes or look at the essay. He had dropped the essay on my desk as the only response to the question I'd held him after class to ask: "What's wrong, kiddo?"

Silence.

"Is that for me, Martin?"

He shook his head. "It was a book report for Mrs. Nero. We had to compare and contrast two books and write a report."

I picked up the paper and tried to smooth it out. The top right and bottom left corners of the report were streaked with jagged lines, the edges of the paper turned inward like it had been held in fisted hands, and the bottom two inches or so of the right side of the essay were missing. The edge of the tear was uneven and rounded—almost like little ears—which made it look like less of an accident than intentional destruction.

"What happened? Who did this?" Visions crossed my mind of a young bully harassing the sweet and smart Martin, who had a tendency to alienate his classmates with long recitations of what he thought were interesting facts and descriptions. Not too long before, he had come to me in tears that someone was calling him a "know-it-all" and didn't want to be his friend. My heart went out to both students—how hard it must have been for them to understand each other, and how sad that each boy had inadvertently made the other one feel out of place. It was too much, however, if it had gotten to the point of physical bullying.

Martin's face was awash with disappointment and that unnamed emotion, but it wasn't for my imagined bully. He shook his head vehemently and said, almost angrily, "I did it. No. Look at it."

I looked again, this time past the wrinkles and rips. His title and name were typed and underlined. The report, which compared and contrasted two common fifth- and sixth-grade level books, seemed at first glance to be well composed without spelling or grammatical errors, and was an appropriate length. His classroom teacher had written a large *A* in purple ink in the top right corner, circled it, and drawn a small smiley face beneath the grade. Besides those rips and tears I was supposed to look beyond, it seemed perfect.

"I'm sorry, Martin. I don't know what you want me to see."

"She gave me an A."

"What's wrong with that?"

His face clouded over. "I didn't read the books."

When Martin had walked in my room that morning, he had 'bad day' written all over him. He seemed angry and distracted. His usually loquacious, outgoing self was shrouded in a one-word-answer kind of shell, a persona that didn't suit the tall, freckle-faced fifth grader. Normally he was the first to come in with a smile and a joke for his classmates.

I don't remember what we were learning about that day. Typically I saw students for small enrichment groups anywhere from half an hour to two hours a week, depending on their level of involvement with the program. The classes were short and broken up among the days to give time to check on student progress, so that the days have blurred in my memory. It may have been anything from Bernoulli's principle of airflow to how dominant and recessive genes work. More often than not, the students picked the enrichment projects, so I've been the overseer of everything from home gardening to a simulation vomit machine.

One thing that remains clear in my mind, however, is how Martin responded when called upon to answer a question. The look on his face was sullen, and he responded with a shrug and a *yes* to something that was not a *yes* or *no* question. When asked to go into more detail, he answered with a deliberate stretch of 10 solid seconds of silence.

The reason I can remember the length of his silence is thanks in part to average wait times. The average wait time—sometimes also called the response time or think time—refers to the periods during classroom instruction where a teacher waits for students to construct an answer to active questioning. The average wait time for a teacher varies, but most educators have a tolerance of silence during the questioning phase for approximately 1.5 seconds.[16] Research shows how little "percolating time" students are allowed to formulate higher-level thinking. When given a wait time of two seconds or less, students can only pull from the absolute surface-level knowledge and basic recall. Generally teachers don't notice because many of the questions they ask are knowledge-level questions rather than a deeper synthesis of their opinions or understanding.[17] Teachers tend to feel—and I've certainly been guilty of this as well—that if students don't have the answer immediately, they probably don't know it, and one should move on or make the question simpler. The silence is uncomfortable, and it can be awful as a young teacher just beginning to get the hang of classroom management to allow so many awkward, stiff silences to invade the classroom. We fear for the students' sense of comfort as well as our own.

To get away from that idea of high-volume, low-level questioning, I practice a slow-count wait time for responses of 5-7 seconds before I'll even call on a student, and then they have another 5-7 before I offer more information or ask them if they (a) want to ask me a question instead or (b) want to call on someone near them to help them "jump start their thinking" with an idea. So by the time I called on Martin—who, by the way, did not have his hand up—I had already waited a long stretch of time.

It is rare to ever count out the full 10, but Martin sat there, staring at me, letting the silence ride. I had a feeling, looking into those green eyes, that he was counting in his head, too, and aiming to let the quiet reach an uncomfortable place. He was angry, and he wanted me to know it.

"Do you want to pick a friend to help start you off?" I asked at the end of the slow count.

"No." He said it sharply, glaring as if to ask what I'd do about it.

The other students, who were already feeling the awkwardness in the room, twitching and moving from their seats like someone had heated up the carpet beneath them, went still again. All were looking at me, to see what I'd say to that one, simple word that had been said so defiantly.

In the end, I smiled, said that it was all right, and asked for a volunteer, since Martin didn't have anyone in mind. More than a few students sent their hands shooting straight up; everyone wanted that moment to be over. We moved on to the rest of the lesson. It wasn't until after class, when I asked Martin to stay behind, that he admitted that he had cheated, and I could understand the root of his anger. Not only had he cheated, but it upset him that he had not been caught.

Why Did Martin Cheat?

Martin had victimized himself with procrastination by throwing his book report together the night before it was due. He described to me how the book report had not been plagiarized. Rather, he had compiled a polished amalgam of skimmed information, sophisticated language, and outright guesses to fill his gaps in information. I looked at the book report again as Martin pointed out some of the falsehoods in the passages, and I imagined how it must have looked to his classroom teacher before the wrinkles and the tears. It was, at first impression, a beautiful two-page book report that gave no indication that it had been hurried. It was typed and had been checked for spelling and grammatical errors. It was modestly spaced at 1.5, was an appropriate length, and above all, the number one thing that freed it from reproach was the student name on the paper: Martin, the sweet faced, clever, perpetual A student. That book report was akin to laying a cereal box on its side and covering it with frosting. If you never cut inside, of course you would think it was a cake.

"I worried about it after I turned it in. I was scared. I thought Mrs. Nero would give me a bad grade or she'd write something on my paper," he confessed.

And instead he had gotten back an A paper—one he knew that he had not deserved.

"How did you feel when you saw what she did write?"

He shrugged in that patented way that kids do when they're asked "Why did you do it/hit your sister/stand up in the bus seat/not clean your room" sort of questions: looking at the ground with sullen faces and shrugs that take the place of the words "I don't know." Martin either didn't know how to give words to his complex feelings or he didn't feel like I'd understand.

"I bet she didn't even read it," he finally said, still not meeting my eyes.

I didn't know what to say. My default teacher impulse was to comfort him. I wanted to say that his classroom teacher had 24 papers to read and grade and that she had just made a mistake. Maybe she had read it too fast or gotten the details mixed up with someone else's paper. Maybe she had not actually read the books or was getting those details confused as well. All of these things I wanted to say, but it occurred to me: Who would I be protecting? I know what it is like, as a teacher, to have a mountain of papers in front of you for grading and to get weary and beleaguered with what seems like an endless task on top of planning for the next day, getting materials together, and considering all of your students' social, emotional, and educational needs. Had I ever seen the name on a student's paper and had a preconceived notion of what the work would be like before it was graded? Any teacher who says they have not is probably a professor in a large survey or 101 college course that has never had the chance to associate names with work—or even faces.

Of course a teacher is never supposed to assign a grade simply because of those preconceived notions, and I knew Mrs. Nero was a good teacher. So what was it? Had she not read the books, skimmed through the essay, saw that it looked good and whole and not bothered to delve too much deeper? Or was it possible that this poorest example of Martin's work really was worth an A, at least perhaps in comparison to that of his classmates or the basic fifth-grade standards?

None of it was fit to tell Martin. Did I comfort him and tell him the teacher was correct—albeit a little confused—and risk not validating how hurt he was feeling, and probably confuse what was expected of him in school? Placing blame on Mrs. Nero risked damaging the positive relationship Martin deserved to have with his teacher, as well as deepening Martin's suspicions that Mrs. Nero either didn't know his abilities well enough to discern when he was cheating or didn't care. The latter may seem like a childish statement, but during a large-scale survey of high school juniors, 47% said that they felt like their teachers ignored cheating; an additional 11% said they felt their teachers knew but didn't care.[18] In addition, in a survey composed of college students, 42% blamed "instructor shortcomings" on their repeated cheating.[19] It is quite possible, then, that Martin would not "grow out" of his assumption that the adults in his life did not care about him or his work without intervention. Unchecked, it was a belief he risked carrying throughout his educational career.

Without knowing what had occurred, I did not feel comfortable intervening with my judgment of the classroom teacher's actions. And as for the explanation that "maybe your work was A quality, anyway," I couldn't bear telling Martin anything that would suggest that all that would be required from him in school—and maybe in life—was the bare minimum, though it seemed from the quality of the essay that it was currently the case.

And what of the lie? Should I turn him in? I did not want that to be the only thing he took away from the episode, because he was obviously hurting. He felt angry and devalued, and I imagined he was questioning every grade he had ever gotten. How much work had he put into assignments in the past to have them overlooked or simply skimmed? What positive comments from papers of old were now being dissected in his mind as being false? How could I, as a person who cared about Martin and knew how deeply he thought about everything in his world, simply stamp an "unacceptable" mark over that day and send him away with a "cheating is bad" lecture? Hadn't the teacher cheated him, even accidentally? And should there be some lenience for the fact that he had not been caught but confessed?

It was not even that he had confessed but that he had done so when there was no suspicion of wrongdoing on his part. There had been no confrontation. If he had never said anything, his A paper would have stood unquestioned. Even in regard to his errant behavior in my classroom, I imagine all he would have had to do was apologize, say he'd had a bad day, and it would have been forgotten about entirely. In addition, if he had chickened out after handing me the essay, he could have agreed that a bully had torn it. Altogether, though, it was absurd to run through any of those *what ifs* because one thing was clear: Martin wanted to be caught. He said as much. Even if he had not put the book report together with the intention of being discovered, a part of him expected it to happen. He thought he would get that paper back with a giant *F* and a comment to the likes of "I'm disappointed in you, Martin. This isn't your best work." Instead, he'd gotten the smiley face and A that had done much more damage to his psyche. It is a unique part of the dichotomous dilemma of bright children; though Martin had cheated, he portrayed the high morality and early sense of moral concern that are typical personality traits of the high-performing population.[20] Though it initially seems contradictory for a child possessed of a high moral standard to cheat, the truth is more complicated. Research shows that there is little relationship between cheating and moral development. Some bright children may be manipulating others because they have learned how to be "showmen," which leads them to measure their sense of self-worth by their impact or power over other people. They may be sensitive enough to realize that they are being manipulative and even feel unhappy about the habit but not know how to stop.[21]

Martin's case felt complicated, rife with moral issues about what was best for the child versus standard practice. The default setting for catching a cheater was to boil the whole affair down to "You cheated; that is always wrong in every circumstance, and you should never do it again." I could have given him a warning and told him he was always supposed to give his best. I could have told him that honesty would always be rewarded and to prove it, I would not have turned him in since he'd been honest about what he'd done. I could have sent Martin away with the knowledge that I had been fair and equitable and that Martin would be better for it. And I would have been wrong.

Martin made a mistake by cheating, but he knew that. He knew well enough to expect retribution, for one thing, and to be surprised and even angered by the lack of it. I am not sure how consciously he tested the barriers of cause and effect, but they were tested all the same. The fact that he was upset by his high marks suggested the inner struggle he was exposed to. According to Dr. Sylvia Rimm, a noted psychologist who specializes in underachievement among gifted students, children will achieve only if they see the relationship between the learning process and its outcomes.[22] With the circumstances of what had happened, it was not possible to assure Martin that his best would always be rewarded and that positive outcomes came from hard work; the evidence suggested otherwise. Why do his best when his "half best" could play that role, throwing on the facade of success and faking it? It was as if he had been painting beautiful masterpieces for years and receiving accolades for his work, only to discover that, all along, his teachers had been colorblind.

What good are our smart children to the world if they believe all that is expected of them is the bare minimum? What are they going to think about themselves and their intelligence? The argument could be made that a teacher never would have made the same mistake on a student's paper who was not as intelligent or who struggled more with their writing work, and with that logic, it could be said that it was Martin's abilities that had allowed him to cut corners. Mrs. Nero was not devaluing his abilities, but rather she was assigning his grade based on what she knew of his performance in the past. After a quick read of his efforts (or lack thereof) the painful truth was that Martin's last-minute, half-fabricated effort still met the standard for mastery on the concept of a basic compare-and-contrast essay. Martin was clever enough that his guesses were close to the mark, and his skimming of the book, though it likely didn't take him more than a handful of minutes, still gave the impression of thoroughness. Martin pulled from past experiences of what he had learned from class discussions, older book reports, and his own unique combination of intuition and previous knowledge. His last-minute effort could have been genuine A work under the current standards. The issue then was that, even if the teacher had not read the books in question, she would have known that something was amiss from Martin's work if she knew what *his* best work was instead of comparing him to his classmates or grading him using standards that he had already surpassed.

Martin was not Arthur. Martin had not lied in order to subvert the rules or to tease out their boundaries. What they did have in common was a need to discover cause and effect in a world that had not given them any causal relationships that made sense in regard to their school-work. Neither had been permitted to struggle or to develop any sense of personal challenge in the school setting. Their relationships with success had not been a causal one; little effort had led to great achievement. Being praised for achievement that they did not feel they had earned led to both students developing signs of a fixed mindset about learning rather than a growth mindset, which is to say they did not accept the relationship between hard work and achievement. To someone with a fixed mindset, intelligence is a limited, instantaneous commodity that is seen to be negated by effort.[23] On the surface, Martin had made an assignment more difficult than its original parameters by rushing it at the last minute. On a deeper level, Martin's cheating—and the gloomy aftermath that followed—was a symptom of his desire to prove that the system would recognize the causal relationship between effort and accomplishment. He expected a poor grade. When his expected outcome was not met, it depressed him and confused his sense of cause and effect.

In the end, Martin, his parents, his classroom teacher, and I came together to solve the greater problem at hand. We became a "Think Tank," each coming to the table as a member of a team-learning process. Martin's teacher and I, in particular, had to take a stance that was strong and fair in regard to the cheating without being overly punitive. During our conference, we focused on the outcomes and goals of moving forward versus establishing winners and losers, fearing that punishment would make Martin withdraw further. We created a process where all parties had to respect one another and recognize that each had his or her own power to affect the outcome. In that process, each individual had to come to a new understanding of what a grade really was, what was being graded, and how we could use pretests and portfolios to establish a baseline for Martin's future performance so that his needs could be met in the classroom. That journey is detailed here so that it may be useful to someone like Martin in your life.

Grades that Are Misunderstood

What we did for Martin was a variation of pretesting and *grade replacing*, which we will discuss later. Before we could establish multiple points of data to determine where we needed to take Martin, however, we needed to relay to him and his parents that grades are most useful to us as educators and learners when they function not as competition or as labels but as a shorthand method of communication.[24]

Many people—students, teachers, and parents—see grades as rewards. Maybe they would not phrase it that way outright, but have you ever heard a parent say that their child "deserved an A"? The very nature of the word *grade* assumes a ranking system, though we should try not to forget that the true purpose of grading is not to assign value to a student as a whole, but rather to place markers on a continuum of curricular knowledge for individual students. In other words, imagine that students are like maps upon which each individual pin represents a different level of understanding. Where you place the pin shows where they have been. That way, you know exactly where they still need to go and what they have already mastered. For people who see grades as rewards, the pinned locations are what they value. For people who see grades as curricular milestones and goals, it is the blank locations that are the most valuable.

Blanket statements about children such as "She is an A student" risk neglecting them as individual learners with strengths and weaknesses and play into the notion that it is the letter that is important. Too many students consider As synonymous with *good* and anything else with *bad* and are never taught what the letter grades actually mean. "I've done a good job, so I've earned an A," or worse yet, "My children worked hard, so they deserve As." Students who buy into the grades-as-rewards mindset are working for the letter itself versus what it stands for in a curricular sense. This can cause students to become competitive and view grades as obstacles that are set out by "them"—the teachers and administration—and band students together in an us-versus-them mindset that further exacerbates collaboration on rule-breaking and plagiarizing, among other cheating methods. Students begin to see cheating as justifiable because they feel they must bend the rules to overcome the obstacles that have been set in their way.[25]

Students are also at risk for misunderstanding the meaning of their grades when they believe they are being used punitively. When factors other than content standards and mastery are being used to grade students or when grades are arbitrarily lowered by behavior issues that do not affect their ability to show mastery, students often develop a negative relationship with not only their grades but also their teachers, whom they begin to see as adversaries. Grades given as punishment increase the likelihood that students misunderstand or lose respect for the evaluation system and engage in classroom power struggles. This may, in turn, increase the likelihood that students will attempt to subvert the system through cheating.[26]

We need to start treating grades like what they are, and we need to teach that new understanding to our children as well. The appropriate use of grades is to indicate the extent that a student has mastered or acquired identified skills, mastered selected content standards, or made progress on specific learning goals. To get an A in fourth-grade math means that a student has successfully achieved a mastery of approximately 90-100% of the fourth-grade math concepts—not that this student is, as many would say, an "A math student." This distinction teaches students to strive not for perfection, only for mastery. "Straight A students" are not perfect students; they may have merely 90% or 95% mastery across the board, depending on what percentage constitutes an A in their district versus an A-. To have an A in fourth-grade math does not mean that students are perpetual A math students. It is an indicator only of where they currently are and where they need to be for growth and learning to occur. Only after we take the issue of identity out of the grading system can we start to see those letters for what they are and how they can be useful for us as parents and teachers. Once that has been established, we can learn how to skip around and beyond those grades when necessary so that we can better serve the Martins in our lives.

How Pretesting Can Help

Imagine a student named John who consistently gets all As on his examinations. Your initial reaction may be that this student's needs are being met adequately and that enough information has been gathered about his abilities to facilitate effective teaching. You likely view this student as a conscientious learner and listener who possesses a wonderful foundation of education for the years and grade levels to come. However, if John has never been pretested, how can you be sure that he had not mastered all or some of that information before teaching ever began? Can you conclude that he learned the information as measured on the post-test in the current class? For that matter, can it even be guaranteed that he was listening to the instruction at all? Getting baseline information on a student is extremely important if you are to establish a pattern of growth. You cannot determine the slope of a line with one solitary point. One data point of information cannot show growth or improvement nor can it help teachers identify the direction in which a student is moving. The primary function of any assessment is for the student and teacher to gain a deeper understanding of what skills and knowledge the student has acquired; using pretesting data supports the importance of assessment for the purpose of learning.

Some teachers, unfortunately, are opposed to the notion of pretesting, but it is the number-one caveat I stress for teachers, as well as for parents advocating for their children—pretest! My exclamation is the same whether or not there are exceptionally bright students in a class: pretest, pretest, pretest! Some don't believe in the validity of pretesting, some say there is no time in class, while others simply aren't comfortable with making data-driven decisions. For those who undervalue the need for pretesting, consider the following: The U.S. Department of Education's report cited that gifted and talented students in elementary school have mastered, on average, anywhere from 35-50% of the curriculum in basic subjects before the school year even begins.[27] Further, the authors of *A Parent's Guide to Gifted Children* suggest that this number may be as high as 75% of material that will be taught in a given year.[28] As a result, high-ability elementary school students are likely to have anywhere from one fourth to three fourths of their class time "left over" after finishing work on basic tasks that they have already mastered, depending on the level of their giftedness.[29]

Perhaps you are like the teacher who once told me that she didn't believe in using pretests because she knew that none of their gifted students were perfect. The reasoning: There is no one who can't pick up *something* from what I'm teaching, so why excuse a student from the unit to do something different when I can prove they still have gaps in their knowledge?

In a way, she was completely correct: High-ability students will learn *something* from their teacher, regardless of how much knowledge they came into the unit possessing. However, the difference between sitting through previously-mastered material and being allowed to work on something more enriching may also mean the difference between students learning what the teacher intended, filling the blanks with whatever they chose, or creatively filling their idle time with plans to manipulate and stir up excitement in order to endure what otherwise would be unendurable. What do you think is the likelihood that they will patiently and happily learn that 5-10% that they have gaps in and sit quietly during the other 90% while pre-mastered information is repeated? The biggest risk in making high-ability students plod through base-level, previously-mastered information is sending the message that school—or at least a large percentage of it—is not worth their time. It is difficult to assert that bright students "are fine where they are" when most are working two to four grade levels below their potential.

That same teacher who refuses to pretest has also shown me students' work and pointed out errors that they made on multiple choice options and offered open-response assignments in which the bright student did not answer deeply or thoroughly enough. This evidence was offered as support for how unnecessary the pretest was and why the teacher would not excuse these students from the repetition. The teacher in question had the best of intentions, but I do not hesitate to say that she was misguided. It is a frightening cycle to teach students that they should not pay attention to the majority of what happens in school by beleaguering them with what seems to them like endless repetition. The result will be non-attentive students with poor study habits and gaps in their knowledge that lead to missed test questions and uninformed short answer responses, leading to further vindication for the classroom teacher that the student needs to sit through the repetition and re-teaching. As time goes on, this cyclical relationship begins to drain on both individuals until you have teachers who do not believe in enrichment and challenge opportunities because the students have not learned how to recognize what is important and zombie their way through school without meaningful learning because they mistakenly believe that none of it is worth their time.

It is hard to argue against teacher-procured work that shows students not living up to their potential, and it is even more difficult to say to a teacher, "They may be working this way because they're bored." I know what a sting it is to a teacher to hear that a student is bored in class. My heart sinks when I hear a parent say, "My child isn't feeling challenged in school." It is hard *not* to take it personally. What I try to stress to the teachers I work with is this: Teachers are not the problem, but they can contribute to it if they are not careful to break the cycle with their students. We will look into this a little deeper in the next chapter, but understand here that pretesting can help stop that vicious cycle of boredom. It is the first step to establishing the needs of these highly individualized learners. Bright children deserve the right to struggle for their learning. We are doing them a disservice if we disconnect the cause-and-effect relationship between hard work and results.

When a student is pretested, the data need to be used to make informed decisions about where to go with that student—not simply recorded in a grade book. Those decisions may include a variety of resources that allow for continuous educational progress, including compacting, which is the practice of eliminating some or all of the redundant curriculum, so that students may buy back their time for more meaningful pursuits.[30] Students may also work on enrichment projects independently or in groups, go to another class (or grade) to work on more accelerated work, or be allowed to work outside of the curriculum, except for those days that their gap areas, as defined by the pretest, are being taught in their traditional classroom. Regardless of which end result is chosen, the underlying purpose should be data collection for the purpose of making meaningful decisions for student learning. The data alone are almost useless.

If we journey back and pick up John, imagine that he has been successfully pretested and the results are all As—he has an A grade on both the pretest and the post-test. As happy as John and his parents may be, the truth is that we still do not have enough useful information about the state of his learning, if learning is defined by what was previously learned and where he is at the present. You may say, "Of course we know where John is; he has an A!" But truly, at best, we can assume that he has an A-level mastery of *at least* the scope of material that they've been tested on. Remember not to label kids as A students, but instead see a grade for what it is worth: An A grade on a fourth-grade math test on fractions means the student has anywhere from a 90-100% mastery of that information. It may not be even a full scope of the knowledge on fractions students are supposed to have by year's end but simply knowledge of that chapter or unit.

If we visualize that map again, replete with all its pins, imagine wanting to place a pin in an exact directed location only to have someone tell you that it belongs "somewhere" in the Northern Hemisphere. It is not a very useful direction if we are trying to be exact. That is all that A scores on pre- and post-tests tell us, however. At best, the combined A pretest and A post-test are an indication that the students' learning is stagnant. Worst case scenario: You have students whose learning is actually deteriorating. That may seem impossible or even absurd, but truly, for all we know, they have actually lost information or skills since we cannot accurately know where their level was to begin with.

For example, imagine asking a champion Olympic swimmer to do a lap in a pool and then testing her on her performance. You then ask her to swim it two weeks later and document that performance as well. The likelihood is good that she will swim that one lap on both occasions with excellent speed, beautiful technique, and a generally impressive display of skill. But if that is all she has been asked to do in the pre- and post-trials, who is to say her true ability, which would be swimming dozens of laps in a highly competitive environment, has not been diminished by lack of practice and attention to her real skill level? Similarly, a student who likes to work on algebraic equations in her spare time but is only ever afforded the opportunity to practice long division and multiplication problems, will undoubtedly score quite high on the latter while sacrificing growth on the former.

When we place intellectually gifted children in academically under-stimulating environments, we run the risk of fostering a pattern of inattention. We are teaching them to underachieve and encouraging them to develop poor study skills and diminished respect for education and learning. Presenting bright students with a built in gap of time and attention is tantamount to asking them to fill their time themselves. This increases the likelihood that students will not have the opportunity to learn the valuable sense of effort they will need to carry them through difficult tasks. Without the coping strategies that develop from effort and continued problem solving, students are more likely to "check out" or attempt deceit in lieu of developing healthier coping strategies.

Consider the Ceiling

There is the case, then, of what to do with those bright students who consistently achieve top grades and have hit what educators call the "ceiling." The ceiling refers to any time a student's scores are artificially restricted by the limits of the assessment; it is not the end of all knowledge available but rather the cap on the house of curriculum that is currently being tested.[31] You have to assume, as a teacher or a parent, that your student has hit the ceiling when they achieve an A grade on both pre- and post-assessments, even though there is a chance that the scope of testing was adequate for the continuum of the child's abilities. For example, a child may be given an assessment that tests the approximate grade level equivalent of their reading ability. The evaluation has the information to place a student's reading ability between first- and sixth-grade equivalent levels. For a child who tests at a lower level than six, teachers can be more confident about pinning in that curricular milestone than if the child tested at a level six. Is it possible that the student has a sixth-grade reading level and nothing higher? Of course it is, but it would be doing the student a grave disservice not to assume that the possibility that the child has "hit the ceiling." It is better to assume that the student has *at least* a sixth-grade reading level. How much higher? We don't know because the test ceiling doesn't allow us to go any higher. Educators must be mindful of the limits of the assessments they administer.

For those who are still in a grades-as-rewards mindset, scores that hover like a balloon at the top of what is being tested at a child's grade level is not seen as a problem. It is the biggest difference between the grades-as-rewards camp versus grades-as-trail-markers camp. The former sees ceilinged grades as something to be lauded and celebrated; the latter, as a sign that a student may be experiencing a learning plateau.

The best course of action for a student who is suspected to have hit the ceiling of the test is to retest using a measurement that goes beyond the current curricular "house"—often referred to as *above-level testing*. Consistent pre- and post-test scores on math chapter tests, for example, might warrant an end-of-year math diagnostic. A student whose writing drafts are superb may be tasked to try a writing challenge from the next grade up, incorporating more complicated topics or themes in the product. The goal is to find an assessment that a student cannot complete easily. In evaluations, a certain amount of struggle is necessary both to clearly abolish the concept of a ceiling and to establish a baseline of a student's actual abilities. Even in subject areas that cannot be as quantitatively measured, teachers can assess using a portfolio of information that is gathered from a student's best works. This way, we can establish a more authentic baseline of starting achievements.

Establish a Baseline

There is less of a problem with grades than there is with *what* is being graded. Grades themselves can be remarkable tools to mark the trail of a child's path through education. Even in situations like Martin's book report where a pretest isn't applicable, efforts should be made to get examples of students' best work to establish their baseline, or a more authentic representation of what their mastery level is prior to teacher instruction. This can be accomplished by creating simple portfolios of students' work that can go along with them to the next year's teacher. Work should be gathered from as many sources as possible; parents, classroom teachers, and specialists can submit best examples of the student's work, as well as tasking the student to create or choose examples, too. Students should be told the purpose of this collection, and teachers should be honest about their motives as well. A baseline portfolio should not be compiled just to make assignments "cheat proof," though it is a natural side effect of the process of teachers getting to know their students' abilities better. As with Martin's case, it should serve as both the student, the parent, and the teacher's reeducation process of how to establish priorities beyond the concept of grading.

Martin's Think Tank

Martin's team—Mrs. Nero, Martin's father, Martin, and myself—met about a week after the book report incident. Each individual brought his or her own role and perspective to the table, and we thoroughly discussed the topics outlined above: redefining how Martin, his family, and his teachers symbolized grades, the value of pretesting, and how to establish a baseline for items where mastery was difficult to show through pretesting. We attempted to create an environment that was collaborative, not only to involve everyone in the decision-making process but also to show Martin that we were all a part of his support system. It is a common misconception that bright students can solve their own problems; however, these children often have not yet developed either the emotional intelligence or the experience to confidently deal with issues that relate to them. In addition, many high-ability children need practice developing persistence, tolerance for ambiguity and frustration, and other coping skills they haven't had a chance to master when prior tasks have come easily to them.[32]

We began with a goal list of discussion topics that gave us, Martin in particular, a road map of what the meeting would entail. The outline let Martin know that although a discussion about the nature of his cheating was on the 'to do' list, punishment was not the main purpose of the collaboration. In addition, it was important that Martin be invested in the planning aspect of the meeting so that he would be similarly invested in the "buy in" that would be needed during execution of the plan.

The discussion of cheating was more thorough than stern for the sake of Martin's mental perspective, and lecturing was avoided. Instead, the adults posed ethical questions and allowed Martin time to think and reflect, rather than repeat rules that he had no part in creating. We asked him what he thought about what he had done and what kinds of cheating he could identify. We posed hypothetical questions about the concept of the ends justifying means, and we focused on the deeper moral implications at hand with how he was using his intelligence and for what that energy would be better served. It was more important that he have a chance to think through the issues and come to his own ethical decisions than to just feed him the expectation that he follow a rule or a punishment would follow. When students do not understand or trust the rule that has been given, or do not have a chance to internalize *why* they are a rule follower or not, they are unable to move to a higher level of moral understanding.[33] In posing questions of ethics and proper use of power, we also wanted to establish that Martin's actions had not *rewarded* him through our attention. By separating the issues, Martin's Think Tank was able to explain that despite *how* he had let it be known that he needed something more, the end result was still the same. He knew we were there to address the underlying issue as well as its symptom—which had been cheating.

Martin was quiet but receptive during the parts of the conversation where he sensed the serious tone well enough to be respectful and listen, and he offered his opinions and feedback to the moral questions, giving more insight into why he had cheated. He cited fear and feelings of not being worthy as well as his concern that his teacher did not know him or care about what he could really do with his writing. He did not blame his teacher, however, and took responsibility for his poor choices based on his fears. When the discussion expanded to how more extensive pretesting could be offered in order to establish a baseline for those subjects that were not easily pretested, Martin offered many suggestions. In the end, a small, file folder-sized portfolio of examples thought to be Martin's best work were collected. Classroom work, enrichment work, and examples of work he had done at home were compiled as indicators of his writing ability. It was not surprising that the clear frontrunner was the piece that Martin submitted himself. Even his father admitted that the work he had chosen for the portfolio—a story Martin had written for him the Christmas before—was secondary to Martin's own submission to the portfolio.

Martin worked on the initial draft of his baseline book report—what he considered an example of his best writing work—for a week and a half. It was a six-page essay about how he thought the deaths in the various Harry Potter book series had affected him and how he thought the author wanted him to feel. His essay was never graded, and it was not part of the regular assignment rotation, but it helped all of us—his parents and teachers—understand where on the map his writing skills were and where he needed to go. Instead of a grade, Mrs. Nero wrote comments on Martin's paper, including this one: "I love how you put yourself in your essay, yet it isn't persuasive. The way you see yourself as a reader makes it seem like you think the author intended you to act that way. You almost suggest that the reader is a character created by the author! This is something called your *thesis*. We will work on this. I would love to see you develop this idea with a few more examples from the book and to focus mainly on this one *main* idea. Can you try and convince me that this is what the author intended?"

Martin worked with Mrs. Nero back and forth over new drafts and ideas for months, and he told me it was the hardest he had ever worked on anything. The first draft of that paper was an almost illegible jumble of half-supported ideas and theories that circled around each other without connecting to one cohesive thesis. It was likely that he had never had the chance to express the true scope of his thought process in writing, and the initial draft was not wonderful, but it was complicated and full of possibility for true growth. Martin read the book series again to search for details to support his thesis. He had been aching for the "beyond"; he did not care one bit that there was never a grade on the paper, only comments and questions spurring him forward. Over the next few months, what began to develop from that initially disorganized nest of thoughts was a polished and very personal piece of work for Martin. In the process, he was willing to abandon the concept of a grade as a badge of honor, which had been a key topic of his original Think Tank meeting; now he was not working for a grade, but rather for the outcome predicated on his own effort.

Barbara Clark was one of the early educators/researchers to conceptualize in literature the need for high-ability students to meet with teachers as a possible alternative replacement to standards-based grading procedures. Many teachers already employ this method of meeting with students to some degree. Teachers can use this structure, with which they are already familiar, as a form of intervention for bright students who are presenting with academic dishonesty or who are showing warning signs. These meetings can occur one-on-one or with a group of students to discuss ways for the group to show growth.[34]

Martin's Think Tank is just one example of an approach you may already be using in your classroom. Please note that the names given to the categories of conference types that will be discussed throughout this text are not technical. As different meeting types and strategies—such as the ones I use with my teachers and parents—emerge and are discussed in the text, I have named them in order to distinguish the varieties and purposes of teacher-student or parent-student conferences. Feel free to replace names as you see fit. Some parents have reported success in getting their bright, creative kids involved with the naming process. Getting student input can result in a student who comes into the meeting excited to discuss his or her "perfect mission" at the "Thursday Battle Plan" instead of sitting unwillingly at the teacher-student "Weekly Independent Project Conference." One teacher I know meets with multiple students at once to save time and, to strengthen group camaraderie, he has a faux-official call to order of the "Superhero's Guild Meeting" in which he reviews the minutes of the last meeting prior to new business. As we distinguish between the types throughout the text, sample meeting write-ups are offered wherever applicable.

The purpose of Martin's Think Tank (a popular name among students for such grade planning) was to encourage Martin to understand what a grade meant and what it meant to ceiling at a certain level. When he discovered that he needed to be learning at his own level, not simply at grade-level curriculum, he worked harder at the work assigned to him because it felt valuable to him. It was important for his teachers to support him where he was so that his grades would accurately represent what he had learned. The first step was finding where he was on the curricular map, ready to pin his knowledge down and make sure he wasn't going to be lost again. The second was to move him forward from that point. He would continue to get As, not as a reward, but because we explained that the grading system for the fifth grade asked that we report to the school, the state, and to his parents how he had performed on that year's standards. To give him less than an A when he had shown mastery would not be fair and, more importantly, it would not be accurate because he would not be working on fifth-grade work anymore. The concept of grade replacing was the most difficult for Mrs. Nero to accept, as it seemed unfair to *give* a student a grade. Even if Martin had shown mastery of the curriculum, it was difficult to accept that he could show mastery without the more traditional, repetitive in-class assignments, homework, and test scores. The key to acceptance was in establishing a way of documenting that Martin had mastered the content area; once it was proven that he had an A-level understanding of the content standards through multiple pre- and post-test data points, the classroom teacher was able to let go of her own concept of "grades as rewards" and began to allow Martin to work at a level that was more appropriate for him.

As with most students, it was easier for Martin to let go of the concept than it was for his teachers. Once he was removed from the idea of the *grade*, he no longer assigned it importance. He didn't feel like he'd been *given* the grade but grew to realize that his performance was at a 90-100% level for the fifth-grade material. Once he had that pin in his map, he was free to travel into unoccupied territory. From then on, the work he did beyond his grade level was remarked upon, edited, and encouraged to improve by his teachers, but those grades did not go onto the report card. The grades on his report cards were all As, as his report card represented the fifth-grade curriculum he had shown to have mastered.

Ideally, Martin would have been in a school where grade acceleration was available, and he would have been able to be graded at his current and appropriate level. Acceleration will be discussed later in Chapter 3 because here, as it often happens, the ideal opportunity wasn't available. Rather than throw our hands up in defeat, we worked with what we had. Martin often worked in a sixth-grade class for many of his projects and assignments, and wherever possible he was working on a much more detailed and thorough version of what the class was learning, but he remained a fifth-grade student who mostly worked on higher-level curriculum. As a result, when he did not pretest out of a unit, he understood that being asked to sit with the rest of the class was not a punishment but rather a way to ensure what gaps he did still have in his understanding would be addressed. Martin was able to attend to the material because he felt like it was worth his time, and more importantly, he understood *why* he was being asked to stay.

Many teachers fear that accelerating curriculum in the classroom means that a student will be working by himself for an inappropriate amount of time. Some independent work is unavoidable, especially in a district where academic acceleration is not supported, but a number of creative strategies can be employed to support this deep level of in-class differentiation. Included at the end of this chapter is a list of valuable text resources that explore this topic more thoroughly. These are intended to be used by classroom teachers, but parents are encouraged to read them as well and to provide resources to your child's teacher whenever appropriate. These resources can help parents and teachers alike who are interested in pursuing additional opportunities for their students.

The argument has also been made that if a student is doing sixth-grade work in fifth grade, won't they be bored in sixth grade? As parents are often told, "If I let him work ahead, what will we do with him next year?" The truth is that these student more than likely would have been bored in sixth grade anyway, especially if they are, like most bright children, working two to four grade levels below their potential. Some of the issue of repeating material can be assuaged by giving students the opportunity to go deeper into their current grade level's curriculum rather than accelerating them outright. Time, most educators would agree, is the most valuable and limited resource in the classroom. Students are being asked to learn multiple subjects and complete lengthy standardized tests as well as working to meet standards for subjects such as physical education, music, and art, which are valuable even though they shrink the amount of time in which any one subject can be explored at length in the classroom. Rather than accelerating a high-ability student to the next year's crowded curriculum, sometimes it is more appropriate to allow them to seize current topics of interest and "unpack" them, taking the time to deeply connect with and draw connections between subjects and ideas.

In the end, there will always be some parents and teachers who will accept nothing less than straight As, whether it is their own expectation or that of society, but I hope that they, too, can broaden their wishes for their students beyond the emblem of A-F. When all students are able to work at levels above their baselines, leaning plateaus will be abolished, and students will have the opportunity to encounter challenge at a consistent-enough level so that they can develop persistence and other healthy coping mechanisms for failure and difficulty. Too many gifted and high-ability students coast for long periods of time, during which they need little effort to accomplish their school work. As they begin to approach where their true learning level has been, in essence, *waiting for them*, many bright students find that they are at a loss of how to cope with the challenges required for forward movement once they finally reach the end of that plateau. Growth beyond that point is precarious without the coping mechanisms that their classmates had to develop years before as they failed and learned how to overcome their mistakes.

My biggest fear was that Martin would lose his faith in the ability of educators to teach him, and maybe even lose faith in learning itself. In the end, I learned that most bright students *can* work with you to help themselves break free of cheating behaviors—but only if they're educated in the "method behind the madness." Trust the bright students in your home or in your classroom who are struggling in some way to collaborate with you to help them through. Teach them what is truly important, and let them know that you are there to support them by elevating them to a point where they will actually be learning. Push them to a point where they find challenge at an appropriate level and reward that with responsive questioning and teaching, rather than with grades. Above all, give your bright kids the gift of making mistakes. And celebrate those mistakes—even those that involve cheating—because growing past them is often where the real learning occurs.

Recommended books that support enhanced use of differentiated methods in a classroom with gifted children:

📖 *Intelligent Life in the Classroom: Smart Kids and their Teachers.* Isaacson, K.J., & Fisher, T. J. (2007). Scottsdale, AZ: Great Potential Press.

📖 *How to Differentiate Instruction in Mixed-Ability Classrooms.* Tomlinson, C. B. (2001). Alexandria, VA: Association for Supervision and Curriculum Development.

📖 *Re-Forming Gifted Education: How Parents and Teachers Can Match the Program to the Child.*

📖 Rogers, K.B. (2002). Scottsdale, AZ: Great Potential Press.

📖 *Challenging Gifted Learners in the Regular Classroom.* Tomlinson, C. B. (1994). Alexandria, VA: Association for Supervision and Curriculum Development.

📖 *Teaching Gifted Kids in the Regular Classroom.* Winebrenner, S. (2001). Minneapolis, MN: Free Spirit.

📖 *Differentiation: From Planning to Practice, Grades 6-12.* Wormeli, R. (2007). Portland, ME: Stenhouse.

📖 *Differentiation in Action: A Complete Resource with Research-Supported Strategies to Help You Plan and Organize Differentiated Instruction and Achieve ... All Learners.* Dodge, J. (2006). New York: Scholastic Teaching Strategies.

📖 *The Multi-Age Classroom: An Inside Look at One Community of Learners.* Maeda, B. (1994). Cypress, CA: Creating Teaching Press.

📖 *Student Assessments That Work: A Practical Approach.* Weber, E. (1999). Boston: Allyn & Bacon.

📖 *Multiple Intelligences in the Classroom.* Armstrong, T. (1994). Alexandria, VA: Association for Supervision and Curriculum Development.

TWO

Terry

Terry was a girl who had what her teachers and parents commonly referred to as "an attitude problem." No one disputed that she was bright; she had received one of the highest scores in her school on a statewide achievement test given to all third graders, and early descriptors of Terry on her report cards were "precocious," "high spirited," and "uniquely talented." However, she rarely used those unique talents on activities that her parents or teachers preferred. She more often chose to daydream, draw in her notebook, or to read openly in class, sometimes keeping the book in her lap or tucked into a textbook if someone threatened to take it away from her. It was easy to spot when Terry was doing something she was not supposed to do because those were the rare calm moments between the energy storms that characterized Terry most of the time. She was a student with a great deal of energy, who constantly fidgeted, kicked, and made repetitive motions and sounds at her desk during every class transition. Giving her extra recess times as a way to help her focus was not successful; she did not enjoy recess or gym class. Her energy came from a mental restlessness rather than a physical one.

Her teachers had other concerns beyond her "stealth reading." Terry's work was rarely completed to satisfaction, with rushed or incomplete answers. In fourth grade, Terry's mastery test scores showed that she was in the 96th percentile for mathematic ability for her grade, but that skill level was not reflected in her mathematics grade of a C-. A large portion of that grade came from a lack of homework scores. Although she sometimes had elaborate excuses for why it was missing, she usually did not bother, answering more honestly with an "I just didn't do it." Terry's educational profile was one of consistent underachievement, which understandably upset her parents and baffled her teachers, who more often see underachievement in students with learning difficulties or a lack of support at home. Terry had neither of these, yet she continued to perform poorly in school.

When Terry did make an effort, it was often in direct opposition to what she had been told to do. She once turned in a 25-slide presentation when her fourth-grade teacher, Mrs. Gold, had expressed that each presentation should only be four slides per student. Mrs. Gold also discovered one day that Terry was not reading but doodling on her Language Arts workbook. After a second reminder to stop, the teacher confiscated the book and continued teaching. It was not until later, when Mrs. Gold looked at the workbook, that she realized that Terry had not only doodled on more than half of the pages but also had completed the entire book ahead of the class. The group had been instructed at the beginning of the year to wait for the appropriate lessons to complete the corresponding workbook pages. This ensured that the teacher could check that concepts had been taught thoroughly before the students attempted the short-answer questions and deep-thinking ideas presented in the workbook. The classroom teacher, fearing that giving Terry a fresh workbook would produce similar results, began to make separate copies of individual pages for each lesson and only gave Terry the corresponding papers that she would need to complete each night. She was distressed that Terry willfully disobeyed and made the extra work for her, both in the superfluously long presentation and by having to forcibly keep Terry on the class's schedule for workbook pages.

Two months after the workbook incident, Mrs. Gold's distress sky-rocketed when she caught Terry cheating on a math test. It was mostly a "skill and drill" exercise, with a page of timed math facts that the students were to complete alone and without any help. Halfway through the test, the teacher noticed that Terry had left a multiplication table sitting out on her desk and was copying answers directly from the table.

The teacher's response, after the initial punishment and calling Terry's parents, was to ask in the teacher's lounge incredulously, "Isn't it so sad? I know she could have done that assignment *easily* without cheating. I would be shocked if she missed even one."

As the other teachers listened and sympathized, understanding Mrs. Gold's confusion and anxiety over the matter, perhaps none of them realized what should have seemed obvious: Wasn't it also sad that, despite how easy the assignment was said to be for Terry, that she was still required to complete it?

Despite how difficult it was for Mrs. Gold to understand how or why a bright child would cheat or consistently underachieve, Terry's profile is unfortunately not uncommon; the only thing that distinguished her case in particular is that her cheating behaviors were witnessed and identified by an adult, which is rare. In fact, she was discovered cheating in two additional incidents over the next few weeks. In the first, she was caught during a vocabulary test having written vocabulary words on the sides and back of her shoes. In the second, the entire opening page of a book report was plagiarized from an Internet site.

It is rare for a cheating behavior to be actively identified in a bright child. In the Parent Institute survey of 2013, only 8% of high-ability students say that their academic dishonesty has been discovered.[35] Though this number is alarming, when compared to the number of students who suggest that they have cheated—upwards of 80%—a greater concern may be the response to the students whose actions are revealed, either by their parent or their teacher. Teachers and parents should address cheating like they approach weed pulling; realize that if you ignore the root and eliminate the surface it will only be a matter of time before the weed re-grows. A child who is caught cheating will not return to the behavior immediately; however, no punishment alone will be effective to prevent or even substantially delay the return of that or another cheating behavior. The underlying causes must be addressed if the ultimate goal is the complete cessation of cheating behaviors.

I will address what to do when a child is caught cheating, both the appropriate surface-level interventions for parents and teachers, and how to solve the issue long term at the deeper roots. Terry's case typifies a very common underlying issue that contributes to a great deal of bright children's underachieving and cheating behaviors—a deep sense of boredom with which they are unable to cope.[36]

Why is Boredom Such a Problem?

Boredom may seem like an easily conquerable challenge, something that we're familiar with on a daily basis. Every parent is accustomed to the oft-heard protest, "I'm bored!" Though boredom may seem innocent enough, in actuality it can be one of the most crippling issues that a high-ability child faces on a daily basis. Bright children may seem to have all the answers, but they are far from indomitable. In fact, their unfamiliarity with appropriate challenges may have left them more, not less, fragile than their peers whose coping strategies are more developed and practiced.

If you calculate the times during a day when boredom strikes you as an adult, you'll find that it is often during waiting periods, the brief transitions between one activity and another, such as standing in line, being placed on hold, or even stuck in traffic. Imagine what it would be like if that bored feeling were reversed, and those brief periods during your day were the only times that you *did* feel interested or engaged by your environment. The rest of the time you were required to sit and listen to information that you either already knew or had lost the ability to see as meaningful, almost as if the language itself was incomprehensible. You might be able to stand it for a day, but after weeks or months you would be overwhelmed by a deep, almost crippling boredom and lack of stimulation. Or as Terry once graphically noted in her writing journal, "I feel like I'm gnawing on my own brain."

Bright children are particularly susceptible to experiencing boredom. At least half of high-ability students report boredom in core subjects because of having to wait for other students to catch up.[37] Some experts even suggest that these students have up to half of their class time left over after they have finished their work or mastered the concepts, which is not surprising considering that studies have shown that some high-ability students come into a school year with a good understanding of 60-75% of the curriculum that will be taught that year.[38] Many bright children, as a result, are able to be tested as working two to four grades below their potential.[39] Even when the performance gap is not so dramatic, all bright children experience some disconnect between their abilities and the pace of curriculum that is taught in the traditional classroom. Because of the slow pace that often has to be set by the classroom teacher in order to express concepts in multiple ways for various learners—not to mention the time needed for the repetition and practice that is required for many students to obtain mastery—bright children are often left unattended with their boredom. What may surprise you is what effect that lack of stimulation has on their forming brains.

Dr. Marian Diamond, an American neuroanatomist at the University of Berkeley, studied the brains of adolescent rats to see what effect stimulating versus non-stimulating environments had on their cortical structures. One group of young rats was exposed to a variety of learning opportunities—ramps, wheels, stairs, and toys. The other rats, though fed and watered in equal measure to the enriched rats, were reared in an environment devoid of such learning tools or companions. After a brief period that consisted only of a few weeks, the rats in un-enriched environments had noticeably thinner cortexes than those that had been offered interesting stimulus. In other words, being consistently bored for only a matter of weeks had a starving effect on the brain. Dr. Diamond referred to the under-stimulated rats, in fact, as "impoverished." The rats that had been challenged to learn had thicker cortexes, a larger number of brain cells, and more extensive and thicker branching of neural pathways, all of which lead to a more effective brain.[40] Even more striking is that dendrite death as a result of a lack of stimulation can occur after only eight days in an impoverished environment.[41] Boredom can not only be frustrating and uncomfortable for children but can actually affect the way they are able to think and learn on a physiological level.

How Boredom Can Lead to Academic Dishonesty

Boredom, though a dangerous hindrance to effective learning for brains that crave motion and stimulation, can become even more troubling when it manifests itself in negative behaviors. These can include daydreaming or other forms of inattention (like Terry's stealth reading), disruptions of class, a sullen or apathetic attitude, or cheating behaviors. Many bright children are adept at finding or manufacturing stimuli outside of the curriculum when they do not find it challenging.

Like it or not, cheating is a very appealing process to a well-functioning, yet bored mind. Cognitive psychologists have shown that the human brain, for all its complexities, is an organ that seeks to simplify processes. Our brains will avoid thinking whenever and wherever they can. In fact, the better the brain is, the better its ability to cut corners, look for loopholes, and generally be a lazy thinker. Bright children have an advantage in these "lazy thinking patterns." It seems extremely contradictory, based on what we know about curious, information-seeking, high-ability children, but the truth is that what we perceive as *thinking* is generally something else: pulling information from working or long-term memory, drawing analogies between new information and things we've already learned, or chunking information to easier categorize it in our brains. Truly deep thinking is an activity our brains like to reserve for rare occasions, preferring a streamlined version most of the time. Cognitive scientist Daniel T. Willingham goes as far as to suggest that our brains are designed to prevent us from thinking whenever possible.[42]

A quote from Stephen King is very apt: *"No one can be as intellectually slothful as a really smart person; give smart people half a chance and they will ship their oars and drift."* [43]

Though that assessment seems bleak, there is yet another loophole that offers more promise towards helping our high-ability students out of their dishonest habits. Despite having brains that seem fundamentally designed to save us from thinking, humans are naturally curious and have a great capacity to enjoy the process of thinking, even if studies show we are not very good at "real thinking." This is never truer than for our bright children, who often possess an innate and insatiable curiosity about the world around them. With the right tools, we can keep our students from shipping their oars in order to drift lazily down the river of thought. Bright children want to learn, and even those—like Terry—who no longer rise to being challenged can fall in love with learning again. The process for igniting this passion is to identify how often students are subjected to boredom and to inject challenge and meaning back into their school day where we can. In doing so, we also have a responsibility as teachers and parents to educate ourselves about the common misconceptions surrounding high-ability children and their needs in the classroom, just as we need to partner with bright children not simply to punish cheating behaviors caused by boredom but rather to seek out underlying causes and reeducate students through careful interventions.

Complications Regarding Punishment

Not much has been said, to this point, about types and appropriateness of punishments for bright children who are caught cheating. This is due in part to the unusual circumstances that often complicate this manner of cheating. Martin, you may recall, came forward to admit to cheating; it's very likely that, had he not done so, his indiscretion would never have been discovered or even suspected.[44] Because cheating can be easily misconstrued, it is often passed off as a misunderstanding or plausible coincidence in many circumstances, which can result in underreporting. In addition, the allegation of cheating is a serious one, and few teachers are willing to address the possible ramifications of falsely accusing a child of cheating unless evidence is clear (if the child was caught in the act, for example). The overwhelming majority of students who cheat are never caught, according to student and teacher reporting.[45] There is also a common lack of resources for teachers or administration to learn how to respond appropriately to cheating: Few high schools and even fewer elementary schools have concrete examples, consequences, and codes regarding cheating in their school or district handbooks. And because school personnel are typically not trained to respond to academic dishonesty in appropriate, consistent manners, cheating, unless it is flagrant, is most often ignored.[46] This means there is often a disconnect between the consistency and fairness of how we deal with academic dishonesty.

Arthur, for one, was punished for his deception; however, it was not a decision that administration and his teachers came to lightly. What might have seemed like an appropriate consequence for another student was difficult to apply to Arthur, not by the virtue of his gifted and talented identification but rather, his motives—or lack thereof. If that seems confusing, answer this: Why is cheating so wrong? At the heart of cheating is the concept of fairness. In fact, the general definition of cheating is any action that affords an unfair advantage to one person over another, generally through deceit.[47] Though Arthur's long-term forgery had not been honest, he had not done so in order to gain an advantage, nor did he ever misrepresent his grades to his parents. What did Arthur gain? If his actions did not afford him an unfair advantage, was it still cheating?

Much debate ensued in digging out the appropriate response to Arthur's actions. Did it matter that he had not gained anything from his deceit? Did his lack of intentions excuse him? Would it send the wrong message to other students if he was excused, namely that *they* had to follow the rules but some students were exempt? It sounds unfair by its nature, but what if the rules did not apply to certain students because of their circumstances? What would be the implications for deciding who is under the domain of which rules, and why? The questions are endless. It is evident that the sometimes paradoxical behavior or motives of bright children and their academic dishonesty can bring up many dilemmas regarding ethics, fairness, advantages, and the nature of rules themselves. To cheat, one must cut corners, neglect to play by the rules, actively exploit a loophole, or take an unfair advantage. Some would say that bright children already have an advantage by their nature—in their large working memories, quick processing times, and various other gifts and abilities. They, perhaps more than anyone, are in the unique position of being able to recognize and exploit loopholes due to the already unequal gifts that they possess. The idea that behavior is wrong simply because it represents something that is unequal or unfair is hard to explain to a group of people who already know that their abilities are not the same as their classmates. Does that make them and what they could do "wrong," too?

Student Perspective on Punishment

Traditional responses to cheating are rarely effective as a method for deterring high-ability students, partially due to the lack of meaningful interventions but also because the concept of punishment itself may be diminished in the mind of the student.

Common punishments for cheating at the elementary-school level are often less severe than the consequences of cheating in middle or high school, though similar patterns are observed. The student is often reprimanded at school and at home, and cause-and-effect consequences are sought and emphasized: no credit for the assignment(s) that were falsified, the need to redo assignments, official warnings, letters of apology, school detentions or suspensions, or other punishments that withdraw a student from the original environment. It is rare that interventions are sought. The one deviation from this pattern is the attempt for a moral intervention, working to re-teach the child how and why the behavior reflects on them and their society. Sometimes, students are no longer allowed to join honor societies or peer counseling groups, or their citizenship or classroom-participant grades are lowered as a result.

Compare the common punishments to these statements bright children have made about how being bored makes them feel:

> *"We review everything. The teacher says everything twice, or three times, or more. It's worse than someone tapping a pencil on the desk over and over."* —Boy, 13

> *"It feels like my brain is asleep all the time."* —Girl, 9

> *"When the teacher doesn't teach me anything new in a day, I sometimes get very angry."* —Boy, 7

> *"I hate school. It's so boring."* —Girl, 10

> *"There's something inside of me that dies when I feel like I don't belong in a classroom. They're not doing anything interesting, or hard, and I feel really out of place."* —Girl, 12.

Which seems like the worse of the two punishments in the following scenarios: failing a test or feeling "like something inside of you is dying"?

Being "very angry" or having to redo an assignment? Feeling "really out of place" or facing detention? Which would you choose? Traditional repercussions at the elementary level for cheating are administered without the realization that many bright children began the cheating behaviors in the first place as a way to escape what they saw as a punishing situation. Taking away privileges is only as effective as a student's belief that they have any control over the cause-and-effect relationship of action versus consequence, which may not be fully realized when students do not see any other way out of the consequence of persistent boredom. If a child feels helpless, no lectures, punishments, or explanations will be successful at preventing future negative behavior.[48]

Consider the word punishment. Beyond the definition—a penalty or chastisement as a retribution for an offense—what is it that makes something *feel* like an effective punishment? It is, to a large extent, subjective. Send two siblings, one a social, outdoors sport-loving student and the other an introverted bookworm, to their rooms after misbehaving and you'll see just how subjective a punishment can be. The introvert likes being sent to her room to read; being sent to her personal space enables her to create a "mini-retreat" to recharge her energy and feel at ease.[49] Similarly, something that is not intended as a punishment can be seen as one by a child. Take that same happy book reader who was more than willing to be "exiled" to her room and see how she fares when her book is taken away at school or at home after bedtime when she is found under the covers with a flashlight. Even actions not intended as reprimands can feel like punishment to a child.

Teachers and parents can inadvertently punish high-ability children without intention and without realizing how it is being perceived by the student. Take, for instance, the level of tasks that Terry was asked to complete. Even though Mrs. Gold had said that she would be shocked if Terry missed any of her multiplication and division facts, she was still required to complete them. In addition, Terry was obligated to do dozens of other assignments on a weekly basis simply because they were part of the regular curriculum. Terry did not have the option to skip these assignments, regardless of whether or not she could prove her level of mastery for that subject. When Terry did finish her class work, she was often given extra work, which was another perceived punishment; not surprisingly, her pace slowed.

There is also the case of Terry's confiscated language arts workbook. The workbook contained grammar and spelling questions as well as deeper-thinking questions that were connected to the texts that students would be reading throughout the year. Terry, as you may recall, finished three quarters of the workbook within the first few months of school, even though she had been directed to keep the slow pace of the rest of the class. The workbook was taken away from her so that she would not finish it early, and copies of the pages that she had already completed were given to her one day at a time so that she could complete them again with the class.

Mrs. Gold did not take the workbook to punish Terry. She was concerned that Terry would not do her best work if she rushed and that her short answer questions would not be correct before she was able to read the texts that were to be covered that year. Of the sections Terry had already completed, 84% of the material was correct. One thing is true: It is quite reasonable to believe that, if Terry worked at the class's pace, discussed the pages, and checked her work with her teacher, she likely would have received a higher average score. The teacher used the same argument; she expected a higher grade from Terry because she knew that Terry was capable of completing the workbook to a higher mastery level.

The classroom teacher had the best intentions; as a teacher who tried to differentiate for her class, she sought higher level work from Terry. What she failed to recognize was that she was inadvertently punishing Terry for being bright by taking away her ability to work at a pace at which she felt comfortable. Instead of teaching Terry to add thoroughness and detail to her work, regardless of the pace, the teacher was bringing Terry back down to a level that she, the teacher, felt comfortable overseeing.

Similarly, imposed maximum limits on how long or how in depth an assignment can be before the teacher feels unable or unwilling to comment in a thorough manner can send very distinct messages to clever children that they have to modify themselves or their abilities to fit what is "appropriate" in the classroom. When a student is asked not to write a longer book report than a teacher feels capable of grading in the time available or is not allowed to tackle an unusual medium for a project because it is one the teacher or parent feels unable to help with or effectively judge, it is very difficult to then require them to "do their best" on tasks that teachers want them to value, such as homework and tests. It is no coincidence that after her long slide presentation was nixed, Terry turned to her workbook to excise her extra mental energy. Not long after that was taken away, her cheating behaviors emerged as a way to alleviate the deep feelings of boredom as they "gnawed on her brain."

Terry did not need a pace adjustment, which she saw as a punishment; instead she needed to be called to whatever mistakes she made and asked to redo them until they were correct. Please note, however, that this method is only appropriate if the material in question is appropriate for the student in the first place. Stressing mastery on assignments that are too easy for students and calling their attention to every individual mistake has the risk of creating or heightening perfectionist tendencies, which we will explore more in Chapter 4.

If bright students perceive the response to the cheating as less harsh than the initial feelings they were avoiding, they will generally continue the cheating behaviors, regardless of their moral compass telling them how wrong the behavior is. The high rate of recidivism for any crime—or even any behavior you wish you could stop but never seem to succeed—can be attributed to the lesser-of-two-evils concept, or of a calculation of risk versus gain. If both the circumstances that led to the behavior and the outcome itself are poor, intelligent individuals will seek the less punishing of the two.

An old logic game, called the Pirate's Gold, is a clear illustration of the calculation of risk versus gain. There are many versions and variations of this, including the Prisoner's Dilemma, but in any case, the game generally goes somewhat like this:

Table 2.1. Pirate's Gold Logic Game

Five pirates attack a ship and return to their own with **100** gold doubloons to split between them. They must decide democratically who will get how many doubloons. Each of the pirates has a different rank, and the most superior pirate (Captain first, Cabin Boy last!) will take a turn at suggesting a way in which the gold is shared. The pirates then vote on the suggestion. If it is a tie, the pirate whose plan it is (seniority) breaks the tie. If it is accepted, the doubloons are shared in that way. But if a pirate's plan does not win the vote, that pirate has to walk the plank! Then the next in the chain of command is allowed to propose a way to share the gold.

The Captain	The First Mate
The Boatswain	The Gunner
The Cabin Boy	

The pirates must base their decision off of three factors:

1. Each pirate is trying to avoid being thrown overboard. Survival is the number one priority.
2. Each pirate wants to maximize the number of coins he receives, assuming that he is able to survive.
3. Each pirate would prefer to throw another pirate overboard so he can get more gold.

It is a fun puzzle, and usually makes for a layered discussion that starts as rank versus democracy even before the students peel back the surface to realize that it is, at its core, a logical and mathematical game. For those interested, the full solution is explained in this endnote.[50] The underlying principle is that, if each pirate is rational, the end result is that the captain would end up with the overwhelming portion of the gold, and all of the others would have one or none of the doubloons but would escape the ordeal with their lives.

One of my students, a passionate, analytical-minded sixth-grade boy named Aaron, understood the concept before his classmates. They had decided to solve the game through role-playing and assigned Aaron the cabin boy role. After reexamining the rules, Aaron explained that he would not vote for anything other than the strategy I have already mentioned—for the captain to receive the vast majority of the gold. When his classmates protested his vote, confused as to why he would not vote himself more doubloons, he explained to the others how the cabin boy would get only one coin, and so would most of the others. When the other "pirates" continued to argue that he should hold out for more money, I remember how frustrated he became as he waited for them to understand, struggling to explain.

"I have two options if we're following the rules. They're both bad things. I either get thrown overboard, or I get almost no gold. I know you want the money no matter which pirate you are, but for some of you, only bad things will happen. You only get to choose *how* bad."

It is a common thread for bright and creative children to feel like they have limited options in a system that does not always understand them. When those options appear bleak, they instinctively turn to the ones they feel are less punishing or less risky. Aaron identified the best-case scenario in what he considered a lose-lose situation in the Pirate's

Gold game and refused to back down from his assessment even when his classmates told him that he was wrong. It is the same when students feel compelled to cheat and risk getting caught to possibly ease the pain of not feeling mentally stimulated; they can see their options as boredom on the one hand or possible punishment on the other. Additionally, as long as the logic that drives a bright child to commit an act of academic dishonesty still holds true for them, proposing a blanket assertion that the student is wrong, even when accompanied by punishment, will have a low chance of reeducating or preventing future cheating behaviors.

The implications of this are not meant to encourage unnecessarily harsher punishments for bright children who cheat but rather to point out that the current method of "punishment as prevention" is flawed. Certainly students do deserve repercussions, but consequences for cheating should function as interventions rather than simply being punitive and ineffective. It is more helpful to separate the cheating incidents you observe into a number of behaviors and actions and to approach them as separate entities. For example, reprimanding students for cheating by telling them that (a) what they did was wrong and (b) exacting a consequence may not be as effective as separating what is wrong (and why) from the underlying *causes* of the behaviors and addressing them each appropriately. An appropriate intervention for an underlying cause of boredom-driven cheating or perfectionism-driven cheating may be curriculum modifications or grade replacements, while a conversation and personal consequence such as a loss of a privilege would be appropriate for the disrespect that their cheating made the teacher or parent feel.

Human minds look to justify mistakes and normalize them whenever possible. As such, when an incident is responded to with a blanket statement of, "You did this bad thing, and you are in trouble," students tend to focus on whatever their initial justification for their actions was. They then are able to dismiss the qualities of the discussion that deal with fairness or right versus wrong because the issue has been presented holistically, and their justification can serve to soften the judgment they feel from others and themselves. For example, when being told that cheating is wrong, students can absorb the repercussions by quietly reminding themselves that they did it to avoid being bored or singled out, or to feel better about themselves. The perception here may be that cheating was still worth it, overall.

A student is more likely to respond to a combination of careful separations that effectively combine both intervention and punishment, where each is required. Though a student might easily disregard an issue that is presented in general terms, it is difficult for a student to ignore when an adult points out what exact components of the behavior have been attached to which consequences. As discussed in Martin's chapter, bright children need to regain a sense of meaningful cause and effect. By separating the emotions from the cause of the action and treating each like a separate symptom, you are far more likely to deflect a student's rationalizations. For example, it is much harder for a child to believe that a lack of feeling stimulated in class is reason enough to make a parent feel sad and confused because one does not directly excuse the other, nor does it represent a rational cause and effect relationship, which is something most bright children crave. Any parents who have ever argued, sometimes futilely, with their clever child knows this to be true, but they also know how challenging it can be to help the child understand it.

Address Emotions Separately

Only after you have separated a cheating behavior into its individual parts—what was done, why it was done, and how it made the individuals involved feel—can you begin to approach those components in appropriate ways. Isolate the emotional responses from the actual cheating behaviors. Good feelings rarely accompany an accusation or discovery of dishonest behavior, and the negative emotions felt by a teacher or parents when confronting a student run the risk of taking over the conversation and turning into the type of reprimand a clever child can rationalize internally. It is better to address your emotional response to cheating separately, though certainly it can be difficult to separate your emotions from the consequences that are imposed as a result of the cheating. Parents are particularly likely to have strong feelings of disappointment, but teachers are not immune to the frustration and sadness of finding a bright child engaging in academic dishonesty and can also use the following recommendations.

Consequences for cheating may include the loss of a privilege, the need to apologize to the wronged party, reflection, and time-out (preferably with a journal or way to record thoughts), etc. Regardless of what punitive response is chosen, the response should be applied as a direct consequence to the negative action in order to preserve the cause-and-effect relationship in the mind of the student, and the punishment should be applied fairly and uniformly. Your emotional response is important, too, and the child needs to know how you feel.

In Table 2.2 are some examples of emotional responses you may need to share with your child. Notice that these are "I-statements" about how the child's behavior made you feel. These examples are not intended as a laundry list of complaints to use with a student. It is better to be direct and honest but not exhaustive about emotions; the emotional aspect can be difficult for both parties. Take care to avoid overwhelming the student or letting the conversation itself become the punishment. That "shaming" holds a real risk of damaging self-esteem or the relationship between the child and adult. The intent of naming the emotions with the child is (a) to address emotions separately and (b) to allow consequences to naturally occur from the resulting conversation. In this way, you are open to treat the underlying causes as something to work on and prevent, which can be difficult to do if the emotions have not been addressed and the distinction between consequences and punishments are blurred. When emotions are high, it is difficult to think in a logical manner.

Table 2.2. Examples of Emotional Statements Associated with Cheating Behaviors

- ✔ *"I feel disrespected because you cheated."*
- ✔ *"I feel that you disrespected the person you copied from or plagiarized."*
- ✔ *"I feel like you took advantage of my trust."*
- ✔ *"I want to be able to trust you, and now I'm afraid that I can't."*
- ✔ *"I feel like you took advantage of your teacher/classmate."*
- ✔ *"It makes me sad that you did something out of character."*
- ✔ *"I am embarrassed because I'm afraid your school thinks we didn't teach you right from wrong."*
- ✔ *"It makes me sad that you did not tell me that something was bothering you and instead decided to cheat."*
- ✔ *"I feel like you invaded the privacy of your classmate." (If the cheating was a copying situation.)*

In addition, this conversation is an excellent forum to begin also addressing the student's emotions that prompted the incident. If children feel that you understand their emotions, even if you do not excuse their behavior, they are less likely to reject your discipline.

Teacher Challenges with Bright Children

It may be true that teachers unknowingly punish the bright children in their classrooms, but it should be noted that I have never met a teacher who actively sought to discourage high-ability students from identifying positively with their intelligence. Nor has there been a teacher, in my professional experience, who has tried to sabotage that self-image through extra work, lack of attention, or requiring maximum limits on assignments. I understand that it can be frustrating and quite emotional when you are working with teachers who do not understand or are not positively challenging your bright child, but it is important to remember that appropriate education is the ultimate goal—both for the child and the educator—and also to know that many teachers have received no special training in how to work with children who are unusually bright.

One Classroom Practices Study survey of 7000 teachers found that half had no training whatsoever in high-ability education.[51] It is rare for regular classroom teachers to receive any detailed training of gifted and talented traits, identification, or service models, and most states do not require any gifted and talented courses in order for teachers to obtain their teaching certificates. As recently as 2013, the National Association for Gifted Children polled states for gifted education requirements and reported that only one state required all teachers to receive pre-service training in needs of gifted children. Even more frightening, only 17 states require (or in some cases, even offer) gifted and talented certification or credentials from the state board of education for those teachers who *specialize* in gifted and talented programs.[52] That means there is an overwhelming chance that a high-ability child lives in a state that does not require classroom teachers *or* specialists to be adequately prepared to meet his or her educational needs.

That is not to say that the professionals in these circumstances are unwilling, only that they have not been offered the opportunities to prepare for the needs of these students. Fortunately, many teachers actively seek additional education and resources through in-service trainings, workshops, and personal research about high-ability children.

In Connecticut, where I have taught and which is also the home to the National Research Center on the Gifted and Talented, there is no certification for gifted and talented teachers at the state level.[53] To become a gifted and talented educator or specialist, one needs only have certification and training to teach a regular K-6 classroom. No specific training is required. Yet I can name five educators with whom I worked in Connecticut who completed that specific training through an advanced degree in order to obtain the knowledge to properly teach high-ability children, even though no such degree was legally required for their position. In my experience, teachers want nothing more than to reach the needs of their individual students, even if they do not have the specific experience to know how to challenge their highest ability students.

Imagine entering a classroom in which one student speaks two languages. One is the language the rest of the class (and you) are speaking. The second is a more complicated language, rich with meaning and subtlety. That second language, in fact, is the one that the lone bilingual student prefers to use when doing something challenging, and those deep-meaning vocabulary words that you do not understand often crop up, either vocally or in writing, when the student is passionate about something. What do you do? Likely, you try to pick up as much of the language as you can through exposure, trial and error, and you ask the student for explanation where possible. Some teachers may ask the student not to speak the second language in school, not because they disapprove of it but because it is difficult for them to feel like they can understand the student unless they are speaking the common language. Some teachers, through repeated exposure, will gain understanding of the new language, but as new students come in with new dialects and slang, it becomes a learning process all over again. A precious few teachers are taught both languages simultaneously as preparation for their classrooms and are able to reach those students in a way other teachers struggle to achieve. However, even they have to build up experience when learning how and when the transition between the two languages is appropriate.

It is in this way that most classroom teachers build their understanding about the gifted and talented students in their classrooms. That second, more complex language is the sum of their gifts and abilities, and teachers learn about the differences through experience, which can be difficult considering that there is no one archetypal high-ability child.

Their profiles vary greatly, their needs span a vast range, and they may be difficult to serve both within and without those needs. As a result, much of a classroom teacher's experience with very bright children is based on assumptions, personal experience, and surface-level information that can lead to misunderstandings and misconceptions about what the true educational needs are.

This language analogy also is useful when explaining why schools should group high-ability children of similar ability in their traditional classrooms whenever possible. Even if a pull-out or separate program exists for high-ability learners, there is something meaningful about having a teacher who "understands your language" on a daily basis. Group common "dialects" together wherever possible, or in other words match students of intellectual abilities or strengths together so that their second language doesn't fall into disuse.

All of this is helpful to teachers and parents as they try to parse out underlying causes of a bright child who is acting out. When looking for "roots," a good place to start is with boredom and lack of appropriate challenge, but there other areas may also need to be addressed, such as feelings of perfectionism, peer pressures, social issues, or avoidance behaviors. In addition, other roadblocks may exist, such as underachievement or inaccurate "worth audits" on the part of the student, and common teacher misunderstandings regarding what bright children need or want. We will address these topics later, but right now our focus is on addressing boredom, as well as common teacher roadblocks, simply because it is the most common principal reason or "root."

Address the Underlying Cause

There is a risk, when identifying underlying causes of cheating behaviors, to pause at a blaming stage and to go no further. It is tempting to say that a child is simply lazy, that the parents are pushing too hard or not hard enough, or that the teacher and the curriculum are not challenging the bright student, and to leave it as something that is beyond your control. However, nothing that a teacher or parent can point to as an underlying cause for cheating behaviors is entirely true, nor does the cause of a situation ever exist solely because of one individual. Shift your thinking away from blame. When pulling weeds, you do not waste your time looking for *how* the seeds arrived there; you focus on digging out the roots.

How do you address boredom? Give students more interesting tasks that challenge them. It sounds so simple, yet it can be one of the most difficult tasks for a teacher due to the many roadblocks that often stand in the way. The teacher may not feel like he or she has the time to address the individual needs of higher ability students, that the high-ability students do not *need* that time, or that they cannot justify the challenge when bright students are not performing up to standard on their day-to-day work. If it were as easy as "give each smart child harder work," it would have already been done. There are many challenging roadblocks and understandable fears that teachers and parents face when looking to challenge bright children. Here are some of the most common ones.

Roadblock #1:

"My gifted students don't need me. They can finish x on their own."

A common and persistent myth that teachers hold is that "high-ability children are so smart that they can do X on their own," or basically, "They don't need me." Unfortunately, this widely held misconception is also reflected in the lack of appropriately sufficient state and federal funds for gifted education. "If they need my extra attention, they will let me know," but bright children may not be as obvious as children at the other end of the spectrum about needing extra help.

When teachers say that the bright children in their class do not need them, they are either consciously or subconsciously comparing them to the other students in their classrooms who may have special needs or simply require more time and repetition to master the concepts taught. In this way, what they mean is, "My brightest students don't need me as much as the rest of my class does." This faulty statement could be corrected with one notable change: "My brightest students don't need the amount of repetition and the same assignments that the other students do." It changes the perspective from "these children don't need me," which isolates them from the rest of the group, to "these children don't need me *in the same way*." Comparison of students and their needs is not only understandable but also natural. The risk is in allowing that comparison to cause high-ability children to be left alone without an advocate in the classroom setting. Although this may come from what seems like common sense to teachers about need and allocation of their resources, it is actually a common misconception about bright students.

Imagine the following: A teacher gives an assignment to their class. Two students finish immediately and correctly complete the assignment. Ten students understand but require clarification on the procedure or are looking to check their comprehension. Another five need extra processing time in order to grasp the concept, and two or three are not at the skill level where they can even approach the concept covered by the assignment yet. As a teacher in this common scenario, it *does* make sense to spend your time on those students who need the extra time with an adult. During this time, teachers are multi-tasking, clarifying other students' questions about the directions and explaining the assignment in a different way to support others' needs. But in this scenario, what of those first two students who understood the directions, grasped the focus of the assignment, and showed that they comprehended the underlying concept by quickly and correctly finishing the work they were given? Most likely, they will be asked to either complete other work, read, perhaps move on to a challenge assignment or an enrichment center, or simply wait for the other students to complete the task. The teacher's assertion that their focus on the high-ability students is not needed is correct because the problem is not in the teacher—or even in the bright student—but in the scenario itself.

Let's try another scenario. This time, you are driving down a one-lane road. If you were stuck driving behind a car that was not able to go the speed limit, or even drove exactly the speed limit but no more, how would you feel? Angry? Impatient? Some drivers experience irritation or even rage when they are forced to go slower than they are capable or are unable to achieve as great of a distance in the amount of time they choose. What if you have plans or want to get somewhere in a reasonable amount of time, and you feel like your speed is being dictated to you by means outside of your control? The impatience, frustration, and waiting that can accompany such a trip mirrors what high-ability learners can feel in environments that do not allow them to go the speed they are capable of achieving.

Of course, this is a flawed analogy in several ways. It would be an impractical and dangerous solution to allow a Ferrari to have a different speed limit than slower cars simply because it is designed to go at faster speeds, yet that is exactly what we should encourage for our students who catch on more quickly. Perhaps a better picture would not be of one car passing another but rather of different tracks, like trains, for students to diverge at different stations. Neither is passing the other or fighting for right of way but merely switching stations and tracks when necessary and traveling the same routes at other times. Just as it requires work on the part of the engineer to switch a train to a new track and to possess the know-how of where to go and when, the teacher can set a roadmap for students that looks and feels seamless while incorporating key ideas of differentiation. I have even seen this analogy used in a classroom via a large visual aid attached to the wall. A teacher turned her scope and sequence (or the plan of what she intended her students to learn and be able to do by the end of the unit) into a visual of a train's trip. At each train station was a key concept that she intended all of her students to learn. Between stations, small chunks of tracks were combined to go in all different directions. Each track had an assignment pinned to it with varying levels according to mastery and two or three per "trip" between stations. Some students were able to skip to other tracks based on demonstrated understanding, and others saw that even if they were "off on Track C" for the first trip, they may be with the rest of the class on Track A or B after the next station, due to pretesting scores. It helped students that there were more than two assignments. When students see every assignment split into two different versions, it doesn't take long for them to identify (even incorrectly) one as being for "the smart kids" and one for "the rest of the class." Because there was a flow of different levels, and their achievement on one determined whether they would get to try track A, B, or C on the next trip, students were less concerned with what their classmates were doing and more motivated to control which direction their own train took.

The problem with the single-assignment scenario is that it was too easy for the highest group of students. If they were able to complete it so quickly and left with that much time at the end, it is unlikely that they learned anything new or gave their brains an opportunity to stretch and problem solve. Give them more challenging assignments to begin with. A common fear is that a bright child will see this as a punishment: Why do I have to do harder work? However, it's important to realize two things. The first is that they see their other classmates struggle, solve problems, and learn at a much higher rate than they do on a daily basis. By taking away their opportunity to do so as well, they can become isolated, which is a far worse punishment. The second realization is this: After a child has completed an easy assignment, what are they then required to do?

Often, as we said, they are asked to finish other work, go on to the next section, or try a challenging assignment or puzzle. As admirable as an enrichment center or challenging extra assignments are, they are just that—*extra*. Additional work can contribute to bright children's feelings of being punished for their intelligence, which may lead to failure to put forth full effort into the base assignments that they are given. Though there are times when additional work can be appropriate for high-ability children—for example when the base assignment is a pretest to identify skill level or a required school examination—the extra work should be something that is motivating and individually fulfilling for the student. Interest projects designed for or even by the student are ideal fits for this.

Roadblock #2:

"How do I make an assignment more challenging in a meaningful way?"

As a gifted education specialist, some of the most common and daily questions I am asked by classroom teachers are these: "How do I make an assignment more challenging? How challenging is too challenging?" It can be a difficult question. It is common for a parent, for example, to ask for something more challenging for their child without being able to give a concrete example of what that might mean.

There are various solutions for teachers seeking to make changes in their classrooms. Existing assignments can be modified; challenges can be tiered in difficulty, as in the example of the teacher with the train stations graphic; or curriculum can be pretested and replaced with the next or deeper level. Additional options are: ability or achievement grouping within the classroom, cluster grouping, and presenting students with conceptually more difficult tasks. A fully differentiated classroom takes some additional planning time, but there are many wonderful resources for teachers to use to ensure that all students have access to learning that is effective and motivates them. One excellent resource that discusses these options in depth is Karen Rogers's *Re-Forming Gifted Education: How Parents and Teachers Can Match the Program to the Child*. In her book, Rogers describes enrichment of three types: (1) *exposure* beyond regular curriculum to skills and concepts not previously encountered; (2) *extension* of regular curriculum in a way that goes more broadly or deeply into the ideas explored; and (3) *concept development* from a concept introduced within the regular curriculum and exploring its meaning and implications fully. No matter which type a teacher may choose, the maxim is "HOTS not MOTS," incorporating *Higher Order Thinking Skills* (HOTS), not *More of the Same* (MOTS).[54]

A fully differentiated classroom uses a variety of grouping strategies, interest centers, mentorships, and other flexible options for all students, including those with high-ability. Tiered assignments, though extremely useful on their own, function best in a classroom that supports all children where they are. Keeping this in mind, let us look at one easy way to create a tiered assignment.

My general recommendation for teachers as they begin to explore options is to begin with simple ways to modify assignments until they discover what works for them. This "tiered" model, which is driven by students' readiness for a particular task, was developed by Carol Tomlinson, an expert in the field of differentiated instruction. She recommends that teachers know the "guts" of the lessons before attempting to create meaningfully tiered levels of them. The first step is to identify the concepts you want your students to understand, the skills they will learn by the end of the lesson, and then compare that to what you already know about your students. The second step is using pre-test or other pre-assessment information to identify student readiness. Next, teachers consider what interests, skill levels, and talents students could use to help them better understand the lesson. The final step is to create multiple tasks that a) each meet the learning objectives and goals and b) each provide different but still meaningful levels of challenge and support to reflect student readiness.

For the differentiation-timid teacher or parent, this final step is where the task can seem overwhelming. Where do you begin in creating these multiple tasks? What to change? What would be appropriate for your high-ability students? Start with a critical eye, and look at the assignment you want the students to complete. What are you asking them to learn and how complex is it? Are you requiring them to complete a page of long division problems? Are they being asked to create a reader's response to a text? Are they creating a science experiment to explain a concept that was just taught? For the knowledge of *what* can be altered, it can help to look at many different examples of differentiated materials and how they differ. The tool in Figure 2.1, a Tomlinson creation known as the "Equalizer" is a compilation of these examples, as well as a way to help teachers chart where an assignment exists on a continuum of simpler to more complex. It helps to imagine a sliding bar that you can place somewhere on the line between each pairing that shows where that assignment exists on the continuum between "concrete and abstract," or "clearly defined problems to fuzzy problems." Use the Equalizer to help you not only chart existing assignments that you want to alter but also to help you create them from scratch by figuring out *what* to alter. One teacher I know laminated a printout of the Equalizer and actually marks it with erasable markers to chart an assignment when she is either assessing an existing assignment or creating one of her own from scratch. The Equalizer strategy can be an incredibly useful tool for parents as well, who may see homework coming home that they feel does not approach their student's learning ability.

The Equalizer has a number of continuums, but an assignment need only be modified in one or two. It is not necessary for each assignment to be on the far right of every sliding bar, nor is it realistic to expect every assignment to be completely rewritten to make the most challenging option possible. Instead, focus on whichever scale seems most appropriate for that individual assignment and make modifications as necessary.

Here is an example of how to create tiered assignment from scratch. The subject is reading, and the entire class is reading the same chapter book. The objective of the lesson is for students to show an understanding of foreshadowing by identifying it in the book and making their own predictions about what will occur in the text based on that foreshadowing. The next step for a teacher, now that the objectives have been set, is to pre-assess student knowledge. This may be an informal or formal process of pre-testing or simply student interviews. Once the student groups have been identified and their readiness assessed, the teacher can now use the Equalizer to create leveled assignments. Look at a few of the "sliders" on the Equalizer to see how they can be used to make elements of the assignment more challenging.

- ✔ Slower to Quicker: Some students may be given more time to explore additional texts for more examples of foreshadowing, while other students are given less time and asked to use only the main text.

- ✔ Simple to Complex: Some students are given more books within the same genre and asked to make connections. Other students may be given additional texts in different genres and asked to discover and explain how foreshadowing differs and how it affects what kind of predictions they are able to make.

✔ More Structured to Less Structured: Some students are asked to mark their predictions in the book with Post-it notes, while other students may choose a creative way to show that they understand foreshadowing.

What follows are a few examples of how to differentiate existing assignments. Remember that regardless of whether or not the assignment is being created "from scratch" or an existing assignment is being altered to be more appropriate, teachers and parents alike should follow the first few steps of successful differentiation: Set objectives and pre-assess student readiness before proceeding. The next step in this process, however, is to use the Equalizer to help you identify how complex the assignment currently is. By identifying where the "sliders" are, you can chart which ones can be made more challenging.

Using the math worksheet example, you may have charted it as an assignment with fewer facets, as there are few parts or steps required in the completion of each problem. In the process of cloning the assignment along the continuum, you may give your high-ability students fewer problems that require more steps. They can even develop these multi-step problems for each other. A reader-response task may chart as "more structured" since students are required to answer a series of questions about the text. Sliding the challenge bar up to "more open" would include giving fewer directions for the student, less modeling on what they should respond to, and more student choice in responding to the text in a personal nature. You may find a science experiment that is "less independent," as it requires the teacher to establish resources, goal setting, and adult guidance. Giving your high-ability students the instructions to create and secure their own resources and develop their own criteria for success can open up the task to motivate the students to succeed while at the same time not sacrificing the students' valuable interaction with the teacher. Remember, sometimes an assignment can be made more challenging by sliding to the *left*. You can make a math problem more complex by making it *less abstract* and *more concrete*. Some ways to do this are to ask students to find a new way to solve the problem, to come up with their own formula or rule, or even to create a concrete, physical model to articulate or prove the math concept.

Figure 2.1. The Tomlinson Equalizer

Foundational _____ Transformational

Information, Ideas, Materials, Applications

Concrete _____ Abstract

Representations, Ideas, Applications, Materials

Simple _____ Complex

Resources, Research, Issues, Problems, Skills, Goals

Fewer Facets _____ Multi-Facets

Disciplinary Connections, Directions, Stages of Development

Smaller Leap _____ Greater Leap

Applications, Insight Transfer

More Structured _____ More Open

Solutions, Decisions, Approaches

Clearly Defined Problems _____ Fuzzy Problems

In Process, In Research, In Products

Less Independence _____ Greater Independence

Planning, Designing, Monitering

Slower _____ Quicker

Pace of Study, Pace of Thought

Figure 2.1. a) "The Equalizer" to chart the complexity of an activity. From: Tomlinson, C. A. (2001). *How to Differentiate Instruction in Mixed-Ability Classrooms.* (p. 47). Alexandria, VA: ASCD ©2001 by ASCD. Reprinted with Permission. Learn more about ASCD at www.ascd.org.

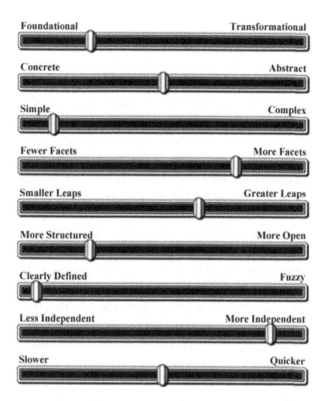

Figure 2.1. b) Here is an example of how sliders can be placed on the Equalizer for an assignment.

There are many excellent resources for teachers and parents about how to differentiate for high-ability children in the classroom. Often it is not the availability of resources that prevents teachers from implementing leveled challenges in the classroom but a lack of understanding of who should be assigned differentiated work, how to implement it, and under what circumstances these challenges can be appropriate.

Roadblock #3:
"If I give them more difficult work, they will miss concepts or have gaps in understanding."

Even after a teacher or parent agrees that having a student start with a more challenging assignment may be more appropriate, there is a fear of what the child might miss. Where do we start, and what do we risk when effectively skipping less challenging work?

If you are concerned that students will miss key concepts, the first and most valuable step is pretesting. Even for assignments that do not readily present themselves with a traditional pretest format, it is not difficult to discover what is important for the student to learn and whether or not the student has mastered the concept and is capable of moving forward. This can be achieved with something as simple as a mini student-teacher conference in which the teacher explains to the student the need to assess what is already known about the upcoming unit and asks a small set of questions. This often takes far less time than developing a paper-and-pencil pretest, and it may be more accurate.

Another strategy is to identify the "five hardest questions" in an assignment—or two, or three.[55] The most difficult, multi-step math question(s) on the page or the deep thinking science question(s) can require them to show that they understand the concepts discussed in a more step-by-step fashion in the rest of the assignment. If the student can accurately answer the hardest of the questions that the assignment asks, then it is reasonable to accept that the student has the ability to skip the rest of the assignment. One teacher I worked with, after introducing this strategy with her math students, complained that it was not working. When I asked what the problem was, she said that her students, excited to skip a whole math lesson, were taking their books home early and studying the night before so that they would be able to answer the hardest questions that she would ask the next day in class. My next question: Were they getting the five hardest correct? When she said they were, I laughed and explained that they were showing that they had learned the concepts. Her fear was that these students who would not naturally be receiving the harder work were obtaining it, but she needed to take a step back and realize that she had stumbled onto something wonderful. Her students were working hard—proactively—to earn the right to skip easy problems and move on to a more challenging assignment. She was concerned about cheating, yet she had to step back and realize that her students were cheating *up*. Regardless of how much work the students had to put in to achieve the goal of correctly answering the hardest questions, they had earned the right to move on.

Keeping communication open with a student is key to the survival of any acceleration or modification plan. When students sit down with you to check knowledge of an upcoming assignment or attempt such strategies as the "hardest problems first," they should understand that the purpose is to have them prove what they know and that you only want students working on something that is new for them. It seems an obvious explanation, but the truth is that most students do not give a great deal of thought as to *why* their teacher wants them to do something. Helping them understand this concept, in fact, making it a classroom rule that "all students work on something new for them," is also helpful toward creating a community of learning. When students understand *why* they are being asked to complete a certain level of work—whether it is an accelerated assignment or whole-class work—they are far less likely to feel like they are being punished. There is a "buy in" when students feel like they have been given the keys to the curriculum and understand why and how certain doors are unlocked.

Roadblock #4:

"My high-ability student isn't performing at a high enough standard to justify moving on. She makes many mistakes and rushes her work. When I do offer her something more challenging, she won't do it or doesn't do a good job."

Frequently, well-meaning teachers say that allowing a student like Terry, who is regularly underachieving, to move to another task or to try something more difficult seems inappropriate. No good teacher feels comfortable accelerating a student without data that support such a move. Even if the intuition is that the child can perform at a higher level, how does a teacher justify curriculum replacement or acceleration to a student who may have gaps in their learning? Truly, "the last thing any educator wants to do is to be responsible for educational decisions that are harmful to anyone."[56] This roadblock can also be rephrased as, "She can't prove what she knows how to do." This can be a very challenging roadblock, and data are imminently important for the purposes of advancement.

It is true that moving a child along the continuum without data to confirm a child's comfort with the lesson is ill-advised. Regardless of their ability level, students who have underachieved for a prolonged or consistent-enough period of time will have gaps in knowledge and understanding. It does a disservice to these students to accelerate them without (a) identifying these gaps and (b) addressing the underachievement before it becomes a lifelong habit.

Terry's teacher's main roadblock—and understandably so—was this data-driven hurdle. Although both Mrs. Gold and Terry's parents knew how bright she was and that she had often risen to the occasion in the past to showcase her intellectual ability, her work was routinely subpar. Also, when Terry had been offered opportunities to do something fun and enriching instead of the traditional curriculum, she declined or underachieved as well. One of the most challenging tasks for the adult in a bright child's life is to see through the child's camouflage accurately, and the most pervasive and sometimes most difficult camouflage to penetrate is underachievement. It is often caused, as in Terry's case, by something that occurs in the mind of most bright students that I call the *worth audit*, a behavior that we all possess to some extent but that high-ability children can become attached to in ways that can lead to underachievement. Understanding this phenomenon and re-educating children how to use it appropriately is the greatest tool against consistent underperformance a teacher or parent has.

Worth Audits

The concept of worth is familiar to the answer-seeking minds of bright children. They are often naturally inquisitive, as well as insightful, and make leaps in understanding that surprise the adults in their lives. This can heighten a greater sensitivity in many areas, including how they perceive the world around them: peer and adult relationships, how and why things work, and what they are doing in school and why. The same children who tie up their parents' minds with seemingly endless *why*isms at home do not suddenly put that curiosity to rest when they go to school. When faced with their daily schoolwork and assignments, the *whys* keep on coming, but the answers are often less available or satisfying than at home.

Generally, a bright child's classmates do not ask why they have been asked to complete an assignment; they accept that because it has been given to them by a teacher it is important or simply that they *should* do it without assessing its value or worth. Of course, there are exceptions, but by and large, most students unquestioningly accept that schoolwork is made to be done and that the teacher knows best. Where many very bright children differ is in the way that they perceive parts to whole—namely, individual assignments versus entire units or concepts within subjects in the curriculum. High-ability children approach curriculum and concepts holistically, with a perspective of where each part fits into a greater whole. They are often less linear than their classmates, which means that for any given assignment they need to feel like it fits into a larger, more connected puzzle. I think back to the bright sixth grader who protested when asked to choose a country in South America and build a three-dimensional map of it as a result of learning about different Spanish-speaking countries, arguing that they weren't learning about maps or art. He did not feel like the assignment connected to what they had just learned or bridged understanding to the next unit topic. Although he was a student who loved both art and maps, he refused to do the assignment until the very last minute. What bothered the student was not the idea of having to do a task he disliked, but one that he did not view as worthwhile.

Gifted and talented students become very frequent auditors of worth: "What is this assignment, why am I doing it, what does it mean to me and my life?" Sometimes, it even goes as deep as "What is the teacher saying about me by having me do this assignment?" Bright children of all ages can perform this audit, though the language evolves as the child's reasoning skills do. "This is no fun" or "I don't want to do this" in kindergarten and first grade becomes "Why do I have to do this?" in early elementary, and finally, to more detailed explanation like that of our reluctant cartographer's. Unfortunately, this can ultimately lead to an "I won't do this." That is when you find teachers and parents confused and frustrated by incomplete or rushed work of a child whom they know is capable of more.

All bright children audit worth. When they are not intrinsically motivated, high-ability students can decide that school has nothing of value for them.[57] That is not to say that they are always accurate in their assessments. In fact, the longer a child is in the habit of dismissing the worth of assignments, the more prone they are to undervaluing those options that could lead to growth, meaning students could be recognized for their abilities and given more appropriate tasks to complete and *still* underachieve. In fact, one of the most common frustrations of teachers is when parents tell them that their children are bored and require more challenging work. A very common response from the teachers of these students is that they have attempted that strategy already and that it produced the same quality of subpar work as the easier tasks.

It is no wonder that many classroom teachers have trouble subscribing to the just-give-them-more-challenging-work mantra. What they do not realize is that more challenging work *is* the answer, but they first have to teach their students to relearn how they audit the worth of assignments. Somewhere along the way, their students have weakened their ability to accurately assess what an assignment is and what it is worth due to a long history of enduring assignments that were far too easy for them. The Land of Challenge is not as difficult to get to as it is to recognize. Many of our bright students who underachieve and seek refuge in cheating behaviors (and even some of those who do not) are stuck on what you might call the "default reject button" in the worth-auditing process.

Let us return to the need to chart the complexity of an assignment so that it can be cloned along the continuum of challenge for a moment. Although this is a skill I want to model and support for classroom teachers, our cleverest students experience this charting every day, to some extent. True, the process is carried out in a less structured and sophisticated way than for teachers, who look for individual characteristics in an assignment and assess its difficulty. Students perform this audit without being able to explain what criteria they use, only that an assignment does not "feel right" to them, "is boring," or they "don't like it." Though a student's assessment of appropriate challenge is often correct in the early stages of school, their accuracy drops as they continue to go for this gut reaction and do not learn to use a critiquing eye when looking at what an assignment's purpose or worth might be. In my experience, the "reject button" effect is addictive. The more times a student feels that the work they are given in school is not right for them, the more likely their brain is to save them time by creating a default "this is a boring assignment" path of recognition in their memory banks. It becomes more and more difficult for any assignment not initially created by the student to "sneak by" this malfunctioning radar.

This helps explain another common baffled response from teachers who attempt to enrich their higher ability students through enrichment centers or leveled, challenging assignments that can be done *instead* of easier classwork. Format wise, these teachers are doing everything correctly: They have identified an enrichment need of a student and have eliminated easier work in lieu of a more challenging and appropriate assignment, yet their high-ability students reject them when given the option. This rejection can either be active—as in, I refuse to attempt that challenge—or passive—completing the work but at a subpar level. Not surprisingly, this often leads to a similar reaction from teachers after numerous attempts to challenge students have failed who say, "These leveled assignments/different reading groups/interest projects are not worthwhile. I will no longer offer these options to my students." In turn, they risk creating more students whose worth audits malfunction.

So how do we help break this cycle? Thankfully, the teacher aspect is relatively easy to address. Once we recognize what is occurring in the minds of our high-ability students, we only need to use what is available in our teacher toolbox to fix the broken audit button. The greatest tools at a teacher's disposal are the bright children themselves. You can teach high-ability students to help you with this process, and in doing so you strengthen their ability to worth audit what they do in school. The second most useful tool is the deep understanding that a teacher has about the curriculum that they teach. Once teachers can vocalize *why* a certain assignment is important, they are able to tackle the worth audits head on through a series of meetings with the student.

Student-teacher conferences have the potential of being endlessly valuable for bright students, because they simultaneously satisfy many different needs in an open and ongoing forum. These talented children should be given credit by educators for what they know, as well as an opportunity to express orally, rather than in written form, what may be a complicated thought process. Additionally, meeting with a student to discuss what is boring and what is not gives a teacher an opportunity to humanize a classroom, which is something that can make all the difference to students.[58]

I begin worth audit re-teaching meetings after I have identified an assignment that I want one of my higher ability students to complete. I come prepared with the reason the assignment fits that student, what knowledge or skills are needed to complete the task, and what he or she will be able to do with that knowledge—in other words, where the assignment leads. Then, I start the meeting with something that catches the student off guard: I apologize to them, as you will see in the example provided later. The highly able brain is absolutely attracted to novelty, as well as to information or things that seem mysterious and incongruous.[59] A teacher sitting a student down in a collaborative yet ultimately casual meeting that begins with an apology has always, in my experience, resulted in a confused yet "hooked" student. Clever children can fall into the belief that they know or can predict what is going to happen, and one of the best ways to attract their attention is to require them to process information they had not anticipated. After the apology, I invite them to forgive me by listening to my explanation and, in some cases, having them offer suggestions. The ultimate goal of the initial meeting(s) is to model correct worth auditing for a student.

Though this process of modeling may seem unnecessary, consider how seldom bright children would have had the opportunity to truly learn what is expected from them or why they are being asked to complete an assignment. It is very likely that a teacher has never sat with them and told them (a) that they have identified what kind of learner they are, (b) what they expect them to achieve as a high-ability student, and (c) why something is important. Why—or how—would bright children put the amount of effort that a teacher expects from them when they may possess neither a concept of what is expected nor the evidence that their hard work will be appreciated or rewarded? Though "do your best" is an often-quoted classroom motto, it means little to a high-ability child who has done his or her best in the past and has not had it recognized. If we ask our children to give us their best, we first have to re-teach some of them what that means, and we have to react appropriately to it with meaningful feedback. Too often, we get stuck on "you are very smart" and then end the conversation with our bright children on feedback that is less than helpful.

There is nothing wrong with being called smart, but it is better to focus on more concrete examples—the action versus the potential. E.g., "I've noticed that you understand things that I teach very quickly, and you write very expressively and with great detail." Encourage students to grow by sharing with them that you trust them. Be very precise with your language, however. I never tell a student, "You shouldn't have any problems with this at all," or "This is easy for you," not because they are not true, but because statements like these suggest that it is *good* for something to be too easy. Students should learn to wrestle with problems, have questions, and struggle towards a goal. In fact, I tell students this. I identify aloud what I know about them in concrete terms based on what they can do, and I do not lie because a clever child will be aware of this and it can fuel discontent with themselves and with you. Robert Marzano, in *What Works in Schools*, cites J. Hattie's comprehensive review of almost 8,000 studies, from which he concluded that the single most powerful change a teacher can make to improve the achievement of their students is to use feedback—consistent "dollops" of it.[60]

After I identify the capabilities I see in students based on their prior and current performances, I explain that I want them to try more difficult assignments by explaining *why*. "Right now the class is going to be working on putting details into their writing. I've noticed that you already have a good understanding of how to do this based on the last few stories you've written for me, so I don't think you have to complete the assignments on learning to expand this skill. I am going to have the rest of the class work on this. It will take about a week. Instead, I want you to try something that fits you better." If the assignment I give is more difficult, I tell them; I do not superficially say that they will "be fine" or "it's not too hard." Students respond more positively when they feel that you are being candid with them. It is helpful to explain that it might feel like a risk to take the harder assignment but that it will be more fun for them. If they get something wrong, it means they are learning, and the smartest kids are the ones who never stop learning.

If students fear that their grades are going to change with the more challenging work, there are two options. One, you can encourage them to go ahead because you know that their final product and its grade will validate their decision to take the risk. Your second option, if you believe their fear is holding them back from the amount of effort you wish to see from them, is to offer a "grade freeze" or grade replacement, such as was discussed in Martin's chapter. "Give" them the A that they have already earned based on proven mastery of the material and allow them to keep the grade as long as they try the riskier assignments. This solution may serve either temporarily or permanently, depending on the level of mastery a student has shown. It may seem counterintuitive, but even habitual underachievers can be prevented from trying their best when faced with the fear that they will try and *still fail*. Removing the fear of a grade can sometimes get a student back on the path of success. This can also function as a special note for your perfectionists. Deconstruct the language you use ahead of the meeting for those students. They need less modeling of what makes a "right" answer and more focus on growth and risks. Grade replacement may also be a good fit for them, as is putting the emphasis on constructive growth versus outcomes.

The final aspect of this conversation, if the assignment is one that is (a) open ended or (b) student-generated, is to tell the student what my expectations are for them. Many teachers skip this step because they want to see what the student is capable of rather than what they can mimic from the example an adult provided to them. However, you have to remember that these students may not just be out of practice from using their abilities to the fullest; they may have never actually had the opportunity to stretch that far. Some students, like Martin with his essay, will at least be excited and willing to get back on that train track towards success, and those are the students with whom you will only need to refine and validate their efforts as they gather speed. Other students, however, will be reluctant and produce work that is still subpar, much to a teacher's chagrin. Don't give up; continue to meet, model, and explain expectations in a way that emphasizes the level of work you expect. Continue to tie it in to what you believe they are capable of and reinforce that you trust them to take risks with both product and process.

Students may not produce quality work after the first go around. That is to be expected, and it does not mean the process is not working. Teacher conferences with gifted students can be brief, but they should be ongoing. Daily or every other day is best, but even meeting with students once a week to check on their progress and firmly but supportively point out areas for growth can cause the student to show exponential gains. Sometimes, students will frustrate a parent or teacher for weeks, only to suddenly "click on" again, as if they understand that you will not give up on them no matter how much they test you.

Below is a conversation that is modeled after the one that Mrs. Gold had with Terry. This meeting took place after the teacher had identified the underlying cause of Terry's cheating as boredom-driven. Note that nowhere in the meeting does it come across as a lecture. When a conversation begins with "Let me tell you why you need to do this assignment" or even phrased more gently, such as "I want to tell you why this assignment is important," it can fall on deaf ears. Just like "Cheating is bad" or "You did the wrong thing" can be absorbed by the justification that a student used to cheat in the first place, simply telling students that they have to do something because "it is important" can create an immediate internalized response of "I've already decided this assignment is not worth my time." The trick is to oppose this in the most direct of ways—by "letting the student in on the secret"—and in doing so, enlist their help and involvement.

> Mrs. Gold: *Terry, I called you over here to talk because I realized I forgot something important I wanted to tell you. I'm sorry. I gave you this assignment yesterday, and I meant to talk to you about it. Do you remember the "Challenge Club" game?*

Terry: *(Tentatively) Yes.*

Mrs. Gold: *I meant to tell you something important about that assignment. I noticed that when the class was doing Geography, you already knew where the states go on the map. First, let me check to see if I was right. How comfortable are you with where the 50 states are?*

Terry: *I can find all of them. I read a book on the U.S. in second grade, and I had my dad quiz me.*

Mrs. Gold: *That's what I thought, too. Thank you for telling me that. I try not to miss when a student shows me that they already know something, but it helps me to hear it right from them. How would you feel about having to fill out the practice maps with the rest of the class as they learn where the states are?*

Terry: *(Shrugs) I don't know.*

Mrs. Gold: *On a scale of one to five, one being "way too easy, give me something else," and five being "This assignment couldn't be more perfect for me. Never take it away!" what number would you give the practice maps?*

Terry: *One. The practice maps are boring, and they're too easy.*

Mrs. Gold: *That's why I wanted to talk to you about the new assignment. I picked out the Challenge Club for you. I was supposed to tell you why I thought it was a good fit and get your opinion, but it skipped my mind yesterday. What do you remember about the Challenge Club?*

Terry: *I didn't really look at it, yet. There was something on there about capitals. And there was a different map of the U.S.*

Mrs. Gold: *Those are two of five games you can pick to do when the class is doing their practice fill-in maps. Each game is worth a certain amount of points. The more challenging Geography games are worth more points. Memorizing the state capitals is worth fewer points, for example, than being able to learn how each state joined the Union and in what order. My favorite part is*

that when you want to do the more challenging puzzles, you are
rewarded with more points. The points tell you how important
the information is, as in how often you will be able to use it later.

Terry: *What do I get with points?*

Mrs. Gold: *That's up to you. You can choose more reading-time*
tokens, you can buy other enrichment games to play when you've
pretested out of a unit, or you can pick something from the class
rewards chart. But even better, in a way, is that you're learning
sixth- or seventh-grade material. Knowing which states were part
of the original colonies and how the others were fought for, won,
or bought is something that students need to learn in U.S. History
in seventh grade. And it makes the historical fiction novels you
like to read come alive, almost as if you're actually there. How
about you get your Challenge Club paper and look it over, and
we can talk about it and I'll answer any questions you have.

(After giving Terry time to look at the assignment again, they discuss
different parts of the task.)

Mrs. Gold: *Now that we've talked, let's go back to that number*
scale. One is "I've already learned it, take it away," and five is
"This is new. I'd love to try it!"

Terry: *I think this is a four.*

Mrs. Gold: *Much better than a one! Let's try this one then, and*
we'll talk again on Wednesday to see if you are ready to test
any of the challenges and see how it's going. What I expect from
you, based on what I know you to be capable of, is to eventually
complete the States' History Challenge and create some new
content for the challenge board based on what you've learned.
I'm excited to see what you come up with, and we'll talk again
on Wednesday.

These individual 'worth meetings' do not have to take a great deal
of time. In Terry's case, she met with Mrs. Gold or me for a brief period
of three to five minutes every other day for about a month, explaining the worth of assignments as they would come up that day. Special
focus was given to those assignments that we wanted to steer Terry

toward—namely, the enrichment or higher-level work that was closer to her actual ability level. However, traditional assignments that she routinely rushed through—such as her reader response journal—were also discussed during the meetings. The main focus was to help Terry identify why the assignment was important and why she needed to have that information in order to move on to something else. If it is difficult to express why the assignment is important, or if the student can show during the meeting that they already *have* that knowledge, take note: Replace the assignment with something more appropriate. As time progressed, the meetings shifted focus to have Terry explain to us why assignments were important. She then had the chance to choose her own learning opportunities and to justify them using what she had learned about worth. In two months, Terry went from a student who did not know what she should or could be learning to one who brought in what she had previously thought of as punishing, extra work and persuasively bargained to be able to complete it.

Strategies for Parents

What if you are a parent and you feel that your child is like Terry? The first step is to identify those assignments that you feel your child is underperforming on. Begin your own worth audit with a critical eye. What is the educational value of this assignment and what does it lead to? Does the homework represent the need to acquire a new skill through research or problem solving, or is it practice work that reflects the concepts covered in school that day? Recognize, before automatically lauding the former and reviling the latter, that each has its place in education. For anything to become easily retrievable or automatic knowledge, it must be practiced. We all understand the value in developing automatic recall for such things as math facts, reading fluency, order of operations, or rules of grammar, among other concepts. Our brains are developed to require practice, and some amount of practice work is encouraged for even high-ability students. Ideally, however, practice work should not make up the entirety of a child's take-home work, nor should it be just "busy-work."

The next step is to enlist the aid of your child's teacher. A simple "I feel like my child is underperforming in school and I would like your help re-teaching her so that she can see the worth in the higher level assignments that we want her working on," is entirely appropriate. Believe me, the teacher will be relieved and revitalized to hear that the cycle can be broken and that a possible root has been identified that both parties can work together to solve. Too often, the partnership between parents and teachers is strained as the stress of not knowing what else to do for an underperforming child builds, and it can inadvertently lead to both parties feeling blamed. Rather than feeling, "If you were only challenging Robbie more in school," or "If only you were not so hard on Robbie at home, he would be more successful," you work toward a common and exciting goal. What comes to mind is "the glory of glasses" story.

I have never met a teacher who does not have at least one story like this. In the many variations of this true story, a child who does not pay attention, complains of headaches, leaves class to go to the nurse, and makes frequent mistakes on homework assignments is eventually discovered to require glasses. Newly-bespectacled students who come back to school are like different children! They can see the board, so they write their homework assignments down correctly. Now that they see assignment instructions and can read the materials posted around the room, their attention and focus soar, leading to higher grades and less acting out. What is more, their headaches from constantly squinting are gone, as are their health-room frequent-flier miles. All that changed was how well they could see, but that one factor affected almost everything about their school performance. Telling a teacher that you found out another way your child has been having difficulty "seeing" the worth in their assignments and that you want to work together to fix the problem will often bring the same excitement that the addition of a pair of much-needed glasses can offer.

The final step is to meet with your child's teacher and discuss the areas in which the student is underperforming. This is a good time to ask questions about the homework assignments that you may have flagged and to ask how he or she would explain the worth of that assignment to the child. Although it is tempting to ask your child's teacher to immediately move the student to something more challenging, remember that without re-teaching how to worth audit, it is likely that the student's performance will suffer even on the more challenging task. The first focus should be to help the student prove what they can do. Only when that roadblock is cleared are students able to achieve at the level at which they are capable.

Ask your child's teacher for help in "resetting the reject button" on your child's worth audit, and offer the support from home to do the same. Give children concrete examples of why an assignment is important by discussing how and why they might be able to use that knowledge, or by showing them that even a simple concept can open doors that lead to more complex ones. Link information into a giant web and show how disciplines are interrelated through exciting projects and opportunities with professionals who can provide even more proof that simple or boring concepts may be important bridges to more meaningful careers. Extension work at home can be just as vital to the success of a child's long-term love of learning as the work given at school, if not more so.

Looking Ahead

Terry continued to explore extension and enrichment work both at home and at school for the remainder of the school year, and as her mood and outlook towards school improved incrementally, so did the level of her work. Terry, like most talented children, thrived in a hothouse of intellectual stimulation, and she came to school excited for the meetings that became a vital part of her day. She prepared for her meetings, looking at homework assignments overnight to assign worth and choosing new assignments she wanted to try that she believed were connected to what they were studying in school. Some of these works were procured for her by her parents, but others had been generated from her own imagination or research.

Halfway through the school year, Mrs. Gold reported that Terry had begun to assign point values to her tasks, even those that had not originally been assigned worth points, and she enjoyed charting them in a logbook that accompanied her to all of her meetings with Mrs. Gold or me. She was not caught cheating again during the school year, nor did she seem to express any interest in internalizing her frustration about rules and regulations she felt were punishing. Her crowning achievement was how she lobbied for the return of her Language Arts workbook. She initially brought the request up at a worth meeting, and she was met with some familiar roadblocks: "You did not complete it to the level I know you are capable," and "What will you do if you are not staying with the class assignments?" Then Terry came to the next meeting prepared with options and possible solutions. Together, they developed a learning contract that outlined stipulations for the level of thoroughness that was expected, as well as a veritable laundry list of alternate assignments and extensions for Terry to complete when and if she was ahead of the rest of the class. Many of these extensions were ones that Terry proposed herself and looked suspiciously similar to the extra work she would have rejected so handily as punishment months before. Without the stigma of boredom hanging over her and clouding her day, Terry could see enriching assignments for the opportunity that they were and not as punishments. Furthermore, she was growing the skills to learn to appropriately dissent when she did not agree with or understand why she was being asked to complete an assignment without internalizing or turning to cheating as a coping mechanism.

When you compare that self-reliant, problem-solving girl to whom she had been several months before—a girl with an "attitude problem" who had been convinced that her only reprieve from "brain-gnawing boredom" was to cheat on assignments to allow herself enough stimulation and challenge to survive in the classroom—it is remarkable to see the growth, but it is not surprising. This outcome is possible when parents, teachers, and bright students come together to form a team that seeks to identify the underlying causes of cheating and overcome common misconceptions and roadblocks to pull the roots of boredom before they have a chance to grow into the unsightly weed of consistent underachievement. The greatest resource for any teacher or parent who is experiencing a problem with a bright child *is* that child. Given the chance with proper modeling of expectations, a focus on constructive feedback, appropriate consequences, and a re-education on the concept of worth, every talented child has the opportunity to succeed without the crutch of dishonesty.

THREE

Amy

Amy was not one of the students I taught, but she was my first foray into the world of high-ability students and academic dishonesty. She and I were fourth-grade classmates. Amy had many friends—almost all of the fourth grade—and a fair number of students in fifth as well. There was much about Amy to like.

Amy was not a permanent fixture at our school. She moved away in the second week of fourth grade, a military brat who was well used to jumping from place to place. She had the easygoing manner of someone who had stared down the frightening eyes of change and realized that she could adapt to anything. She was a beautiful little girl—tall, quiet, with a big white smile and cute, colorful outfits. She was also an accomplished gymnast and a member of the school chorus. She held the record for fastest mile run by a girl for three months before a fifth grader broke it by three seconds. Amy was an only child, but her mother bred and raised Australian Shepherds, and I sometimes saw her walking a pack of five dogs when I biked through her neighborhood. She talked about them at school like they were her siblings, and she would bring her friends home to meet the new litters. She helped train the dogs and spoke like an adult when she talked about their care or how they were bred for different traits. Everyone knew that she was smart; kids always seem able to identify who the "smart ones" are, but generally she didn't speak much.

Amy and I shared both a traditional classroom teacher and a TAG group, that is Talented and Gifted, one of the many common names for enrichment programming that exist right now in the U.S. The program in our elementary school was typical of many enrichment programs both then and now in that it was underdeveloped and not supported by necessary resources such as trained staff, appropriate curriculum, or consistent identification procedures. Amy had been formally identified as gifted and talented in her previous school and then tracked into the TAG program at her new elementary. Once every other week, students who had tested as having a 130 IQ or higher left their classrooms to go to the TAG Resource Center, which was located in a back room in the library, where they worked on independent projects. The lack of direction from the well-meaning but ineffective staff member who oversaw the program was evident in the lack of enriching activities that had any connection to the traditional curriculum. To my recollection, the only thing that I ever remembered hearing from the teacher assigned to the room was her oft-repeated question: "Do you have something to work on?"

At that point, students had one of two responses: They either said yes, which meant they would begin working on their independent project, or they said no, which meant that they would be sent back to class until they had an interest project to work on and a plan for implementation. Needless to say, the projects students designed looked good on the surface but were gutted of substance or effort. Most were little more than busywork to ensure that the teacher did not send students back to class. To ask for help or feedback was akin in her mind to not being prepared. She never graded or commented on projects, and I never remember any TAG student—including myself—presenting what they had been working on. Most students worked alone and did not speak to the other students in the Resource Center for fear that they would be sent back to class for not working on their projects. It was a confusing place that told us that we needed to be isolated from our peers, but that we should not collaborate with one another or discuss *what* made us different, or how. Students were left to draw their own conclusions.

Looking back, I regret building a farce of a Viking ship scene out of Popsicle sticks and colorful pompom people when I could have been writing, or painting, or trying to learn how to play an instrument. I wish I had read the books on entomology I was obsessed with at that age, or drawn plans for the mini villages my sister and I used to build out of acorns and stones for the imaginary fairies that lived in our backyard. It never occurred to me to do those things because I was never told that those could be interest projects or that they would be accepted in school. Looking back, I can understand how students with potential can squander it if they are placed in something labeled an "enrichment opportunity" that does not celebrate or excite the idea of a challenge. We TAG students got the message that we were to look busy. If we had to work on our interest projects, we should do them quietly and independently and then take them home without celebration or critique. At the time, however, all I could see was that I was the bad kid who was breaking the rules, and out of fear and shame, I never told anyone that I was not working on anything important. I had not researched Vikings or drawn any plans for the "Good Ship Popsicle." There was no justification for the thing's existence, except getting and keeping me out of class. I assumed that I was the only one that was perpetrating this farce until I met Amy.

To this day, it is Amy, the shy, sweet little girl I knew in fourth grade, who is possibly the most brilliant cheater I have ever met. Though I have encountered many high-ability cheaters in my career and made a point to study their motives and their methods, Amy is the only one whom I saw from the perspective of a fellow classmate. Generally, when researchers study student cheating at any level, their most common method of gathering information is to ask the students themselves. Self-reporting, of course, carries its fair share of inaccuracies, and actually witnessing behaviors gathers far more precise data, but as we have seen, most students—particularly those with high abilities—are seldom caught in the act. Self-reporting is often the best tool we have to begin to identify the types of cheating that are occurring, how frequently they are used, and by what kinds of students.[61] I doubt Amy is actually the most prolific cheater I have ever encountered, but she does represent the only opportunity I have had to witness clever cheating on a daily basis, particularly before I possessed the judgment of an educator.

Amy was the only other TAG student I knew (besides myself) who cheated. At least, she was the only one to admit it to me. Amy did not cheat for herself; she cheated to help her friends, and it was only after she offered to help me learn those tricks in order to become more popular that I discovered them at all. Otherwise, I likely would have remained ignorant of the other cheating behaviors around me. I did not take Amy up on her offer; where Amy craved social interaction, I was afraid of it. But the offer did become the catalyst for a year of watching her, fascinated with her daily tricks and elaborate strategies to use her gifts, if not to be just like the students around her, then at least to secure herself a place in the social schema of our world.

Amy's Tricks of the Trade

Above all, the one thing that was important to know about Amy was that she was a champion note passer. Amy was so good at the subterfuge and creativity required to exchange notes without being caught that she even passed them for other people. Her signature move was the most simple in her retinue: the paper loaner. She would write a note on a perfectly flat piece of paper, and rather than folding it into a small square as most students do with clandestine notes, she would leave the paper in its original form. Then she would put it beneath a piece of blank paper and signal to me by tapping on her desk that it was time.

"Amy?" I would say softly, but not so quietly that the teacher couldn't hear me. "May I borrow a piece of paper?"

She would make the motions that she was rustling around, then hand me the faux loan with a smile. If I had something to write back to her, I would simply repeat the process and return the note, saying, "Thank you, but I did not need the extra. Here is your paper back." We were never caught with the paper loaner; it was too common for kids to share supplies, and as long as you were obvious about what you were (ostensibly) doing, the teacher never suspected chicanery. In fact, any time a friend failed to notice Amy's signal, she would turn to the person and prompt with, "Here's the paper you wanted to borrow," and even that would not arouse suspicion. Amy had identified the common procedures in the classroom, which was to note what teachers would pay attention to versus what was seen as commonplace. It is another example of talented students being able to assess their environment and identify its elements in respect to how they fit into a whole picture. Bright children can often be superb actors as a result of this keen awareness of their environments and the ability to mimic what is considered to be normal.

A variation of the paper loaner was the "pen roll." Amy would gut a click-top ballpoint pen by unscrewing the two pieces of the body and removing the spring and ink line from the interior. To make a pen roll note, she would write on a small square of paper and then roll it between her palms until she had twisted it into a long, thin stem, which she would then feed into the empty cavity of the pen. Once the pen was put back together, the same procedure as the paper loaner was followed: Amy would either give a signal or just hand the pen over with a suggestion that it was what her classmate wanted to borrow. The pen roll only worked for a short note, but I imagine that she did it more for the challenge than anything; sometimes a pen roll note would arrive and I would unfurl it only to see a smiley face with a tongue sticking out of it staring back at me. Above its head in an oblong bubble, she'd write something small, such as "Hi!"

A popular way for students to pass notes was (and still is, incidentally) "the drop." Rather than wait for a split second of teacher inattention to meet hands over the aisle, which risked the teacher seeing either the exchange or the quick hand pull away that marked guilt just as sure as a visible note, students would drop the note on the floor and kick it towards their friend's desk. It was fine in theory, but in practice the kick could send the note too far—or worse, not far enough—and leave it stranded out in the aisle, and everyone knows that aisle debris is akin to a homing beacon for a teacher's eyes. Amy had several improved variations of the drop, most of which included a hidden note (pen roll, tucked into a reading book, textbook, or simply folded and snapped into a pencil case), which was then dropped into the aisle. The trick was to not look like it had been done it on purpose. Amy would always manage to look impressively embarrassed, even apologizing if the sound had been particularly noticeable. The receiver of the note would offer to pick it up for her. The Good Samaritan would then retrieve the note subtly before handing back the dropped object with the natural dialogue: "Here you are, friend. Be sure to be more careful next time." "Oh, thank you. I will."

She experimented with stranger things: writing on the bottom of her shoe, writing notes big enough to see from far away, and, in one particularly bold venture, designing a location-based tapping message system that she abandoned when it became too difficult for people to follow. It was too obvious that other students were staring at Amy's desk, struggling to catch up with her quick code as she thumped on the four corners of her desk in rapid succession. Amy was, without question, Note-Passer Queen, but she saved her greatest creativity for her more dramatic—and traditional—cheating behaviors. They often overlapped.

When Amy cheated, she did so for the benefit of her friends and classmates. Although it is possible that she also cheated for the purpose of bettering her own grades, I neither saw Amy engage in cheating behaviors where she was the benefactor, nor heard her tell of any such occurrences. One of Amy's common moves was the "go ask teacher." Amy would go to the teacher's desk during a test to ask her a question, thereby distracting her while neighbors cheated from Amy's paper. The "go ask teacher" was also an opportunity for Amy's friends to have a quick, clandestine check of their notes or to look through their books for an answer.

Occasionally, Amy would directly correct a friend's work. In one iteration of this cheat, she would ask the teacher if she could retrieve her previously turned in paper, apologizing as she did so for not putting her name on it. Sometimes the teacher would rifle through the pile, but occasionally, she would allow Amy to go through the stack to find it herself. In those instances, Amy would pick the pile up, keep it facing her, and then pull out the friend's paper so that the name was not visible. Under the pretense of taking it back to her seat to write her name on it, she would quickly change a few incorrect multiple-choice items or true or false questions before returning the friend's paper to the middle of the pile.

The "pass your paper forward" was a much more common cheat for Amy. When students were instructed to send their papers to the front of their row, Amy would hold onto the ones that had arrived from behind her and quickly write in the correct answers to multiple-choice questions that had been left blank before sending them forward. I remember being amazed at how much work must have gone into fine-tuning the process of the "pass your paper forward" cheat. Consider the amount of challenge that even a simple cheating behavior such as this must have required. First, there was the need to complete her own test; accuracy must have been vital for Amy because she would need to be reasonably sure of the correct answers in order to help others. Then, she would need to assess which questions might be considered troublesome, as well as discover which friends were having trouble with which questions. Then, she had to plan which method she planned to use to help them, some of which required quick memorization. For example, true and false questions often come in clusters of 5-10. Amy would memorize the order so that she was able to fill in empty spaces for friends behind her during the "pass forward" cheat. Sometimes Amy still remembered short answer questions or patterns from tests weeks after they had been completed, so committed had she been to being able to quickly and efficiently helping her friends.

What made Amy so daring was that she hid her cheating, in a way, by *not* hiding it. She deciphered which behaviors and actions were accepted by teachers and classmates, and used that detailed observance of her environment to mimic what was considered normal and acceptable behavior: passing notes in the guise of sharing supplies, taking another student's paper out of a pile instead of your own, or just taking advantage of how normal it is for students to ask questions of a teacher or pass papers ahead. In order to manipulate her environment, Amy had to become an expert on its daily functions.

Amy's cheating became something that I learned to look out for. I would watch her superb acting skills, her effortless transitions between honesty and dishonesty, and wonder how I had ever needed her to tell me what was occurring; it happened every day, right under my nose. It taught me a valuable lesson about how attuned high-ability children can be to their environments that allows them to be so manipulative. Some students use their skills to become passive observers; others, chameleons; and some, like Amy, to engage in academic or personal dishonesty. Amy's shy exterior held a very proud and creative little girl who desperately wanted friends and for people to like her for what made her special. Without a medium to safely express her intellect and problem-solving abilities in a way that would be celebrated, Amy could not risk alienating others or causing them to feel threatened by her gifts. For another student, underachievement and refusal to acknowledge their abilities may have been their "answer," but for children like Amy, the fear of disappointing others makes underachieving unappealing. Some students cheat in order to disappear, but some cheat because they already feel invisible.

Invisible Girl

Imagine, for a moment, what life might be like if you woke up one day and were invisible, actually and truly invisible to everyone around you. What would you do? When asked, people inevitably choose forbidden things that they would never do—or be unable to do—in a world where others notice them. Common answers are often spying on others, stealing money or goods, playing pranks on others, and other things of that nature. It is difficult, in fact, to find someone who would not choose something taboo or downright illegal. Why do you think it is that no one chooses to use their invisibility to do good deeds? Putting aside the disappointing possibility that perhaps individuals are just looking for an opportunity to cheat without being caught, there are other reasons that may be more revealing. Perhaps using one's abilities for manipulative and dishonest purposes is a cry for help, a way to prove that they exist, or maybe it is that they would see their ill-gotten gains as compensation for not being able to be normal. The nature of being invisible does suggest that something—one's ability to fit in with others, for example—would be lost, or sacrificed, for this gift. But why cheat, steal, and lie?

Dishonesty is often born of desperation. If someone feels unable to be seen or to be perceived as the same as their peers, it may be easier to loosen the standards and morals that the "normal" group is held to. Stealing and playing pranks in an invisible state would be fun for a time, until individuals just wanted to be seen again. The invisible men or women would use their "power" to get something that others could not have, but that connection with people that they craved felt out of reach due to their ability, which they might even see as a disability due to its isolating qualities. Is there anyone who believes that being invisible would always be worthwhile and fun? How long do you think you would last before even the pranks you pulled could no longer make up for the fact that you felt alone?

Now, imagine I have told you that your intelligence seems to be invisible to those around you, since it is treated as if it is nonexistent or unimportant. Those around you do not talk about it; they do not use it or even seem to see it. You know you possess it, but it is unrecognized, uncelebrated, and difficult to use to its full potential. How would you take advantage of that gift? For Amy, no matter how much popularity she strived for, and ostensibly obtained, she was the Invisible Girl. Even if everyone who came into contact with Amy knew she was smart, it did not help matters if her talents were not also discussed or celebrated. As a result, they were underused and underdeveloped. In lieu of that, Amy used her invisibility to gain something she felt she would otherwise be unable to have—popularity. Cheating became something to use to gain friendship and recognition. Many extremely intelligent individuals, when they do not receive support and guidance, can feel emotionally isolated and very, very lonely.[62] When bright children are not supported and their intelligence goes unrecognized, their social and emotional development suffers.[63]

I wish I could tell you how Amy's story ended. She was never caught cheating to my knowledge, though a note or two were intercepted. A month into our fifth-grade school year, her family transferred away, and I never heard from her again. As an educator, however, Amy has remained alive to me in the students I meet who crave deep connection and social interaction with others. I am reminded of her altruism and friendship when I encounter others who use deception in order to benefit their peers. I thought of Amy when I encountered the two best friends from third grade who had to be in separate classes because they would otherwise turn in identical homework assignments. I was reminded of Amy when one of my fourth graders confided in me how much his friends had frustrated him. He told me that he *had* to teach them how to plagiarize because they had been trying to turn in work that had been lifted from easily searchable sites like Wikipedia. He wanted them to do a better job at plagiarizing so that they would not be caught; he saw it as his personal duty to help them cheat because he was their friend and he wanted them to continue liking him.

It is these students and others that tell us how much support and modeling are needed if altruistic cheating is to be prevented in our gifted youth. Amy deserved both a better outlet for her creativity and intelligence and the opportunity to be a part of a supportive group that encouraged her to be herself. By changing the social atmosphere that surrounds our bright children to one that is inclusive of all talents and gifts, as well as de-emphasizing competition and ranking among students both in and outside of the regular classroom, we can help prevent students from expressing their raw talent in destructive ways.

Altruistic Cheating

Altruistic cheating is a form of dishonesty or cheating in which the intended benefactor of the deception is not the person originally engaged in the behavior. Amy did not cheat in order to elevate or misrepresent her own scores but to aid other students in the class by falsely enhancing their grades. All people, not just high-ability children, are susceptible to this very social form of dishonesty. Dan Ariely, a leading expert on behavioral economics, has led numerous studies that show that individuals are more dishonest when others can benefit from cheating—even if those individuals had never been introduced before the opportunity to be dishonest arose.[64] Even complete strangers can benefit from this form of social utility, the very human quality of having empathy towards others that leads us to help where and when we can. When a clear opportunity to cheat presented itself in a circumstance in which another individual would benefit from their dishonesty, participants in Ariely's studies overwhelmingly engaged in this kind of altruistic cheating, even at potential risk to themselves. Not only are bright children not immune to altruistic cheating; they may be even more susceptible to it.

Later on, in Chapter 6, we will discuss how emotional intensities, which are often endemic to high-ability children, can result in a deep need for these students to connect with others on an emotional level.

This keen awareness of others' emotions can result in a sensitive child who prioritizes the needs of those around them. This habit of taking on others' struggles at their own expense is something that emerges out of a deep need for friendship, even if it means that one sacrifices his or her own needs.[65] High-ability children, when presented with the opportunity to engage in academic dishonesty in which a peer would benefit, would likely be doubly tempted—first, by the nature of their empathy, and second, out of their deep desire to connect with others.

Altruistic cheating is as dangerous as it is ubiquitous. It may also be one of the most socially acceptable forms of cheating, at the very least from the perspective of those who practice it. When the gain to be had from cheating is not borne by the students themselves but by a friend (or, according to Ariely's research, even a stranger), it is easier to feel that the behavior is justifiable, even noble. It is easier to rationalize cheating behaviors when they are seen as purely altruistic. The greater the ability to rationalize or justify one's behavior, the lower inhibitions are when engaging in the personal choice of cheating. In fact, higher levels of justification lead to lowered inhibitions whenever a new opportunity to cheat for others presents itself.[66] To some extent, this feeling of a noble cause is reminiscent of the well-known tale of a merry band of thieves who stole from the rich and gave to the poor. In this socialized "Robin Hood Effect," crimes committed do not prevent others from seeing the dishonest person as a hero because the crime was altruistic in nature. In Amy's case however, the question is this: Who was really being robbed? Though the students may have believed it was the teacher or the system, the truth is that students who cheat for their friends not only rob themselves but their beneficiaries as well.

Amy's classmates didn't learn from her clandestine notes (even when they held test answers or instructions to help them through the next assignment). Their inflated test grades were false indicators of any knowledge that had been gained. If anything, Amy did her classmates a disservice, for the grades they were presenting to their teacher were false indicators of their understanding of the subjects that were being assessed. Those inflated grades served as false positives that prevented teachers and parents from spotting the gaps in their knowledge that Amy's cheats seemed to smooth over.

For authentic altruism to take place, the beneficiaries must actually gain something from the action or interaction. Keeping this in mind, a teacher might think that a better strategy for an altruistic individual like Amy would have been to encourage her to tutor students prior to the exams, but I caution teachers from utilizing this strategy. Teachers often use their brightest students as tutors for their classmates without realizing that it can define the relationships that the students have with one another. It is true that some talented students are uniquely talented and willing to work with their classmates, playing the role of educator in the teacher-student relationship; however, students also can become alienated from possible friendships if peers find relating to them difficult. It can be threatening for students to feel like their weaknesses are being highlighted by peers who not only have no shared gaps but also have enough ability to teach the concept.

Using high-ability children as teaching resources is not supported by research. Studies suggest that it is a poor choice to pair clever students with struggling peers with the intention of increasing the latter's achievement. Although students paired with the higher-ability children often work at a significantly quicker pace and are able to produce more work, they do not show marked increase in achievement. In addition, the social self-concept of a high-ability student's "pupil" or teammate can often decline after working cooperatively with them.[67] This may be due to the fact that it is far more difficult for individuals to build positive relationships where a power differential exists. Though I meet many parents of very bright students who are afraid that their children may be ridiculed by peers who are jealous or immature, it is more often the problem that many age mates of bright children do not seek out deep friendships with them because it is difficult to relate to or understand the discrepancies in ability levels. Teachers and parents can help by avoiding power differentials in student placement and by strengthening and celebrating all students' talents.

Social Cheating

A case could be made that Amy did benefit (or at least sought to benefit) from her cheating behaviors by acquiring and maintaining friendships, which brings into question the nature of how altruistic *any* cheating can be. In many cases that involve altruism-based cheating, a possible personal motive might explain the cheating behavior, even one as simple as the pleasure the student derived from feeling useful. It is easy to get lost in the nature of altruism.

Some people suggest, however, that all altruism is false; that all individuals require a personally beneficial motive to act, even if they are not aware of it. I have no doubt my students and I could debate this fascinating philosophical issue for days and not come up with a clear answer, so let us assume that if there *is* a motive for why one student would cheat for another individual and that it is not purely altruistic, then the motive logically has something to do with the nature of the relationship he or she would like to have with that person. In Amy's case, it could be said that she was both avoiding a negative relationship with her peers (in regard to how she perceived they would treat her intelligence) and seeking positive relationships by proving how useful her talents were to others. In this way, altruistic cheating could simply be known as "social cheating."

Working to fit in, some high-ability students engage in social cheating by mimicking behavior patterns and assimilating to the attitudes about work that peers follow. This is especially true of the most socially adept bright students—the leaders who know how to make friends and be cool with a crowd. Their friends may know that they are bright, but the true range of their abilities is not displayed beyond a sort of "safe zone." Some high-ability students, in fact, face the issue of acquiescing, which is to say that they attempt to conform to the norm of classroom and social behaviors, as well as levels of achievement.[68] Though many bright children have experienced some manner of attempting to "normalize" themselves, the greater the gifts, the more difficult it becomes to downplay their potential enough to avoid being recognized or singled out from their peer group. Some, like Amy, are "outed" by being identified for special services or grouping strategies, or simply by the extent of their ability in compared to their classmates. There are so many aspects of intellect and ability that are visible throughout a child's day. The amount of willpower and, yes, intelligence, required to keep such a big secret can be exhausting. The price of keeping up the façade is sometimes a very high one, and students can conform to social pressures, such as playing into the desire to be liked.

Though high-ability children commonly share many traits and strengths, it is important to remember that every bright child is a separate and unique individual. Two puzzling, opposing stereotypes exist about how sociable gifted children are as a whole. In other words, it seems just as common to have a teacher or parent describe the typical gifted child as being well liked and well adjusted as it is to find an individual who describes gifted children as shy, introverted loners. In addition, though some literature suggests that gifted children are actually *more* likely to be well adjusted and popular than their non-gifted peers, there are as many texts that point out the unique social difficulties and isolation often experienced by this population.[69] Neither is universally true.

Though there will always be bright children on both ends of the social spectrum, the truth is that most are often a combination of these two extremes. As well-liked and admired as Amy was, she was still terrified of being singled out in a negative way for being smart, and that it would preclude her from having friends. For many smart children like Amy, being smart is far from a guaranteed prescription from isolation. If anything, their heightened perception can lead to a greater understanding of the differences between them and their friends. At an age where any variance from the majority can lead to a fear of being rejected by one's peers, many bright children struggle with the issue of conformity.

Challenges with the Gifted Identity

Peer influences and expectations of dominant social groups begin to affect student interaction most during the preadolescent period, often fourth and fifth grades. During this time of conformity tug-of-war, gifted students particularly begin to recognize and describe their feelings of not belonging.[70] When popularity depends on conforming to a dominant group's norms and tastes, gifted students are often, by nature of their divergence, excluded. Loneliness and alienation can be strong forces on a young, gifted child's decision-making process. From their first words, motor skills, and behaviors, children begin learning as infants by observing patterns and gradually assimilating them. Assimilation is the foundation of learning for all children; they are naturally predisposed to learn by adapting and mimicking cues from others. As natural as this process of observation and assimilation is, without intellectual peer groups and appropriate role models, gifted children are susceptible to a type of assimilating that may require them to adjust or regulate their talents and gifts to fit into *normal* patterns.[71]

The gifted identity can be a difficult one for students to relate with positively, particularly if they fear it distinguishes them from their peer group. Even if they do not highlight or identify their own differences, peers often remind them. How many times has a gifted child heard, "You're smart. Do this math problem. Spell this word. Show me how to do this"? It is an intimidating moment for gifted students to simultaneously be identified with and challenged to live up to that persona, and it can happen on a daily basis. The process of identifying how to fit in with a peer group is one of the more challenging aspects of gifted children's development, and it can largely depend on what kind of connection they have to others.[72] This is particularly true of gifted girls, who may be more susceptible to choosing their relationships with others over their own personal growth.[73]

In one recent study, researchers noted that gifted girls tended to perceive their self-regulating behaviors as simply being a good friend rather than seeing them as compromising their intelligence or identities. The students who regulated their giftedness by not "performing" around their friends or not sharing their accomplishments with others did not feel that they were doing anything negative. They explained that by being intelligent and getting good grades while not advertising or "showing off" to others, they were able to maintain friendships and a sense of balance.[74] Although there is a valid argument to be made that gifted children who isolate peers with show-off behaviors may also deprive themselves of meaningful social development, the greater danger is in downplaying gifts and regulating their abilities instead of developing their own potential.[75] In Amy's case, her abilities were adjusted and regulated—not by force, but by direction. In other words, Amy did not dampen or falsely portray her abilities, but she did use them primarily in the service of others rather than herself, hoping to validate her intelligence in a way that kept her safe from ridicule as being a teacher's pet or a show off. Even so, one could say that fundamentally, such bright children are lying, manipulating, and cheating.

There is an irony to Amy's avoidance of showing off in this manner, as of course her cheating behaviors were quite dramatic. Stealing another student's test directly in front of a teacher was an extremely impressive display; it more than showcased her capabilities to her knowing classmates. However, the very nature of what it was—a dishonest act and a very punishable offense for *both* parties—was enough to keep students quiet and in awe about Amy's capabilities. Amy feared that her identity as "Tutor Amy" may have been ridiculed or avoided, but she felt validated that "Cheater Amy" had been accepted by her peers by cheating on their behalf.

Addressing Social Cheating

Social cheating is often the most difficult to identify, namely because the students who engage in it are doing so in order to fit in or to help others. Consider how difficult it is to identify high-ability children cheating in normal circumstances and add the complication of the traditional profile of a social cheater; often, they are some of the sweetest, most likable students in the classroom. Picture the student who is afraid to have anyone dislike him or her, the social, empathetic friend. The student may have the moniker of teacher's pet.

It is particularly difficult to deal with cheating for social reasons in ways that focus appropriately on underlying causes of dishonest behavior. As discussed, the most effective way to address cheating is not to focus primarily on a punitive response but to aim for prevention by addressing the underlying cause of dishonesty. For example, students who cheat because they are bored may need their stimulation increased appropriately. When they cheat as an outlet for their emotions, it is important to address and explore their feelings and situations. When their cheating is an avoidance strategy, counseling to demystify or lessen the fear of what they are avoiding does wonders. But when a child cheats in order to have friends… What to do? We cannot give our children friends or popularity, as much as we might wish these things for them.

The most appropriate way to address and prevent social cheating, then, is to ensure that the social and emotional environment of a bright child is as inclusive as possible. A nurturing, inclusive environment for highly able children is one in which flexible grouping strategies and positive outlets for creativity are prioritized and where risk-taking and community celebrations of gifts are emphasized. In addition, adults can learn how to start the conversation with students about their note passing and cheating behaviors. Social cheaters are not likely to out themselves, particularly to adults, as the outcome that they seek cannot be obtained from anyone other than their peers. We cannot rely solely on self-reporting of social cheating behaviors, nor can we be confident that parents and educators will be able to identify the social cheaters in their care. We can, however, learn how to start the conversation with students and how to encourage students to share their cheating behaviors through a gateway discussion, for example about the social activity of note passing. Positive and open communication with bright students is key to creating an environment in which they feel safe and validated, and the most productive way to ensure that social cheating does not occur is to create an atmosphere that is as inclusive as possible of the social and emotional needs of high-ability children. The social and emotional components of gifted education are as important as their academics; in particular, addressing these sensitive topics can help them feel secure and valuable enough in their environment that the lure of social cheating loses its appeal.

The Problem with "Patch-On" Enrichment Services

Underdeveloped enrichment programs that do not adequately serve the social, emotional, and academic needs of high-ability students have a potential smokescreen effect. They can give the illusion that the students are more enriched than they actually are, which can lead teachers or parents to fail to provide mentors, intellectual peers, and meaningful activities that could serve as creative outlets. Though Amy went to the TAG resource room every other week, she was not provided with any modeling of what she could be learning or creating, nor was her work monitored, her learning encouraged, or her products celebrated. While I faux-toiled away at the Good Ship Popsicle, Amy drew pictures of her Australian Shepherds and told the teacher that she planned to turn them into a how-to book about their care and breeding. Not surprisingly, that book never materialized.

The kind of "patch-on" programming that Amy and I experienced is an unfortunately common way that school districts seek to solve the gifted education "problem." By creating and identifying a service model, however inadequate to the academic and social needs of their high-ability population, school districts can be comforted that they have served the needs of all of their students, regardless of the program's effectiveness or how it aligns to the general curriculum. Not only is the overall infrastructure of these programs often weak, but the programs continue to fuel charges that enrichment programs are elitist and overly specialized.[76] Some schools err on the side of less intervention versus more, out of a fear that their gifted and talented services will be seen as elitist, their highest ability kids singled out for jealousy or teasing, or that the community will not support a program that does not benefit all students. Unfortunately, this often strengthens the illusion that enrichment programs for high-ability students are limited and overly restrictive.

Although Amy's school appeared to offer more enrichment services than most in that it sought to identify and serve high-ability students, the program did nothing to address her academic or social and emotional needs. What the token TAG program taught her was that she had to be labeled and separated from her peers by being taken out of the class every other week. In my experience, no one other than the few TAG students themselves knew what happened (or didn't happen) in the Resource Center, which meant that the opportunity to connect what was happening in the classroom with enrichment challenges and vice versa was lost. Classroom teachers never asked about TAG time, and it was not unheard of for students who had never visited the small Resource Center to tease those who did attend for "living in the nerd closet." The culture was not one that celebrated the talents of all students, and classroom enrichment and pull-out enrichment were not connected. This possibly came out of an administrative fear that, by highlighting the fact that some students were different, it would acknowledge that students had unique learning needs that would need to be served. The opportunities that come from serving those needs can lead to fears that elitism and inequality will arise.

In the end, the TAG program was much less effective as a true means of support for the students who were pulled from class. By not developing the program to the extent that it could have meaningful connections with the classroom, the administration unfortunately stranded these invisible kids in a situation where classmates were unaware of why certain students were isolated over others. Students like Amy, who took the social component of her school environment very seriously, then sought to find ways to prevent themselves from seeming like outsiders. For Amy, this included joining every team or activity that would have her and cheating for her classmates on a regular basis.

It is not only the relationship between gifted children and their average-ability classmates that can suffer when students' enrichment programming requires them to attend a patch-on program that does not align with what is being taught in the classroom; the relationship between highly able children and their teachers can also deteriorate. When specialized program personnel in schools ostensibly serve the gifted children, classroom teachers (who may already feel inadequate in their knowledge of gifted education) may see those students as adequately taken care of by the program and that can lead the classroom teachers to feel even more ill-prepared to provide consistent and appropriate challenges to their high-ability students. When communications between an enrichment program and the rest of the child's school experience suffer, the overall consistency of service and outcomes for the student are seldom met.

Enrichment services should be a continuum of services that encourage talent and support growth for all learners, rather than singular programs that seek to exclude or isolate a select few from their classrooms without meaningful supplementation of their core curriculum.[77] Additionally, the use of flexible and appropriate ability grouping of high-ability children wherever possible can extend the speed or depth at which they are able to tackle the curriculum. Resource rooms can still be extremely valuable places for peer collaboration when they function as a place where students can go to connect with like peers as well as receive adult guidance when working on independent projects. Resource rooms should not, however, function as a patch to cover a gap where effective grouping strategies have been absent.

Grouping Strategies

Traditionally, students are grouped by age into grade levels and sorted into classrooms in a process that seeks an equal distribution of demographics across the board. Depending on the district, class sorting is done either by administrators, classroom teachers, or a combination of both, but the process is often the same. Deborah Ruf, an expert on grouping and services for highly gifted children, likens the usual process to a card game wherein the highest ability students are "dealt from the top" and separated into different classrooms to ensure that each teacher has an approximately equal number of high-, middle-, and low-ability learners to create a sense of balance.[78] Unfortunately, this not only poses difficulties for the teachers, who now have widely heterogeneous groups whose wide-ranging needs they will have to address, but also for many bright students who find themselves stranded without academic peers with whom to identify. Age sorting alone does not accomplish this since age-mates may not actually serve as peers for high-ability children in regard to many of their needs. However, if students are exposed to a variety of individuals and groups with whom they can identify or share interests or abilities, they are then able to develop good self-concepts and become more tolerant of others' differences.[79] After school age, it is completely normal for individuals to identify with and spend more time with others who are dissimilar in age, yet many call for grouping based on more than age in school-aged children, particularly when it involves grouping by ability.

Ability grouping has gotten a bad reputation in the past few decades in America. Ability grouping is sometimes mistaken for, or used synonymously with, tracking, wherein learners are labeled as above average, average, or below average, and accordingly attend classes only with those students who have been identified as having the same overall achievement level.[80] Arguments against tracking have included fears over students being incorrectly identified or pigeonholed as one kind of learner, the limits of a tracking system to identify and develop talents, and possible segregation based on culture or socioeconomic status. The apprehensions surrounding this all-or-nothing approach are understandable, and the call for a more child-centric approach that recognizes that the needs of an individual may call for multiple groupings, whether in a tracked group or within a heterogeneous classroom.

Ability grouping differs from tracking in its flexibility. Ability grouping emphasizes that students are able to move between various groups according to academic and social needs. Where tracking calls for an overarching judgment about students' anticipated performance, which can be extremely difficult to accurately gauge, ability grouping responds to what they are currently able to do and begins instruction at their level. When students are able to be grouped and regrouped according to their individual educational profiles and needs, they are more successful.[81] For example, rather than identifying talented students as belonging in the tracked "college-bound" group and allowing them access to the most rigorous curriculum at all levels, they may be grouped with other high-ability math learners in one setting, allowed to work on an interest project with (different) students who have similar interests, and then involved in a pull-out group that connects quick readers from multiple classes to work on a literature circle or book project.

Very bright children often have a variety of peers based on their abilities and interests and may have different groups that are composed of various ages and abilities for their math ability, reading interests, musical aptitude, etc. When students are ability grouped for enrichment, they experience substantial academic gains not only in general achievement but also creative and critical thinking as well.[82] Although all students who are schooled in homogeneous groupings according to ability appear to experience positive effects to achievement levels, bright children, particularly minority youth, experience even stronger positive effects.[83] By allowing all students to flow through a variety of need groups, rather than being singularly tracked or identified, not only are they afforded a broader spectrum of challenge and social and academic groups, but many of the issues of fairness and arguments of elitism are alleviated. Note, however, that a sensitivity to open communication between all parties—students, teachers, parents, and community members—is vital if the purpose of the program is to be understood and celebrated as something that can help all students experience higher achievement.[84] Schools should stress with teachers and parents that students should not be viewed through a lens of gifted or non-gifted for the purpose of labeling and separating them into groups. Instead, students should be seen for their individual collection of abilities in various areas which can be strengthened and capitalized. No student is universally strong in every subject or undertaking, and ability grouping can help identify and compensate for weaknesses in even the most able student.[85]

Whenever possible, students should be grouped with academic peers in the classrooms that they spend the most time in. Bright students should have the opportunity to regularly interact with not only their peers of like age but also intellectual peers; parents and teachers should recognize that these may not represent the same age group.[86] When bright students are exposed to other academic and intellectual students, particularly those with similar ability levels and interests, it is far more likely that students will identify with that social group rather than engaging in social cheating where they acquiesce or regulate their gifts to fit into another peer group. To this end, the most ideal form of grouping is a full-time enrichment or gifted program. This may include a specialized magnet school, gifted classrooms, or even a fully utilized Schoolwide Enrichment Model or School-Within-a-School type program.[87] In the absence of these options, however, the recommendation is to offer specific grouping and instruction to talented children according to individual strengths and knowledge, either within or across grade levels.

The beauty of grouping bright children by ability is that there are a variety of different grouping methods that are appropriate and no one size fits all. What might work for one school district in resources and scheduling may be unmanageable for another. There are many ways to serve students through flexible grouping, and few additional resources are needed beyond careful scheduling, flexibility, and a desire to work with talented children at their level. Often, a combination of strategies is used. It may take some time to find what works best for your students, but a sample of support options are available in this chapter. Above all, take to heart the words of Deborah Ruf:

> *Everything that a gifted child needs is available somewhere in the typical school system. If a school can be flexible enough to allow a child to go to another teacher, building, or group of other learners who are ready to learn at his or her same level and pace, the child's needs can be met.*[88]

Within-Class Grouping

Clustering students based on ability within their traditional classroom is the most commonly used grouping tool since it requires little additional resources. It is rare that achievement-based grouping is used for a full school day. Typically, students remain mainstreamed in the traditional classroom until they are grouped based on their instructional level for a core content area, for a specific lesson, or for a collaborative learning opportunity. Within-class grouping is commonly used for literature circles, curriculum compacting, and learning centers, but it can be expanded to include students who group together for an entire subject or topic, either to compact, accelerate, or enrich the existing curriculum. Grouping students by ability is not recommended if students are working on the same material at the same speed or complexity as that of their classmates. Ideally, when students move into ability groups in a classroom setting, the work should be differentiated for each group to reflect appropriate learning, either through variations of process or product. Note again that flexibility is key. Bright students may not always fall into the highest group depending on their ability to master new concepts in that particular subject, and that is okay. Grouping should remain fluid, allowing students to move up or down depending on how needs evolve. Teachers should be wary of allowing groups to become rigid because it can lead to students labeling or ranking one another based on ability level.

Within-class grouping can be especially beneficial if tutors, para-professionals, aides, or outside mentors such as community members or parent volunteers are available to work with individual groups. In this way, within-class grouping can take on many of the benefits of a full-time gifted class in that students are not always tasked to work independently.

Across-Grade Grouping

Across-grade grouping is very similar to the process of students being grouped with like-ability peers in their own classrooms, except that students are grouped with students from other classrooms. Students who are intellectual peers may be composed of a single grade level or exist in a cross-grade group. One challenge with grouping students with intellectual peers can be finding appropriate partnerships in a smaller sampling of students such as their homeroom classroom; the differences between a high-ability student and a gifted student—or a moderately gifted student and an exceptionally gifted one—can be profound. Unless careful planning went into the original class lists, giving consideration to creating appropriate ability groups, it is rare to find students of equal ability with only one classroom's worth of students from which to pull. It is often the case that a wider net must be cast to find appropriate peer groups.

Again, flexibility should ensure that students are able to move into and out of not only groups but physical locations as well. Students in one grade who are in need of enrichment in a particular subject area can be grouped together under one teacher's care to access their differentiated curriculum during a particular block of time (daily or weekly). Similar to within-class groupings, outside mentors and volunteers can be pivotal in providing children with feedback support between check-in meetings with their teachers.

Pull-Out Enrichment Grouping

Students who are grouped for a pullout enrichment program are removed from class anywhere from 2-4 times a week, on average, for short blocks of time to work on extension or independent work. On the surface, the TAG program that Amy and I attended was a pullout program model; however, the work that went on in the group was anything but research supported or well managed. Used alone as the sole grouping strategy for bright children, pullout enrichment represents one of the least effective way to appropriately challenge students or to increase overall achievement.[89]

The most effective way to use a program such as an enrichment resource room is to use it as an opportunity for a mentor or teacher to supplement the work that students are doing in the classroom. One option is to ensure that the material covered is in direct extension or replacement of the curriculum that would have been covered during that time in the classroom. The other is to cover material that represents hands-on learning and experiential tasks (such as simulations or skill building) that develop specific talents. Pull-out time can also serve to introduce different career paths or experiences, often through speakers or mini-workshops. Many excellent school enrichment programs, such as the Schoolwide Enrichment Model or the Parallel Curriculum Model, often include pull-out classes or workshops as a component of their overall program.

Acceleration

Acceleration is the act of advancing a student to a higher level based on academic readiness or appropriateness. A student may be accelerated a whole grade (i.e., grade skipping) or transitioned into another grade level for either single or multiple subjects. Another form of acceleration is a multi-age classroom, in which students are grouped by achievement level in subject, rather than grade or age, or they are regrouped by achievement for different subjects. Acceleration achieves what other groupings can sometimes fail to achieve: providing qualitatively *different* work as opposed to additional work. When students are accelerated to more advanced content, it is often a better fit for their abilities.

When acceleration is an option, it is often the most effective one—according to some studies, the *most* effective.[90] Accelerated children outperform non-accelerated children substantially—in academics by nearly one year on a grade-equivalent scale. In addition, students who are accelerated, either by specific subject or by whole grade, have been shown to benefit not only academically but socially as well. It is a misconception that bright children suffer socially when they are accelerated. Social problems actually often improve after acceleration, and existing problems rarely worsen. For more information about accelerating students, refer to *A Nation Deceived: How Schools Hold Back America's Brightest Students*, by Nicholas Colangelo and *The Iowa Acceleration Scale*, published by Great Potential Press, to determine whether or not a student is a good candidate for full grade acceleration, single-subject acceleration, or other mentoring or grouping options.[91]

Even when the most effective grouping strategies are not available for high-ability children due to the policies of individual school districts, some level of academic peer grouping can be always be accomplished. Depending on the available resources, this could be through pull-out enrichment programs, in class (or inter-classroom) groups that are based on ability or interests, or even student run clubs that allow them to explore common interests during or after school. The intention is to allow these students the opportunities to be exposed to multiple groups, not only to match their ability levels and offer them intellectual peers but also to make multiple social and intellectual opportunities available to them. Very bright children have unique social and emotional issues that are not found in their age-mate peers, something that is often noted by parents and teachers who work with them.[92] When high-ability children are mainstreamed for their entire day and only grouped with age-peers, they may feel very different from the main social group, which can cause feelings of isolation.

As we have seen, the act of trying to fit in can lead gifted children to deny their gifts, underutilize them, or even employ them in the act of deceit. Amy constantly sought alternate peer groups through a revolving door of extracurricular activities, looking for a connection that would have been more easily obtained if she had been regularly grouped in an interactive environment with students who reflected her ability level. If Amy had been grouped with students of like ability, the need to cheat in order to help them—or to fit in—likely would have been alleviated. Grouping strategies can be a simple way to expose students to a variety of differences and commonalities, as well as to offer other peer groups with which they may identify. What is more, if Amy's enrichment program had reflected her need to collaborate with other high-ability individuals, to share her talents, and celebrate her achievements with both her intellectual and age-mate peers, it would have gone a long way toward addressing her social and emotional needs.

As a Parent, How Can I Use These Grouping Strategies?

Parents are almost always the first line of advocacy for their bright children.[93] Parents who believe their child's school district is not offering a challenging curriculum can lobby for a community of learning in their schools. Administrators and teachers of those schools may not be aware of the different grouping strategies, curriculum compacting, or differentiation techniques that can easily be employed. A good place to start is to make a specific request about placement for a child and to bring the available research on the appropriateness of flexible grouping strategies for high-ability children to the attention of a teacher or administrator. Parents can ask around, look at how other school districts in their state are serving high-ability children through grouping strategies, and bring success stories to their own district. Sometimes all it takes is a success story and "this is how they did it" to get a school on board to try something new. As for the schools that do offer some manner of programming, it behooves parents to become involved, to ask about the curriculum, and to offer support through volunteering or mentoring work to ensure that students are receiving quality opportunities rather than a patch-on program.

Even when resources are not available in your child's school for a full continuum of enrichment programming, parents should encourage opportunities for bright children to have relationships with intellectual peers, even if they are not linked age mates. Lobby for a bored or socially-focused student to skip a grade, if only for one subject. If high-ability students are not already grouped in one classroom, request more opportunities for like students to spend time with different peer groups in school, under the care of a teacher, resource professional, mentor, or volunteer. Seek out role models and mentors for your high-ability students, particularly those students who seek to please others and who choose social fulfillment over personal enrichment. Parents can employ tutors, find mentors for their children, and investigate summer or weekend institutes for the gifted, talent searches, supplemental advanced classes, or even advanced curriculum programs available online that they can do with a friend or neighbor so as to not lose the social component and risk associating true learning with being alone.[94] There is nothing that says that learning ends at school; bright children can benefit from a home environment that is highly enriched and encourages additional learning.

Unfortunately, parents will sometimes find that the path of advocacy is a rocky one and that they will need to become more involved, more insistent, and well-equipped with research, ideas, and the support of other parents of high-ability students to in order to obtain better options for their children. For more ways that parents can improve communication with teachers (and the school, in general) to help support the needs of a bright student, and to keep that communication positive and collaborative, read on to Chapter 7. Nothing but good can come from improving the communication between the most important people in a child's academic life: their parents and their teachers. That improved communication reduces the likelihood of power struggles, deception, lying, and cheating.

Amy's case was pronounced by the lack of available peer groups to which she felt that she belonged. Though she was involved in many activities such as chorus and gymnastics, she always feared that she was too different from others and that they were judging her for her inability to blend in. Amy's issue may have been compounded by her lack of siblings, but all very bright students—especially those focused on social fulfillment—are susceptible to choosing to acquiesce or adapt to the prevailing social group. This is like a social form of code-switching, the ability to speak or behave like the more dominant group or to adjust in order to be acceptable to their peers.[95]

When only one social group is available for students, there is a greater likelihood that they will attempt to adjust to the social standards of that group. In fact, contrary to the "shy, introverted, smart kid" trope, Terman's studies suggested that gifted and talented students may find it easier to adjust and grow socially well-adapted than their peers.[96] Amy, like many gifted students I have known, had more personal resources than her peers for being able to fit in and adapt to her group. What she lacked were options. Though our TAG group could have presented her with a more appropriate social group with which she could identify, a group for whom she would never have to cheat in order to fit in, the nature of that underdeveloped and unstimulating program precluded this scenario. Unused abilities can make students feel invisible and strive to be seen and recognized by their peers and, as stated previously, just because a highly able brain may be capable of working harder does not mean it will unless it needs to do so. When presented with more appropriate peer groups, these socially adept students seek the company of those most like them and select a group that more closely resembles a student's abilities and goals. Generally, too, they will opt for the group that requires the least regulation and acquiescing—as long as the social standing of the group is accepted or respected.

That is not to say that high-ability children have nothing to learn from their average-ability peers, or that there are not valuable peer relationships to be had in mixed-ability friendships. In fact, much is to be gained from an environment that includes all learners and which supports and celebrates challenges, strengths, and talents no matter what form they take. When this sharing and collaboration exists, it is very possible to allow for and to admit that all students are not equal, and yet still have happy, well-adjusted students who do not resort to cheating behaviors to mask personal insecurities or to fit into the dominant social group.

Start the Conversation about Cheating

The act of secretly passing notes is not necessarily a cheating behavior, though it shares much in common with academic dishonesty. Both cheating and the act of passing notes require secretive behavior, planning, awareness of one's environment in order to manipulate it, and violation of classroom rules. Beyond even those similarities, however, the act of note passing warrants a mention as part of the larger discussion of academic dishonesty among high-ability students—and not just because Amy's notes often held answers or cheating strategies for her friends. In fact, note passing has been, in my experience, one of the easiest ways to begin the conversation with students about cheating.

Studies of academic cheating generally show that students talk among themselves about their cheating behaviors.[97] Although these clever students may tell a few friends about their experiences with dishonesty, they only gradually and uncomfortably become willing to explain their behaviors to their peers and to adults. A certain amount of trust and familiarity is required before a student will feel comfortable enough to tell others how they have cheated. It is important to let students know that they have a safe environment to report cheating behaviors; otherwise, the loneliness and boredom they feel that are directly connected to those cheating behaviors may also go unexpressed.

If you think it unlikely that you could tell children that they can safely tell you or their peer group how they have cheated and have it result in an open, honest conversation about academic dishonesty, you are right in being skeptical. Of the students whose stories are recounted in this text, only half self-reported their cheating behaviors. The stigma of cheating is clear; students are taught from a young age that deceit is morally wrong and that punishment is a natural consequence of cheating.

When I began to uncover cheating behaviors in the students I taught and asked point blank questions about their cheating behaviors, the questions unequivocally resulted in denial even after I assured them that they would not be in trouble. However, when I asked them to detail their note-passing tricks and cons, most students were far more willing to divulge their own personal methods, as well as those of classmates. Note passing seems to be categorized as a form of *acceptable* deceit: harmless and common; most students will admit that they have passed notes in class even as they agree that it was a breach of the rules. Similarly, most adults would be willing to admit that they drive above the speed limit. When a rule is commonly broken, it becomes easier for individuals to justify that it is not meant to be followed or that they are simply following the normal behavior of their social group.[98] Note passing is an easy starting point for parents and teachers to begin to uncover just how much creativity and dishonesty the bright children in their care are practicing on a daily basis. The discussion about note passing as a widely accepted form of deceit can then be the jumping off point for a larger conversation on cheating and dishonesty.

As a disclaimer, I realize that many teachers and parents may be surprised at the thought of such an exchange of unethical ideas and perhaps dismayed that it was allowed to take place at all. Yet it is important and all too rare for high-ability children to feel like they have an outlet or a forum where they can express their feelings. Bright students may have few chances to ever share their experiences with intellectual peers, which is why gifted resource rooms can be an excellent place to start the discussion to encourage the social and emotional development of high-ability students without censuring discussions beyond requiring that students remain respectful of one another.

It is tempting to compel students to be positive, but unless we allow children to commiserate over what bothers them, we are not able to see when larger, more systemic problems—such as cheating behaviors—affect our creative and talented youth. If I had not allowed students to come forward to me about their cheating behaviors, it is extremely likely that they would have joined the overwhelming percentage of high-ability students who cheat, are never caught, and are expected to simply grow out of their cheating behaviors. Without addressing the underlying causes of cheating behaviors, students cannot resolve the fundamental issues; they will continue to be lonely, or bored, or angry and are not likely to suddenly learn the coping skills needed to tackle challenge appropriately. Though it may seem unwise to allow students to come forward and openly discuss their cheating without fear of reprisal, the purpose of such a forum ultimately should be to help students in the long term.

Generally, it is easier to start the conversation on hypothetical terms, or even personal terms: "When I was your age, I used to pass notes like this," or "I have heard of students passing notes in very creative ways. What are some of the ways you have heard of?" Even though note passing is often seen as akin to a speed-limit rule, I have found that beginning the conversation in hypothetical terms can maximize the students' feelings of comfort and willingness to open up about the actions of "their friends." As students become more comfortable, they will often feel more open to saying "*I* have done this," and that is when the conversation is best able to shift to include other cheating behaviors. In these circumstances, teachers and parents should strive to listen and not judge. Questions that ask for elaboration are acceptable and can help a student feel comfortable with discussing specific details about incidents in which they have seen friends cheat or cheated themselves; however, resist the urge to punish or lecture a student. Also refrain from celebrating the lies, even though you may find that some are particularly clever, creative, or funny. The goal is to provide students with a safe place to express themselves and to begin to consider the reasons for their cheating and manipulative behaviors as well as alternatives, including reporting their own cheating. When students feel like they are being listened to without judgment, many *will* self-report.

It seems counterintuitive to say that any individual would confess his or her crimes, but time and time again I have experienced just that— bright students detailing how they have lied, cheated, and conned, not only in the past but also what they routinely do in their traditional classrooms or even in an enrichment opportunity. Some begin to recognize and describe *why* they did it, while others remain blind to the underlying cause of their behavior. It is difficult to speak to why this is often the case with students, but the majority of the students whose stories are detailed in this book self-reported their cheating behaviors to an adult with whom they felt safe and had a rapport, and their self-reporting made it easier to begin to focus on and change the cheating. These stories were chosen not as exceptions to the rule, but as representative of the many students who admit to engaging in academic dishonesty.

Address Creativity

Even though Amy's purpose for cheating was altruistic and social in nature, she persisted in adding to the number and complexity of her cheats as it became evident that her dishonest actions could also serve as an outlet for her underutilized intellect and creativity. Amy's impressive array of note-passing strategies, as well as the attempted development of the elaborate 'desk-tapping' system, was more than what was necessary for their original purpose: to help her peers get a better grade. Amy was a highly creative child, yet she had little opportunity to exercise those talents in ways that felt fulfilling (i.e., recognized and celebrated).

Though the link between intelligence and dishonesty has yet to be adequately explored in the literature, the connection between creativity and cheating are well studied. Dan Ariely suggests that this link is related to our ability to tell ourselves the best stories about who we are as people and that the key to dishonesty is to be able to think of ourselves as honest. Those who are less able to justify shady behavior are less likely to engage in it, whereas those who can creatively explain their actions or tell themselves better stories can continue to think of themselves as being moral even as they engage in cheating behaviors. In addition, the more creative the individuals are, the more they also are able to envision unique ways to circumvent the rules, which is yet another facet of how creative individuals are often better problem solvers. In this case, the problem creative individuals seek to "solve" is simply how to manipulate the truth.[99] We will explore this connection between creativity and dishonesty more in Chapter 8, but understand for now that the more creativity a student possesses, the more likely she may be to resort to academic dishonesty, particularly if that creativity does not have a positive outlet for expression.

Encourage Community over Competition

As mentioned earlier, teachers should be wary of using their brightest children as little teachers. Bright students function best when they have outlets to share their abilities in an environment that does not pit or rank classmates against one another. Certainly, competition can be a healthy aspect of a child's development, but there should be some reprieve from constantly being ranked. Teachers who outwardly value certain skills over others are unconsciously encouraging ranking among their students. Teachers also inadvertently encourage a ranking system when they praise one skill over another or give more value to certain gifts by telling students that they identify with them. A classroom should function as a community where all skills and abilities are valued and celebrated in a way that emphasizes difference as a good thing. This, in turn, encourages children to take creative risks with their learning as they work to develop their individual talents. Some students will continue to rank their individual gifts, suggesting, for example, that being smart is better than being good at kickball, but teachers should actively discourage this.

Another way teachers unwittingly sabotage a celebration of skills is by not taking it any further than the act of sharing. In the absence of a clear direction or purpose for a sharing assignment, students will either dismiss it as having no purpose or assign one according to their own interpretation. This increases the risk that the "gift share" becomes another competition.

The easiest and often most effective way to achieve a sense of community talent and cooperation is to have them take ownership of their community by sharing their gifts and abilities with one other, and when it comes to bright children, make it tangible. Tell them why they are learning something, make it real, give them the history, connect it to the future, and paint a holistic picture of why they are undertaking something. Rather than just hoping students will realize from the assignment that they are all valuable, make the intention tangible. I am not suggesting that you say to them, "You should see how important all these skills and talents are together." Instead, guide students to draw their own conclusions with questions that engage them in the process. My first question after a sharing session is to have students help me paint that big picture.

"What kinds of careers could Kareem do since he has shared with us that he is good at and likes math?" or "Abby is a good soccer player. What could she do for a living?" These are examples of questions I ask the entire class. We then all participate in naming various excellent qualities of our classmates.

The next step is to prevent students from stopping at the obvious answer. A leads to B: Abby plays soccer, so students will inevitably answer that she can play soccer for a living. After they get the knee-jerk answer out of their systems, ask for help breaking a larger talent down into *skills*. What do you have to do to be able to play soccer well? You have to be a team player, listen to others, have good coordination, and be willing to keep practicing and trying. Then ask the question again. What could Abby do for a living? The new list might include a manager, a coach, a pilot, a fitness instructor, a physical therapist, or a surgeon, and, yes, professional athlete will probably still make the list!

The next step is to let the original student pick a favorite from their classmates' brainstormed suggestions of jobs. That then becomes his or her highlighted "job" for the month, or however long you choose the display to run before you cycle through it again. After all the students have chosen their possible future professions based on their skills, they build a class map on the wall, a simple collection of squares in the same configuration of their desks to represent a town. We call it "SkillTown" and mark it according to what jobs have been chosen by whom. This month, Abby's desk represents the doctor's office. Joel runs the local theater, and Ang's desk is the sports arena.

Note that even non-academic talents and gifts should be celebrated. One student who left the classroom for most of the day for special education resource work was praised by fellow students for "always sharing and listening to other students during recess," and he chose to be, from the jobs that followed in his classmates' suggested list, a school psychologist. It helps students to realize that the world of adult professionals is made up of "once upon a time" students just like them and that those students individually showed very different abilities and talents. Not every doctor, lawyer, painter, or firefighter was a perfect student, but they possessed some skills or talents that helped to prepare them for their future. In a cooperative environment where everyone has something to offer and students can see how they are interconnected in a visible community built out of mutual pride, there is less need to rank or to out-compete one's classmates in regard to whose gifts are better. For the high-ability children like Amy who crave social acceptance and who fear that their intelligence sets them apart from their peers, it can be enlightening to hear their classmates excitedly collect their good qualities and then project a possible future based on those gifts.

Students will be excited and surprised to hear what positive things their classmates have to say about them. It can be easy to fall into an assumption of who does or doesn't like you, as well as to imagine what others think of you. Even adults are guilty of negative self-talk. Once, I discussed this strategy with a group of parents and teachers at a workshop and had them try creating a SkillTown themselves. I was worried about how well it would work, as I was largely unfamiliar with the community and could not tell how well the individuals at the workshop knew one another. They had come in with little cross-talk or discussion and sat without much socializing. Still, I forged on with the example, telling myself that individuals could fill in more skills and talents about themselves as necessary. In the end, I need not have worried. One woman was collectively identified by the other adults as "passionate, organized, an excellent mother" who "had sophisticated taste buds, had an eye for beauty, and was quick with numbers." Some of the jobs that followed as a discussion of those skills were accountant, painter, fashion designer, office manager, chef, food critic, and owner of an interior decorating company. This same woman, who in actuality worked at a local deli, was amazed at what others in her community thought or even knew about her. She had been volunteering for the PTA for several years and had helped organize their flower drive, decorating the school's front lawn with beautiful patterns of flowers to form simple pictures or words in order to encourage sales. One man, who didn't know her name, remembered her as "the mom of one of the students in my son's class last year who made the amazing crumb cake squares for the bake sale."

SkillTowns can be run with groups as small as two students or as large as a full class. It is important to engage the entire group in the brainstorming process, however, in order to reap the full benefits of celebrating skills as a community. The most wonderful consequence I have seen arise from SkillTown is the year a group protested the map. One student brought up the concern that the map did not make sense due to their seating chart. In the room, desks were grouped in clusters of four where the students faced inward toward their seatmates. These clusters were scattered throughout the room in a way that allowed all students equal vision of the front of the room. The individual groupings were based on a combination of alphabetization and classroom management needs—in other words, which groups would make the most non-disruptive seatmates. The result of this was a town in which buildings were clustered in groups of four. The contention among students was not the grouping itself, however, but the lack of meaningful themes. After one student brought it up, others protested. It did not make sense, they said, that the doctor's office and the mechanic's shop would be in the same cluster as the library and the railway station. The mechanic's shop and the railway station would be too loud for the library, they said, and the fumes and oil might make people even sicker at the doctor's office! It would make more sense, they said, if they moved the seating chart to reflect a more appropriate town layout.

Rather than dismissing their suggestions, even though many of them were said in jest, the students were allowed to take more ownership of their SkillTown and were permitted to change their seats on the stipulation that it would be a trial basis to see if the new groups would be disruptive or cooperative. The teacher of this class was very wary but allowed the students to move after having another group discussion. One month later, the teacher was amazed and pleased to report that the students had, for the most part, grouped each other based on similar skills—the doctor and the physical therapist were in the same "desk complex," as were the inventor and the mechanic—and that they had been working together with not only ease but also engaged to find that they had more in common. Groups that had never attempted to be friends together now formed new mini social groups. What is more, students were excited the next time SkillTown discussion rolled around. They had another opportunity to share other things that they were good at or liked and to choose new jobs to try for a month. Cooperation was valued over the competition of who had the better job because every student believed *he* had the best job, and half of the fun was bonding with new social groups as they realized what they had in common and what they could celebrate about their classmates.

SkillTown is just an example of ways that teachers can encourage positive associations between classmates and put an emphasis on cooperation over competition. It is certainly not the only way to create a classroom community that is based on mutual respect and celebration of individuality. Regardless of the method you choose to support your students in this manner, it is important to remember that all talents and skills have their place in a greater community, and students should be praised and encouraged to develop them all. When children have a sense of ownership and participation in their daily lives, when they feel valued, and when they understand the reasons for what they are doing, then there is little reason for them to cheat—either themselves or others.

When teachers neglected to praise or even mention Amy's skills and abilities out of fear that she would be isolated from her peer group, it became a self-fulfilling prophecy. When students are taught that standing out leads to social isolation or lack of social functionality, they will strive to connect to others by blending into the social group that is most readily available or desirable to them. By creating more social groups with which to identify, such as those with common skills in a SkillTown simulation, as well as other flexible grouping strategies, bright students are better equipped to relate to their peers and to socially navigate their academic experience.

What I Wish For the "Amys"

My wish for Amy is that the school to which she moved offered opportunities for her to meet and work with students who had things in common with her. I wish that her social groups were varied and ever-changing, reflecting the different hats she wore throughout her day. I see her in a math class where she was able to work with sixth graders who did not need as much repetition as her fifth-grade classmates. I can see her staying after school to write for the school paper, where she worked with other writers to express her creativity and use her problem-solving mind to conquer layout issues. In this vision, she also used her acting skills in the drama club and made friends with the other TAG students. They all met twice a week in the resource room to practice their individual or group presentations and get feedback from mentors before sharing their hard work with their classmates. I wish for her that she was celebrated and that she saw that her talents gave her a place in the grand scheme of her community. I wish that her classmates realized this because of the hard work of the parents and teachers in that community, and that they all felt like they had a place, too.

I wish for Amy that she continued to have many friends but that she never felt the need again to have to *earn* their acceptance through academic dishonesty. I wish that she had the chance to identify with students with whom she was not tempted to acquiesce or regulate her giftedness. I wish that she was able to focus her abilities on her own dreams and goals and to use the full strength of her skill set on activities that would further her love of learning. I wish that wherever she is, Amy grew into a person who accepts herself for who she is and not simply on what she can give to others.

The "Amys"—the altruistic, social cheaters who often hide beneath the guise of the perfect student and friend—can be supported to be themselves and not have to earn the friendship of those around them. Create an inclusive environment where all students feel valued based on their abilities and skills and where social and emotional needs of high-ability children are addressed by allowing them to move flexibly through a variety of groups and educational opportunities. When students are the greatest outliers, either academically or socially, in their group, it stands to reason that they would feel that they would need to regulate themselves, or normalize, if social standing or acceptance is their goal. By offering high-ability students a glimpse of how different students socialize and work in a variety of grouping strategies (including ones where they work with like-ability peers in cooperative situations) they are less likely to feel that they are the *most* different of all and that they must change themselves in order to be more like their peers. Social cheating may be one of the most difficult forms to identify, though starting the conversation with your students about cheating behaviors can help them feel safe to self-report. The best way to tackle altruistic cheating is to be proactive rather than reactive. When a school functions as an environment where all students are valued and are taught to value one another for their skills and their differences, every student benefits from the sense of community that is instilled.

Four

Gus

"I hate writing." This was from Gus, a sixth grader.

"What did you get on the essay?"

"I don't know yet. I haven't finished it."

Gus's friend, a fellow classmate who was working with him in the resource room on a project unrelated to the essay, seemed startled.

"Gus, it was due last Friday. You're going to get an F."

"No, I won't. I do this all the time. I don't turn it in, and then I ask Mrs. Peters where mine is when she hands them back out. She thinks she might have lost it or left it at home when she took the papers to grade, and I get extra time to work on it."

"Yeah, but when she finds out *you* have the paper, she'll know you didn't turn it in."

"I do turn it in, just late. I just slip it onto her desk or I turn it in to another homework bin that it doesn't belong in. It looks like it got turned in to the wrong place or she lost it, but it was on time."

"But you still have to do it. Why not just turn it in with everyone else?"

"Because I need more time. I'm so bad at writing. It's not like math where you can check your answers. You can spell everything right, and the grammar is good, and still only get a B or a C on an essay."

Gus went on to detail several other late-turn-in tricks, including how he would turn in the first page of an essay or an assignment with a staple in the corner, but the back pages are missing. You can say that the rest of the assignment got torn off in the pile or in your own book where you put it for safekeeping, he explained. A teacher would not suspect that a student would staple only one piece of paper, so the rest of the pages *must* be missing. Gus started to talk about his preferred plagiarizing methods but was cut short by the end-of-the-day bell. The boys headed back to class to pack up for the bus, and on their way out, project in hands, said goodbye to me. The entire conversation had occurred with me in clear earshot; I was less than 10 feet away from the boys. Though some may find this remarkable, to me it was a direct result of Martin's confession of almost a year earlier.

Martin's and Arthur's actions had opened up my eyes to the possibility that high-ability children were not unlike their classmates in one respect: At least some of them were part of that 85% of students who have engaged in academic dishonesty during their school careers. Not long after Martin's and Arthur's actions were discovered, I set out to discover the different ways that bright elementary-age children were cheating. The majority of students who admit to academic dishonesty also specify that they are not caught doing so; presumably, this figure also accounts for the bright students within that population who cheat.

Since it seemed unlikely that much data would arise from waiting for my students to be discovered cheating, I explored a different avenue—namely, self-reporting. This resulted in the institution of a no-fault reporting zone in the enrichment resource room, called Safe Space. Although the students in my care delighted in teasing me about the nature of the no-fault policy and questioningly battled a variety of hypothetical loopholes regarding what they could do and get away with, they gradually accepted the policy and its boundaries. One, normal classroom rules and their natural consequences still applied. Two, students could discuss any behavior that they engaged in outside of the enrichment room safely, without fear of punishment from the resource room teacher, as long as the action discussed did not involve themselves or another person being harmed. And finally, the third component of the policy was that there may be a teacher response to what was reported, but it would not be a punishment. "Expect response, but not punishment" was the way the rule was displayed in the resource room.

There's an old saying along the lines of "You find what you look for," but for almost a year after Martin's profession of guilt, that was not the case for the Safe Space reporting zone. Although it had been instituted with the intention of encouraging students who would be unlikely to be caught cheating to come forward, in the first year of Safe Space's existence, there were zero confessions of cheating behavior made. However, Safe Space remained; its no-fault reporting policy seemed to fulfill another need of the high-ability students who visited the enrichment resource room—the need to safely and openly discuss their problems. These disclosures ran the gamut from questions about themselves, to problems with their teachers, to fights with and confessions about their friends. It was almost a year to the day after Martin had handed me the essay he had crumpled in anger before another student self-reported their cheating behaviors. That student was Gus.

Gus was a longtime enrichment student; he had been identified as gifted and talented in kindergarten and worked with me primarily in enrichment math. Gus was well liked, had several close friends, seemed to identify very positively with his abilities, and was not afraid to act smart around his classmates. Though I had never suspected that he was engaging in cheating behaviors, his confession did not surprise me, as it spoke to an issue that Gus's parents and I had been working on for several years: Gus was a perfectionist. He had imposed a very detailed set of rules upon himself that dictated what behaviors, actions, and grades were acceptable, and he held himself to these stringent standards on even the most seemingly minute details. When he missed a word on the grade-level spelling bee one year, a two-hour-long meltdown followed where he refused to come out of the boys' bathroom. In another particularly memorable incident, Gus's parents contacted the school regarding the harshness of the comments written on their son's papers. The notes ranged from "You're not smart," to "Failure," and "No one else in class got this wrong." Their concern shifted when the comments, written in large, angry red letters, were discovered to be Gus's own words written to himself after receiving the work back from his teacher.

Fast forward to the overheard conversation in which Gus told his friend how much he hated writing, and his cheating behaviors were not a surprise, based on his history. Like most perfectionists, Gus had a fear of ambiguity, which included open-ended response questions and any writing assignment that was not strictly factually based. He was afraid of the grade that he would receive if he turned the essay in on time, so he had developed a cheating ritual to compensate for his perceived weakness.

Perfectionism is one of the few underlying causes of cheating that results in a type of academic dishonesty that fulfills the traditional definition of cheating, which assumes that individuals engage in dishonest behavior for the purpose of obtaining a higher grade. Consider Arthur and his three-year forgery operation. His behavior, though fulfilling the stipulation of being dishonest, did not result in a higher grade (nor was it ever his intention to do so). Martin may have originally intended to get a better grade through deceit, but the anger that resulted from his easy A suggested that it was not actually what he wanted. Terry's boredom-driven cheating also qualified as dishonest; however, her underachieving profile and growing disinterest in her grades suggested that her goal was not to obtain better marks. Amy's cheating behaviors did fulfill both stipulations for the traditional definition; however, consider the added complication that her own grades were not affected, only those of her friends and classmates. Clearly, most high-ability cheating behaviors are engineered in a way that complicates the original, limited view of what constitutes academic dishonesty.

Gus's case is more of what we think about when we imagine a child cheating in school. He was dishonest for the direct intention of getting a better grade. What is more, he believed that his cheating was necessary to prevent failure. Fear of failure is one of the top reasons cited for cheating.[100] Unlike other forms of cheating undertaken by bright students, the motives and intent of which are often difficult to discern or understand, Gus's actions are at least understandable. Students who feel great pressure to succeed and who feel like they do not have the confidence or the skill set to do so honestly are susceptible to academic dishonesty. We cannot excuse cheating behavior in any form, despite the motive; however, it is vital to understand the cause if we are to prevent and respond to it.

Perfectionism's Two Heads

The desire to be flawless is a characteristic not unfamiliar to the gifted child. According to some, "Giftedness and perfectionism are soul mates."[101] This does not suggest, as it seems to, that one inevitably accompanies the other but rather that they are both abstract concepts that are difficult to define, as well as having both positive and negative characteristics.

It is true that perfectionism, the desire and attempt to meet internal high standards, is seen in many high-ability individuals. The incidence of perfectionism in bright children as opposed to the general population suggests that it is at least as prevalent, if not more so, in the gifted community, though studies suggesting that it is *more* frequent in the gifted community are mixed. One study of 112 gifted and talented adolescents in grades 7 and 8 revealed 87.5% as possessing strong tendencies toward perfectionism, a rate that was higher than the general population.[102] In another study of over 350 honors and gifted students, a whopping 89% responded that they engaged in perfectionist behaviors such as procrastination.[103] If those numbers seem fearfully high, remember that not all perfectionism is maladaptive. We want our talented children and adults to set high standards and to achieve them. In fact, perfectionism can present as either normal or neurotic, and students who possess a healthy amount of normal perfectionism often benefit from the strong work ethic and desire to succeed that normal perfectionism provides. Perfectionism is often found in both competitive and successful individuals; alone, it is not an inherently negative quality.

Perfectionism only becomes a concern when it impairs how individuals function or prevents them from recognizing or appreciating their own competency.[104] Normal perfectionism, which is characterized by a positive, self-oriented perspective that allows students to take pride in their successes, can be a very positive characteristic. What is generally discussed, and has therefore taken over common contextual use of the term, is the negative variety—the maladaptive form of perfectionism known as neurotic or dysfunctional perfectionism.

Many successful individuals possess some measure of normal perfectionism, which encourages them to look ahead to the future, learn from their mistakes, and maintain good work habits in order to complete tasks to their satisfaction. Students with normal perfectionism appreciate their own sense of competency and hold themselves to high standards but are not afraid of failure to the extent of becoming neurotic, or even self-destructive, about their inadequacies. Normal perfectionism does not generally cause cheating behaviors, because the tremendous fear of mistakes is not present in those individuals.

Students with normal perfectionism face forward, striving to achieve their goals and to control their lives, whereas students with neurotic perfectionism face backward, concerned with their mistakes, punishing and judging themselves.[105] The five main characteristics of this maladaptive form of perfectionism, as named by Miriam Adderholdt-Elliot, are procrastination, fear of failure, an all-or-nothing mindset, being paralyzed in the face of a challenge, and workaholic behaviors.[106] All of these carry a greater risk of leading to underachievement than the likelihood of producing perfect work, thus making the situation worse and increasing the student's self-criticism. In fact, neurotic perfectionism and destructiveness often go hand in hand.[107] When a desire toward excellence is driven by an inner motivation to succeed, students are able to gradually grow and learn in order to meet their goals. However, when the desire for excellence is driven by the fear that they are inadequate if they do not succeed, the fear of not being good enough is often enough to cripple the process of growth. Stress and fear are not conducive to learning. Students actually can make themselves sick trying to maintain their excellent grades, procrastinating to avoid being seen as inadequate, feeling guilty and dissatisfied of their work, judging themselves harshly, and cheating to maintain the illusion of control.[108] When students are excessively anxious about mistakes and simultaneously lack the coping strategies required to change their negative mindsets, cheating can be seen as an appealing self-defense mechanism to protect their fragile self-concepts.

Roots of Perfectionism

What causes perfectionism? There are many possible sources, any combination of which can result in perfectionist tendencies. External factors, such as a pressure to succeed, teacher or family expectations (either real or imagined), social modeling, and media portrayals of success and failure can all contribute to perfectionism. In addition, the asynchronous nature of very bright children can result in children creating unrealistic goals that do not match up with their abilities. It can be difficult for children of many ages to accurately judge their own diverse capabilities when setting goals, especially when their aspirations are high.[109]

Perfectionism can also be caused or reinforced when quality work is praised and prioritized over the process required to complete it. Competition among siblings and friends, either self-imposed or encouraged by adult role models, can create a "superkid syndrome" where students are encouraged to be engaged in a plethora of activities and scholastic endeavors. This lack of moderation can lead to the expectation of overachievement, either in reality or as perceived by the student. Although it is unlikely that elementary-aged bright students are afraid of not doing well enough to get into a good college or to reach future career goals, age does not preclude any school from potentially becoming an increasingly competitive environment. Even if students do not yet see poor grades as a career setback, the message they may be getting from home, teachers, or other students is that they are being judged based on their performance and must succeed in order to be valued.

Some children show perfectionist tendencies from a very young age, younger than when many of these external influences would have had a chance to exert themselves, which suggests that there are innate qualities that contribute to their development. Some parents of talented children have reported that their child would not walk or talk in front of others until they had learned to do it well, surprising adults by going from no apparent verbal skills to full sentences. There seems to be an inborn quality to certain forms of perfectionism. In addition, regardless of external stimuli that can reinforce perfectionist behavior, many perfectionists share a very internal quality of their perspective on learning—namely, a fixed mindset as opposed to one of growth. These mindsets were described by Carol Dweck, a researcher who specializes in how individuals cope with failure.[110] Individuals with a fixed mindset view characteristics such as intelligence and ability as static, meaning that the amount is predetermined and that you only possess a finite amount of intelligence. Those with a growth mindset perceive of learning as a continuum and believe that intellectual characteristics can be obtained through learning and growth. These mindsets, and how they influence perfectionism, will be discussed in greater depth later in the chapter. For now, it's important to realize that the cause of perfectionism is not always easy to pinpoint because internal as well as environmental factors play a role.

Dangers of "Being Perfect"

Though it may seem counterintuitive that striving for perfection could lead to self-sabotage and self-destruction, considering the original intent of the student is to better themselves, perfectionism can be an increasingly damaging pursuit. Students have to compose their understanding of what would constitute an ideal level of achievement for their behaviors. For some, this may be achieving straight As. For others, their journeys extend to their daily behavior, interactions with others, and excellence in extracurricular activities, such as Gus's attempt at the school spelling bee. Perfectionists are often hyper-sensitive to how they imagine others perceive them, which can lead to harsh self-judgments, rules, and rituals. Perfectionists commonly strive not only to feel perfect but also to be unimpeachable by others, as though they need to protect themselves. Maladaptive perfectionism often leaves individuals extremely susceptible to these judgments and opinions, and many live in fear that they will be exposed as worthless. Students who have reached this dysfunctional stage are increasingly agitated about the mistakes that result from their high and sometimes impossible standards, and they begin to identify themselves by how they perceive others see them.

If bright children have other emotional or physical intensities in addition to perfectionism, this narrow level of thinking can lead to any number of cognitive distortions, leading to a skewed view of the world and their interaction with it. The world explained by a perfectionist often sounds like a very regimented, rule-oriented place with little to no room for gray areas, and perfectionists are often ruled by a very narrow black-and-white, all-or-nothing pattern of thinking. When they view other people as either loving or hating them, or a test grade as either perfect or an utter failure, they transform even small negative experiences and interactions into devastating occurrences—a cognitive distortion known as magnifying. In addition, because ambiguity and flexibility are not options in this distorted reality, the cognitive distortion known as catastrophic thinking, or "catastrophizing," can also occur.[111]

Catastrophic thinking is rarely based in truth or pulled from the evidence of a student's actual experiences. Many parents and teachers with bright children have seen this firsthand—children feeling that terrible things will happen if they do not succeed at tasks they have set for themselves, citing that they will be "in so much trouble" or "everyone will hate" them, even if there has been no expectation or precedent set regarding the consequences of their actions. Even gifted adults can be guilty of this. One mother was struggling over the decision of whether or not to let her son get a pet. In the course of the discussion we had, she laid out her hypothetical fears: She thought that her son might not take care of the animal to the right degree and that it would escape or die, thus causing her to have to comfort him, him to need therapy, and her to be simultaneously worried about him and upset that he did not take care of the animal properly. Before she had ever gotten the pet, she had already plotted the poor thing's demise and subsequent devastating response from her child and herself. She was guilty of catastrophic thinking, as well as a common perfectionist coping mechanism, which was to avoid possible consequences by not attempting a challenge in the first place. Perfectionists often lack reasonable coping skills; the longer they practice avoiding and postponing difficult situations, the more difficult it will be for them to either proactively respond or react positively to challenges as they occur.

This lack of coping strategies to deal with failure (even perceived failure) can lead to increased negativity, as well as a constant desire for approval.[112] It is this fear that can lead to avoiding disapproval through cheating and other self-destructive behaviors, partially out of self-flagellation and punishment, and partially as collateral damage in the process of students continuing to fix what they perceive as their imperfections. When students are driven by a need to excel and simultaneously believe that mistakes will show them to be wrong, incapable, or unintelligent, obsessive behavior that supersedes the fear of not being successful can result. Examples of obsessive behavior can include not completing work honestly, procrastination, or not completing work at all because it cannot be done to their standard.[113] Obviously a student cannot be successful or seen as perfect if her work is late, subpar, or never turned in, yet these non-perfect behaviors are often a direct result of the cycle of maladaptive perfectionism.

Similarly, many physically self-destructive disorders stem from perfectionism, though it should not be assumed that all individuals with academic perfectionism are also physically self-destructive. Excoriation, the habit of picking at one's own skin, and trichotillomania, the compulsion to pull out eyebrows or other hair, stem from the anxiety experienced by perfectionists. This often results in larger blemishes, wounds, and other flaws that then trigger additional obsessive and compulsive behaviors, and the cycle becomes self-destructive.[114]

Likewise, when students set unattainable or unrealistic goals for themselves, it can trigger a cycle of inevitable failure, which leads to depression, self-punishment, guilt about one's ability or performance, and harmful coping mechanisms. This can also help explain how some academic perfectionists can be difficult to identify, as the cycle of striving for a perceived perfect ideal may have resulted in procrastination, poor grades, and overall underachievement. These students are often precluded from enrichment programming as a result of their chronic underachievement caused by perfectionism. It is important to remember that not all perfectionists paint the picture of the overtaxed, overachieving teachers pets with straight As. In fact, some of the most challenging cases of perfectionism are those students whose "wounds" may be hiding their deep desires to be perfect.

Cheating as a Coping Mechanism

Not long after overhearing Gus and his friend's conversation in the resource room, I met privately with Gus. I let him know that I had heard what they had been talking about and that, true to the Safe Space policy, he would not be punished. I would not tell his classroom teacher about the incident, but I did want to talk about it. The discussion that followed was a long conversation, not only about the types of cheating that he had engaged in but also about how he felt about his abilities in school, both writing and otherwise.

What emerged was a picture of a student who often used tricks and ploys to turn work in late, to gain extensions on assignments upon which he was afraid he would not succeed, and who commonly plagiarized writing work because his "just wasn't good enough." For Gus, cheating and procrastinating were both coping mechanisms to deal with his fear of not doing well on his assignment. Academic dishonesty and procrastination are "buffer-zone" coping mechanisms, meaning that they are reasons students can give to distance themselves from the grade they received and the grade they would have gotten if they had put their full effort into the assignment. Excuses and rituals such as these help to remove students from their failure by one degree of difference. Perfectionists seek out buffer zones, excuses for "if I did not succeed, then *this* was the reason, not that I'm not good enough."

A distinct link between procrastination and perfectionism exists. Procrastination is often caused by stress, and students who appear to simply be putting off work may actually be paralyzed by the stress that is brought on by fears that their work will be inadequate. To students who are highly competitive with themselves or others, risk and effort are two things they feel will cause their weaknesses to be uncovered by others. Higher competition leads to greater pressure to succeed and with it, the temptations of cheating. We have all experienced how, when our fear or worry surrounding a certain task is too great, worrying can replace the task itself. This can result in a pattern of hiding behind these self-perceived inadequacies. These threatening feelings can prompt students to invent or discover new rituals of manipulation to prevent them from putting out their best effort.[115] For Gus, as well as others, this can mean turning to cheating behaviors.

Maladaptive perfectionism is rife with contradictions. Perfectionists unconsciously build in excuses for failure—reasons why they did not, or even could not, succeed. Maladaptive perfectionists fear that if they try their hardest, they will not succeed and will be valued less. However, despite this deep fear of being discovered as a phony, the easiest way to identify a perfectionist is to listen to what they say about themselves and their work. For a group of individuals who spend so much time and effort preventing the possible negative perceptions of others and hiding their inadequacies, they out themselves to an extraordinary degree. Like cheating, perfectionism is often discovered through self-reporting. Although students seldom will say directly that they are perfectionists, their actions and their words about their work often describe clear signs of perfectionism. Gus self-reported his perfectionism early, not only with the disparaging comments that he wrote on his returned work but also from the breakdowns he would have as early as first grade when exposed to difficult tasks. He internalized all defeats, however slight (or perceived), and would let others know periodically what he thought of himself, sometimes with shockingly negative language. Even his confession in the enrichment room, telling his friend that he needed the extra time because he was "so bad at writing," was a confession of his perceived inadequacies.

Another contradiction that occurs commonly with neurotic perfectionists is telescopic thinking, also known as filtering, which can become another cognitive distortion. The way that perfectionists view their accomplishments can be likened to looking selectively through either end of a telescope lens. When looking at goals yet to be accomplished or perceived failures, perfectionists view the incident through the magnifying lens and amplify it, overwhelming themselves with self-doubt, pity, or punishment. Similarly, they have a tendency to view their positive accomplishments through the minimizing lens and discount their achievements as insignificant or undeserved.[116] Thus, they filter out the accomplishments and only see the negative in many situations.

Gus was overwhelmed by not graduating to the next level in the spelling bee, so much so that it paralyzed his ability to move past the loss; all he could see was a magnified "I failed." He had filtered out the two previous wins that had allowed him to get to that level of the competition and was unable to see them as true accomplishments because they were "just the little competitions." Likely, if he had won the school spelling bee and moved on, his poor coping mechanisms for failure and success would likely have minimized that accomplishment as well.

Neurotic perfectionists need healthy replacements for the negative coping mechanisms they have developed, such as cheating, procrastination, and other built in measures of failure, if they are to be truly productive and experience growth. Some of these replacements are learning positive language and perspective in their thought process, as well as a shift from a fixed mindset to one of growth. It can help students, too, if they understand that even if others see their inadequacies, they are more valuable than their current self-imposed belief that they must consistently be perfect and produce perfect products.

The road to overcoming perfectionism is not easy, and it requires support from all individuals who work with a student, including classroom teachers, specialists, and parents to solidify the message that they are worthwhile. Some professionals suggest that perfectionist characteristics never completely cease; there will always be a tendency for those high-ability individuals to be overly critical of their own work. However, even gradual steps for students like Gus can help decrease and even eliminate many self-destructive coping mechanisms. The goal is to work on eliminating maladaptive perfectionism and to work toward developing healthy perfectionism.

Fixed Mindset: The Perfectionist Perception

As discussed earlier, students with maladaptive perfectionism have a common fixed mindset or perception regarding their abilities rather than one of growth, and this mindset profoundly affects the way individuals process their ability to learn, as well as how they perceive their abilities. Individuals who believe that their qualities, such as their intelligence, are "set in stone" have a fixed mindset and believe that they are either intelligent at a certain rate, or they are not. Students with a fixed mindset particularly often feel the need to prove themselves or that they're fooling others. They fear that any mistake proves that they are not very capable and that if they have to work hard toward a goal, it means that they are not really smart. Risk and effort both may reveal inadequacies.[117] Children with fixed mindsets are afraid of being discovered as being phonies or that they will be unable to maintain their identity as "the smart kid" when they are faced with something they are unable to do well.

Those with a fixed mindset are often more susceptible to cheating behaviors; it is in fact one of the few evidences of high-ability cheating that can be seen in research on bright children. Perfectionists who feel like their identity is at stake, or that they do not have the time or the ability to perform, may cheat in order to maintain their identity, even if they perceive it to be a false one (i.e., "I'm not that smart.").[118] Dweck likens it to a poker game. If you believe you are limited to the hand you have been dealt, you will try to convince yourself and others that you have a better hand. This "bluffing" in the context of a school environment can often take the form of cheating behaviors. For Gus, that meant using dishonesty to elongate his deadlines and plagiarizing his work, but for other students it may include other cheating behaviors. These may include cheating on tests, using unauthorized notes, copying from another source or student, or any other form of academic dishonesty that represents a way to avoid what they fear would occur if they relied on honest work and studying.

Because they feel that struggle and effort are equated with unintelligence, students with fixed mindsets often have very poor mechanisms for studying and achieving. They believe that other good students learn instantly and that if they were smart, too, their intelligence would yield immediate results. Cheating seems to be an easy way to achieve that instant result without needing to study or develop knowledge based on persistence, trial and error, or growth in the area. Rather than working with his teacher to improve his ability to answer open-ended questions or challenging himself to work on essays that required him to collect information and make a thesis statement—something that did not come with a singular correct answer or format—Gus chose to create a buffer between himself and his fear of failure. Putting himself out there with the possibility of failing was not an option for someone with a fixed mindset who saw it as "nothing ventured, nothing lost."[119]

In contrast, students with a growth mindset believe that their characteristics and qualities are cultivated, not inborn, and that they can achieve through effort. They perceive failures not as proof that they are incapable but only that they have yet to learn the skill set necessary to achieve the task at hand. Learning is a series of goals to be obtained, and students with growth mindsets believe that they can grow through work and practice. This is not to say that anyone can become a prodigy or to perform any task at the highest level, only that one's true potential is unknowable and must be cultivated, not reached or "maxed out."

It is important to recognize that there is something tempting about a fixed mindset for individuals, even as it risks veering into a self-destructive cycle. As Carol Dweck explains, "It seems to promise children a lifetime of worth, success, and admiration just for sitting there and being who they are."[120] Who wouldn't want the universe to grant them everything they desire based solely on the virtue of who they are and on their innate worth? It also frees you from responsibility, e.g., "I cannot do X, so why try? X was not my fault because I know what I am capable of; the test/teacher/world was flawed, or beyond my reach." Unfortunately, as tempting as it may seem, there is one problem: Fixed ability is a lie. It may be the biggest lie that bright children and adults tell themselves—first, that they are instantly endowed with a given amount of talent, and second, that their endowment will or should write their ticket for them.

Surprisingly enough, parents and teachers unwittingly nurture this fixed mindset in a child by referring to the student's potential as if it were an existing, tangible concept. We often say "You *have* so much potential, and you are not using *it*," or "I know that my son is not working *up to* his potential." Whenever I hear phrases like that from a parent or teacher, I imagine potential as a shelf with a golden box on it, affixed at high level on a wall of a very tall room or tower. Children must climb up to reach their golden box where it waits at a fixed, set point. Although the term potential is positive and suggests that something is possible—a level of capability that can be developed—it is often used in a way that supports a fixed mindset. By believing that children have potential that needs to be reached, you inadvertently suggest that there is a fixed point, a level that they have not earned, but that belongs to them by virtue of who they are. That high shelf becomes a point at which they feel they should already be or innately deserve. They *belong* at that high level; they simply are not there currently. It is less scary to think that way and even may initially be comforting; any lack of success that a child experiences is a faux failure, and it puts the child at a disadvantage because a fixed mindset implies a lack of personal responsibility.

The truth is scarier. If your child is not learning and not showing—or learning how to show—what they already know because he is cheating or using other coping mechanisms, he is at an actual disadvantage. When Gus cheated his way through his writing assignments, he was preventing himself from true growth. He was not learning how to correctly research, cite source materials, or learn how to express his own thoughts in writing.

Sometimes talented children are given a pass for cheating, or the seriousness of the action is downplayed because they could "probably do that task well anyway." At the heart of those assumptions is the very fixed mindset-based assumption that children have the capability and knowledge already, rather than the scarier truth that they are sacrificing actual growth through their actions. From a growth perspective, it is not enough to rely on the assumption that students have the capability to perform. Instead, they have to learn, develop, and perform.

With a growth mindset, however, there is a tradeoff for the lack of comfort. There is no promising instant payoff as seems promised by a fixed mindset, but something greater is to be gained. If we return to the analogy of the potential shelf, we see a different perspective under a growth mindset. There is no such thing as a potential shelf, or a level that waits for you to catch up to reach it. There is such a thing as potential, but it does not wait high above students. Their potential is always in their pocket, and however high that student climbs, it is their companion, compelling and encouraging them to continue to climb. This is the true meaning of potential as it exists as an agent for growth. Where potential is concerned, it is far scarier not the higher up you are, but the closer you are to the ground.

Helping Gus

Identifying the underlying issue or cause is the first step in developing a support and response team for a student with cheating behaviors. For Gus, his underlying cause was quite clear. As a result, it was no challenge to form his team of teachers, parents, and support professionals, considering that his overly perfectionist behaviors had been well documented. Even without the inclusion of the cheating behaviors themselves, the team readily agreed that Gus needed structured support to help change his mindset to one of learning and growth.

Although it was positive that his response was so immediate and that the team was already informed of Gus's particular issues, I caution you not to see this as an ideal. That Gus's perfectionism had gotten to such a serious point was an indication that we had not done enough previously to help him combat his issue. Even though his parents and teachers, myself included, were aware of his neurotic perfectionism, we were guilty of a common misconception that he would grow out of it and learn how to manage his perfectionism in healthy ways on his own.

It is not uncommon for the parents and teachers of bright students to afford very capable, often mature children a great deal of trust and leniency; however, it is important to remember that they are still children, and they still need to be taught, particularly when it comes to developing manageable and healthy coping mechanisms. We had inadvertently allowed Gus's perfectionism to reach a point where it was self-destructive. Many underlying causes of cheating, such as boredom, avoidance, and perfectionism, have this in common—that they will not be surmounted without proper guidance and modeling.

The track we took to address Gus's perfectionism was individualized to his needs, but several components—such as home support, changing the way we praise our talented students, and increasing the amount of coping mechanisms students use to deal with failure and challenge—are applicable to many individuals with neurotic perfectionism. These methods, documented here, may be useful in the journey of your own perfectionist. There is no one-size-fits-all approach to transforming a child's perfectionism to that of a healthy, self-appreciating level, so the best recommendation is to explore different options for children whose underlying challenge is perfectionism. Unaddressed, it may or may not lead to negative coping mechanisms such as cheating behaviors, but the prognosis that a child will outgrow their issue on their own is bleak. As the author of *Freeing Our Families from Perfectionism*, Thomas Greenspon, remarks, "Perfectionism is a wound; it is never healthy, and it may never heal entirely."[121]

Undoing the Fixed Mindset

For students like Gus, it is most important to teach them how to break their cycle of fixed thinking; undoing this mindset was forefront in his team's "battle plan." Brain research has shown that fixed thinkers are individuals who focus on only the product, rather than the process of their learning or growth, and that they pay less attention to information that can improve their learning. They are hyper-focused on the outcome and do not attend to information that was given to help them succeed the next time.[122] What this often means for perfectionist thinkers is that they show interest in material only when they succeed immediately. When tasks are more challenging, they "check out," feeling, unlike a growth thinker, that there is shame in working to understand a difficult concept.

Parents often describe how their bright children once started a new activity that the parents believed would be a perfect fit for their interests and ability, only to have the child quickly show disinterest and quit. What confused parents do not realize is that perfectionism can lead to early withdrawal when students are presented with a challenge that is unfamiliar or seemingly too difficult for their conceived fixed amount of ability. When the fear of having their inadequacies illuminated by continuing and possibly failing is too great a risk, many high-ability perfectionists feign disinterest and quit. As one of my students loves to say, "I don't play any game I don't think I can win."

A particularly effective strategy teachers and parents can employ is to change the way they praise their students because it is actually the *type* of reinforcement that makes the greatest difference in a student's self-esteem and ability level, rather than the *amount*. Adults should praise students not for their outcomes or end products but for the process of working or the amount of effort that the student put forth. Certainly, the end result can be praised as well, but it should be praised only through the lens of the student's work rather than ability level. For example, rather than saying, "I am so proud of you for winning first place in the spelling bee," the parent can say, "I am so proud of how hard you worked in the spelling bee. Your studying really paid off." Although many adults recognize that the former praise statement also implies that hard work must have taken place, it is difficult to tell whether or not that message was conveyed to the student. As discussed earlier, high-ability children, particularly at a young age, often exert little to no effort in order to achieve impressive outcomes. Their ability actually prevents them from understanding the normal relationship between effort and outcome.

Parents and teachers cannot rely on their bright students to understand this concept without the aid of modeling or firsthand experience. Furthermore, they cannot expect bright children to have the coping strategy of "If I work harder, I will likely do better" already in their toolboxes for when material becomes more challenging down the road.

In another study performed by Dweck, hundreds of adolescents were given challenging problems from a nonverbal IQ test. When told their overall score, some students were praised for their ability and were told "You must be smart at this." Other students with similar score profiles were praised for their effort: "You must have worked really hard." Not only did the ability-praised students report less enjoyment when given additional challenging problems, but they scored lower on these additional problems than they did on the initial test questions, even though the original questions were more challenging. Effort-praised students both enjoyed the additional challenging problems and performed better on the additional questions than they did on the original test measure. What was even more telling was that when the students were then given the opportunity to share the problems and their scores with other students, almost 40% of the ability-praised students lied, misrepresenting their scores as higher than they had actually earned. Simply by labeling a group of random students in a sample as "the smart ones," researchers greatly increased the inclination of those students to cheat.

Students who feel they are being judged based on their achievements can put undue pressure on themselves to be continuously successful in an attempt to maintain their status or identity. For the students in Dweck's study, all it took was a one-time, random label as "the smart ones" for some individuals to risk cheating in order to keep that label from being disproven. What then of the bright students who are continually categorized based on their abilities? How ingrained into their consciousness and sense of identity has the smart-kid label become?

Students with this must-achieve mentality also have the tendency to reject creativity and risk-taking in their work, fearing that it will not be what the teacher wants. Gus, for example, was assigned a book report that required a visual component to his final presentation. As long as the final product had all of the required information, the format of the visual component could be anything of the students' choosing. Some chose to create computer-based presentations complete with videos and graphics, others built models, displays, games, and one student even created a movie poster. Gus, limited by what he knew would be successful based on past efforts, was one of the few students who came with the traditional poster board with information typed and glued in neat, succinct sections. Even with a free pass to try something creative, Gus was reluctant to take a risk of not receiving praise and recognition for his product, and so he went with an old standby.

The lack of creativity and innovation that can come from the praise of product over process has potential long-reaching consequences. Imagine if the leaders of any artistic or scientific movement through history had decided that they ought *not* to take a risk or try something new because it might not be understood. What if Einstein had limited his work to equations and theories that he could easily prove? If Thomas Edison, who reportedly had to try over a thousand different filaments in his quest, had been afraid that he would be mocked for his mistakes, the light bulb may never have been improved to what it is today. The world needs risk takers and creative minds who are not afraid to push the envelope and try something that might not be immediately understood. The first step is to let your students know—loudly and clearly—that you value their work ethic more than the product.

Use this language every day, both at home and at school. Find reasons to positively reinforce the amount of work that students exert with their schoolwork, their creative endeavors, and their work habits.

Do not praise students randomly or without cause; telling students that you are proud of their hard work when they did an assignment at the last minute will only reinforce poor studying skills. Rather, you can show interest in the process of work as it happens. Have an open-ended discussion with students, encouraging them to teach you how they solve their math problems. Ask them to show you the steps needed to finish a science diorama, just because you are interested in *how* they are working. Encourage students to take risks and be creative, giving them access to interesting materials, junk boxes, and a variety of other mediums. Let students know that they have some "sacred time" that is all theirs to create. If they show you the end result of their creation, focus on *how* they did it; praise how much time, commitment, attention, or thought went into it. Both parents and teachers can show their students that they respect them as thinkers and creators of unique and individual pieces, rather than how they often view themselves—as students who seek prized product perfection.

Another way parents, in particular, can help is to show their children a behind-the-scenes look at their own success. We all have a hard-times story where we are particularly proud of how we overcame a challenge: the work we put in to finish college, an invention or a creative project, a challenging course we passed, or a long journey to be promoted at our place of work. Share with students when you make a mistake, or made a mistake in the past, and how you relished the opportunity to learn from it and overcome it. Place your hard-earned journey to success in the foreground rather than presenting only the end result to your children. Parents can show their children that they can live with mistakes and are not ashamed of them because they do not expect perfection either from themselves or their children.[123] Mistakes help us improve.

By the same token of not hiding mistakes, do not feel that you need to hide your stress levels as long as you are willing to think out loud—and "work out loud"—about your stress. Encourage children to model your behaviors as you identify sources of stress and prioritize responsibilities. Help students recognize that a moderate level of stress can be both manageable and even beneficial for peak performance. Sylvia Rimm recommends creating helpful outlets or therapy in the form of physical or enjoyable activities, as well as being a supporting and empathetic listener to a child's stress.[124] Humor can also help defuse emotionally stressful situations.

I often see parents of perfectionists who are baffled that their son or daughter puts so much stress on themselves. They insist that they do not require perfection, and they cannot see how telling students expressly that they do not seek perfection will help their student. What they do not realize is that their too-frequent praise that emphasizes superlatives and perfection can be a subtle source of stress.[125] I do not blame parents; it is incredibly difficult not to respond enthusiastically to the exceptional achievements of their talented children. When a child wins first place at a gymnastics meet or makes the honor roll, it is natural to exclaim and celebrate and tell them how proud you are, and you still should. However, remember that many high-ability children may have achieved these things without working as hard as their friends and age-mate peers did, and they may not have learned fully to associate hard work with success. In fact, seeing this pattern repeated too often can actually have an opposite effect, in which students begin to associate hard work with failure, or as an indication that they are not as good if they have to try. That model of what they see in their lives as they compare themselves to others can become their new cause-and-effect relationship, where having to work hard means that you are not as talented as those to whom it seemed to come naturally.

It is not enough to tell perfectionists that you do not expect perfection only after an incident has arisen. Anyone who has ever been told to calm down when they are upset knows that the command often has the opposite effect; it can generate more stress into the situation. Instead, encourage hard work and valuing the process for the sake of learning. Expose your perfectionist students to the message that their intelligence is ever-changing and that growth and working through the process are more valuable than the product. This will help them to develop confidence and not be afraid to take risks when they feel that, regardless of the outcome, their efforts will be appreciated by the ones closest to them.[126] What matters most is how students feel about their abilities and how they have internalized their ability to achieve successful outcomes.[127]

Overcoming Procrastination

Another strategy to use with perfectionists and underachievers who wait until the last minute to produce ultimately unsatisfying work is to give them tight mini-deadlines. Individuals with a tendency to delay work often perform better when there is little time or room to either second guess themselves or to lose themselves in the many excuses they can fabricate as to why they were unable to finish a task.[128] Have some of these deadlines take place during school, where the teacher presents a challenge to students and gives them a mini-deadline that does not allow them to take the project home. This forces them to not only abandon their excuses and get right to work but also to trust their own creative instincts—something they likely give themselves little opportunity to explore.

Here are two approaches for this strategy. First, build students' tolerance for deadlines by assigning challenges that are not connected to a larger project. Assigning a question to research or tasking students to create a geometric shape out of a net before the end of the day are examples of mini-deadlines. This version of the mini-deadlines strategy is easily implemented by either teachers or parents. The second method consists of breaking down larger projects into smaller, more manageable mini-deadlines. The process of transforming large-scale projects into forced mini-deadlines, which can be used by either teachers or parents, helps students develop healthier work habits. It is the second method that was particularly useful for Gus, who had developed a negative ritual around procrastination—so much so that he had not developed the skills to use his time productively.

Assigning long-term projects to a student with procrastination issues is often a recipe for a stressful all-nighter the day before the assignment is due. Although it may help to offer in-class time to complete projects, perfectionist students will often claim that they "are working on it at home" and have left their materials there. It is important to remember that the procrastination is a ritual, a built-in excuse in the event that they do poorly. Offering a student who wants an excuse to fail more time to complete a project, an open timeline, or more guided support are usually unsuccessful strategies because they allow more procrastination.

Mini-deadline meetings can be beneficial. For example, rather than telling a student that I will have them working on an interest project for two to three weeks or giving them an open time frame, I sit with them and divide the project into tasks. Each mini-deadline is marked by no more than a 5-10 minute mini-meeting. It is often more efficient for the teacher to group multiple students together for their check-ins. This forces students to use the entirety of the time they have been assigned to complete the assignment, and it helps them break their ritualistic cycle of procrastination. Here is an example of such a meeting.

Examples of Mini-Meetings

It is important to ensure that bright children do not spend the majority of their school experience working independently without the benefit of guidance, particularly if they are engaged in alternative curriculum, individual activities, or long-term projects. These children need a structure that enables them to meet with an adult who can support and guide them, and these periodic check-ins help to engage students in genuine learning experiences as well as to maintain the quality of the projects. This role can be filled by a parent, teacher, teaching aide, volunteer, or mentor.

The first step is for the facilitator to help the students divide their tasks into smaller sections and deadlines. Plot through the entirety of the course of study, identifying clearly marked expectations for what will be due at each checkpoint. For each checkpoint, set an appointment for a mini-meeting. The facilitator and student both should keep a copy of the expectations, the appointment calendar, and details of what will be due at each mini-deadline.

It is vitally important for facilitators to always keep the appointments they have made with students, even and especially if the students have not met the deadline. If you reschedule a meeting, it is often a relief for the student that elongates the procrastination and encourages their existing rituals. Breaking up a larger task into smaller chunks helps many students—not only bright procrastinators—because it increases the manageability of tasks. For clever students, however, who can power through an assignment in one night or on the bus en route to school, mini-deadlines do less to support making a project more manageable than they do to encourage the kind of quality work that comes from not leaving work to the last minute.

Teachers often ask what they should do when a student is not prepared at a deadline meeting. My response to teachers is that, at least at first, this is more of an inevitable *when* than *if* occurrence. Sometimes students simply forget, but for a student with a habit of not coming prepared, you can be almost certain that there is something other than a forgetful mind at play; don't be discouraged. Remember that there is an underlying dysfunction that needs to be addressed, and as with any deeply engrained process, it can take time to resolve. My second warning is for facilitators of the meeting to avoid the impulse to lecture students about their late or incomplete work. Almost like a tape recorder turning off, student minds will stop recording what lessons you are attempting to impart to them if they sense a lecture is forthcoming. This gives students the opportunity to lapse into justification mode: "This is why I did not complete my work, and this is why it is okay—to me." Students will come in expecting to be punished or lectured and are prepared to rationalize this to themselves. The cost-versus-benefit model, as simple as it may be, comes back into play. If what they are avoiding seems less punishing than the consequences for not completing the task, it is unlikely that they will initially come prepared. Again, the recommendation is not to increase the punishment for not meeting a deadline, but to reframe how the student views the work.

It is likely that students will come to the first few mini-deadline meetings unprepared. Do not be deterred. Start, as a parent or teacher, by restating what was going to be discussed on that deadline and remind the student of what was due. Then say, very simply, that the deadline was not met and read off the next deadline and what will be due. Set a new deadline for the missed assignment, but schedule it *prior* to the next appointment. In other words, do not let the entire deadline schedule get pushed back because of a missed assignment.

The next important thing, the next cardinal rule after "Don't lecture" is to utilize the whole meeting. Start by telling the student, "We already have these five minutes scheduled to talk, and I think it is important to keep our appointments. What do you think we can talk about to make sure this time is not wasted?"

Resist the urge to help the student work on or finish the project on the spot, even if it is what they suggest as a way to fill the time. Even if they say they just need to do a few more things, calmly tell them that the meetings are special times that are set aside to talk and solve problems, not to work on assignments.

It is difficult to have a tolerance for empty space or silence, but you need not worry about the meeting not being productive. More often than not, just by insisting to the student that you keep your appointments, you send a message that you will not give up on them, regardless of how many times they come unprepared. Even if the meeting turns into checking on something unrelated to the project, which has happened with a few of my students, they generally come in prepared for their next meeting. And to the teachers who fill the silence with suggestions when their students do not offer talking points, don't. When asked what they want to talk about to make sure their meeting is productive, most students respond with a shrug and "I don't know." They wait for the teacher to take control of the situation. Many students are not used to being given control, not only of what they do in school but also of what their teachers will do, and it takes time and modeling for them to accept that you will not fill the silence. Only once, in my experience, has a student come unprepared for a mini-meeting and sat in silence for the entire five minutes.

In the case of silence, either slight or prolonged, I sit across from the student with a pleasant smile on my face and hands folded on the table in front of me. I do not shuffler papers or look at my calendar; instead, I look at the student, not expectantly, but calmly, as if he or she were talking and I were listening. The ball is in their court. Usually, it only takes 10-15 seconds of this for the student to talk about the project or another subject such as the book they are reading, etc. And what became of the one student who did not speak? He sat, staring back at me for five whole minutes. I do not know what went through his mind during that time as we played our game of "Who's going to talk first" chicken, but it was, to me, a five minutes well spent. Even though we said nothing about the missed mini-deadline or any other assignment he was working on, he came to the next meeting prepared, ready to share his work and talk about it at length as if nothing had happened. He never came unprepared to another meeting again.

When a student comes unprepared to their mini-deadline meeting, it in fact becomes a "blank meeting," so named because the key to blank meetings is resist, resist, resist the urge to fill in the blanks for a student. After 15 seconds of silence, they will say again, "I don't know, Ms. Maupin." Unlike common practice in teaching, I do not encourage them with prompting cues such as "Just think of anything," "How about we talk about X?" or any other guiding prompts. I make sure that I state the instructions at the start of the blank meeting, and I check to see if they are understood. Past that point, when students ask questions such as "What should I say?" or give excuses such as "I don't know what to do," it is actually a strategy to prevent actual thinking. You will be surprised how quickly even the most vocally helpless protesters will come up with a plan when they are finally convinced that you are not going to do the thinking for them.

Once, one of my students came to my desk for help on a challenge assignment and asked a question to which she already knew the answer. She was just seeking to check her work against the teacher, rather than using her own problem-solving skills, so after she asked the question, I simply smiled at her pleasantly. After she realized that no words were forthcoming, she looked concerned and asked, "What does that mean?"

Then another student, overhearing, sighed loudly and answered, "Oh. I know that smile. It's her 'I am not going to just tell you the answer' smile. I hate that smile."

"It's okay. I know how to figure it out anyway, I think," the girl replied and returned to her seat. She finished the assignment correctly without any guidance.

To this day, it is one of my favorite student exchanges. That student may have hated the solve-it-yourself smile, but he read it perfectly. He knew what I expected of him and the other students, which was to take the risk to accept their own discoveries. Being correct 100% of the time is less important than creating a classroom where all students have the permission to be creative. A non-creative classroom is one in which the teacher is preoccupied with giving information over allowing students to come to their own understandings and discovering for themselves.[129] In the end, it is a far more useful skill for students to learn.

Other Ways Teachers Can Help

Schools and classrooms are often the battleground where the greatest perfectionist battles are played out. Though parents can recognize perfectionist behaviors of their children at home, the competitive school environment often exacerbates the symptoms of perfectionism. Because school becomes associated with schoolwork, grades, and ranking, all components that can trigger that polarized all-or-nothing perfectionist thinking, teachers typically see the greatest evidences of perfectionist behaviors. Students become hyper-sensitive to the fear that they will be seen as either a success or a failure.

Even though perfectionists often feel safer taking risks in a home environment, the elements of safety can be mirrored in the classroom setting through some easy steps that teachers can take to create an inspiring, inclusive classroom where risk is expected and safe. One way is to design assignments that are challenging, encourage creativity, and have multiple correct answers. If students are graded on these exercises, the grade should reflect their amount of work rather than the end product. This reduces the pressure students often feel to dominate or be labeled a failure. Have students design a science experiment, invent something using limited materials, explain a dream, write a story using made-up words, or undertake any other creative, challenging tasks that require them to think and process but without anyone judging how correct they are. This does not imply that bright children should be given easier tasks, but rather that work should allow them to experience both challenge and problem solving. Ruth Duskin Feldman, who as a child participated as a "Quiz Kid" in the popular 1940s and 1950s radio and television series, wrote that when gifted children are "accustomed to easy success and … are praised for work requiring modest effort [they] may not develop discrimination or learn to meet a challenge. When these children grow up, they seek applause constantly without knowing how to get it."[130]

Perfectionists traditionally have low tolerance for coping with ambiguity because of this reason; if they do not think they have a right answer, they fear that they will be unable to be praised or valued through their success. Teachers can be pivotal in helping these students develop a taste for open-endedness. Just as my students have come to recognize my solve-it-yourself smile, teachers can encourage their students to be problem-solvers and broad-thinkers by allowing them to make their own choices and, by extension, through the possibility of making their own mistakes. This happens dozens of times a day, sometimes in small ways: Students will ask where the stapler is, what side of the paper they should write their name on, what they should do next, etc., and my response is to point to a flag I have on my desk that reads, "You have permission to problem solve." What this means is that I will accept whatever choice they decide is right. They are allowed to make a choice and live with the consequences of that choice. Please note that this is only acceptable if there *is* no one right answer; if students must turn their work into one particular bin, they should be instructed to do so, for example. Then for any answer that students have the ability to discover on their own or choose from multiple choices, let them.

It may seem like a small thing, but perfectionists often seek continual reassurance that they are doing the right thing, which can lead to seeking comfort from adults regarding even the most minute of choices. They do not trust themselves to make choices because they internalize negativity and question their own judgment.[131] Students with perfectionist mindsets crave one right answer, and multiple choices can lead to a fear of being called out for being incorrect. Gus once stood at my desk for several minutes, quite frustrated that I would not tell him whether he should turn in his multiple pages of work stapled, loose, or paper clipped together.

His frustration rose when, after he finally made a decision, I would not tell him where the paper clips were. We had a very small room, and the paper clips were located in three separate, clearly marked locations in the space. Gus was fully capable of finding them; he was only afraid that he would not be able to and that he would be judged for it. Of course, as soon as he turned away from my desk, he located a paper clip, turned his papers in, and now makes his own decisions about how he wants to turn in his work. He needed his own reassurance that he was capable of making decisions and solving his own problems far more than he needed my help with two inconsequential pieces of information.

This permission-to-problem-solve mentality can also be extended to the type of work a student produces. Create open-ended, variably answered tasks whenever possible, and give students clear feedback that encourages process over product. Ask them to explain their thinking, to show their work, and to value that process over the grade. One way to accomplish this is to allow students to redo assignments for a different grade. This is one of the best ways for a teacher to communicate to a student that the learning process is the most important aspect and that they are not judging the student based on the quality of a student's first attempt at a goal.[132] Allowing students to grow and improve helps set a framework that you believe in a child's ability to be resilient and encourages them look past their perfectionism to take academic risks. For Gus, this was one direct application that the team used to encourage him to attempt even the scariest of writing assignments and to negate that all-or-nothing mindset of failure or success.

Whenever possible, I try to present my students with challenging work, often more challenging than they can complete correctly in one sitting without some ongoing feedback and discussion. I encourage them to try wacky problem-solving, make mistakes, and take academic risks because they probably will not get it right the first time. They receive their work back with feedback; we discuss their progress in meetings; and we celebrate their creative choices by having group creativity shares. I explain to students that if all their schoolwork is perfect, they may not be learning, and that the goal in school should be to always learn something, even if it is a way *not* to do something.

Student outcomes are greater when they seek not grades, but communication from their teachers about their progress and abilities. Students generally dislike the word potential, as it is often abused and used only as a reprimand, as in "You are not meeting it," "You are wasting it," or "I don't understand why you are not succeeding because you have so much of it." Potential is a beautiful word, and it should be used not as a motivator or a reprimand but as a descriptor of progress, such as: "The way you explained yourself here shows me great potential. I can see where this might go," or "I like how many potential options you can take with this assignment. Which will you choose?" Teach students to be explorers, allowing information or options that may have been filtered out in their perfectionist state instead to be investigated and attempted. The hyper-focus of some perfectionists can cause them to sacrifice the fun, relaxing aspects of learning that can lead to creativity, but they can also learn to use that focus to passionately explore areas of interest.[133]

It also can help if students feel like a part of a team or group, either through school pairings or in after-school activities that involve teams. Teamwork can help parents and teachers in rehabilitating the perfectionism, as well as helping bright children who are experiencing self-isolating behaviors to branch out to a variety of social groups. Children need to learn both how to win and how to fail, and to internalize the concept that every challenge does not become their own personal victory. They need to accept that all individuals have strengths and weaknesses, and they need to learn to work collaboratively with others whose ability levels are different than their own. For Gus, this meant that his parents offered him the chance to pick one team sport or activity to do after school. To combat the common "interest drop-off" that perfectionists can have with an activity that becomes too unfamiliar or difficult, Gus was allowed to try up to three different activities, but at the end of a set period of time he was required to choose at least one to continue and complete. This not only prevented Gus from being able to drop out by citing disinterest but also let him know that his parents required perseverance from him and that they valued the character and process of his journey.

Teachers and counselors should not completely discourage perfectionist behaviors because they can benefit a student when managed healthily and with reasonable expectations.[134] Instead, help students channel their perfectionism toward positive, specific goals, and teach them the value of process over product.

Throw in a Little Grit

It takes bravery and unwavering commitment for a child who has learned to hide behind perfectionism to be willing to risk failure. Coping mechanisms of any kind are difficult to abandon, and no one can snap his or her fingers and transform from neurotic perfectionism to a healthier form overnight. Throughout the process of growth, students will be challenged, and what students need is a character trait known as grit.

Paul Tough, author of the bestselling book *How Children Succeed*, stresses how vital it is for students to develop grit, as a quality of perseverance and fortitude, and how it may be even more important than having opportunities, including even their natural ability.[135] When students score high on a simple, 12-question "Grit Scale" to measure their dedication to finishing tasks and not allowing setbacks to deter them, not only is that scale a remarkable predictor of success but also a predictor of entrance into challenging colleges. In addition, students with higher grit scores fared better at the National Spelling Bee.[136] And, not unlike a growth mindset, which tells us that abilities can be malleable, grit also can be learned, practiced, and, better yet, taught.[137]

Parents and teachers should praise grit and perseverance as attributes that are valued over outcomes. The former are the building blocks of the latter. Gifted and talented students may succeed early in life, but a high number of them drop out of school, fail to complete college, or do not lead eminent lives. Natural ability will not always protect a child from challenges, competition, or self-doubt, but grit can. Together, grit and talent can do great things, but we should be wary of putting the cart before the horse. Positively reinforce the building blocks—the grit, endurance, effort, diligence, and other skills that lead to positive coping mechanisms—and praise them. Help your children develop them. Celebrate the outcomes of that work, but try not to have them become the focus—either yours or your child's.

For years I have coached a competitive problem-solving program known as Future Problem Solvers. In this difficult yet rewarding team challenge, students research current world issues, extrapolate how the issues will evolve in the future, and in the culminating competitions write challenges and solutions and develop criteria to judge their solutions. Students then write an action plan to solve creatively a futuristic (hypothetical, yet plausible) issue. The entire process (sans research) is completed in a two-hour, timed window. Every year at my current school, we have had at least one team qualify for the state-level championship competition, but usually several teams progress and face the challenge of competing against the other teams from their school for the first time.

It is an agitating time for most students who struggle with their desire to win compared to their knowledge that only one—if any of them—will win. As a result, I have dealt with tears, anger (often at themselves), and self-doubt at every awards celebration. Last year, however, was the first year that I was amazed by a team's reaction. After the awards ceremony was completed, and the lights in the massive auditorium went up, I turned to comfort the team that was leaving empty-handed, only to find them wide-eyed and smiling.

When I asked them how they were feeling, one girl answered that they were excited.

"That's great to hear. You should be," I said, without having any idea why. Did they not understand that they had not won?

"Our moms promised we'd go out to Dairy Queen to celebrate after the awards ceremony."

"And what will you be celebrating?" I asked in my best "teacher already knows the answer and is just checking to see if you know" voice.

"How hard we worked to get here," one team member exclaimed.

"I wish we'd won," said another, "but some of the other teams put in more work than we did. They deserved to win."

As they filed past me, happily headed towards frozen treats, one turned to me and said, "Don't worry, Ms. Maupin. The team decided we're going to do this again next year. And we're going to do even better."

Later, when I spoke to one of the mothers of the students on the team, I discovered the root of her child's attitude. Their family strove to instill the quality of grit in their children. They did not give false praise where it was not due, and they never said that their children deserved to win or get a greater accolade when they did not. They focused on the work and celebrated that hard work regardless of the outcome. The attitude had been infectious. Just one child on a team of four had been excited about their celebration and proud of the work they had put in, and it had spread to the other three. They were all proud of themselves but realistic about the amount of work they had put in compared to the other teams who had performed better. Even though they walked away empty-handed, I have rarely been more proud of one of my teams than I was then.

Gus came back to visit me recently, having progressed to middle school the year after he self-reported his cheating. He told me that he was on the soccer team and that he was working on a science project that he found very interesting.

"Gus," I said, carefully steering the conversation, "how is writing going for you? Still finding it hard to turn writing assignments in on time?"

"No, I turn everything in on time. I don't do *that* anymore. I have a B in language arts right now. That's mostly because of the writing."

My eyes widened. The Gus I knew would have been panicking if he had less than an A in anything. Furthermore, I knew that with a grade like that, he likely thought that it reflected on his actual ability, since he would have instigated his various cheats to cover up that "failure" of a grade otherwise. That B was perhaps the first honest writing grade he had ever received. He was finally acquiring the skills and strategies for writing that his classmates had been learning while he was using cheating behaviors to cover up his fear of failure. I asked Gus how he felt about that grade.

"It's fine. I'm not as bad at writing as I thought I was. It's just not my strongest subject. I have an A in everything else. My parents say it's okay, and as long as I'm doing my best I'm not in trouble or anything."

I told Gus what a terrific attitude he had and how proud I was of his hard work. He was turning in assignments on time; he was open and honest about his grades, and realistic about his strengths and weaknesses. He no longer professed what a terrible writer he was, but rather was able to see his abilities relative to his other strengths and weaknesses. Gus was learning to take risks to be on a team sport where he would not get to have singular successes and could not control the outcome of games or standings. He was persevering through topics that were of interest to him, and he seemed happy and calm. I have little doubt that the greatest change was implemented at home and that his parents are to thank for his attitude shift. They came away from our initial battle-plan meetings ready to shift the focus in their household from one of outcomes to that of process and effort. Their focused praise and support of Gus had produced a young man who is succeeding on his own merits and working to improve his writing without punishing himself or turning to cheating as a coping mechanism. The changes that can be made in the lives of perfectionists are sometimes subtle but can have dramatic results in the scope of their futures.

FIVE

Marie & Joaquin

Marie

Mr. Carver had a great idea for a "teachable moment." His sixth-grade class had been dreading an upcoming math test on statistics, something they had been studying for two weeks. It wasn't long before something about the combination of probability, graphs, charts, averages, and calculations had the class feeling unsettled about the complexity of the subject. After several straight days of students begging for an extension of the test, Mr. Carver came up with a proposal. He would grade the test on the curve, he said, enjoying the opportunity it gave him to teach the concept to his students. He explained that statistically, students fall in a certain range of scores on any given test measure, and that grading on the curve was a way to statistically "reshuffle the deck" of scores to reflect the group's understanding relative to how the highest scorer performs.

The students' relief was short-lived. When the test came back, one student—a bright little girl named Marie—earned a score of 100%. Although Mr. Carver had debated using the next highest score—81%—as the top of the curve, he decided that the class had done well enough overall to justify letting the teachable moment stand. He discussed this with his class and mentioned the two highest scores without saying who had received each one. Marie tried to hide her grade and even reported to some classmates that she had gotten a C, but the class blamed her anyway. She had been identified as gifted in the first grade—a fact that none of her classmates would have known—but she was an exceptionally bright young girl, and her classmates knew that. They accused her of ruining the curve.

Over the next few weeks, Marie noticed students whispering to themselves and looking at her, or sometimes students in a conversation would go quiet when she came near. She spent recess alone, and during quiet reading times, she was afraid that every whisper was about her. She started to miss classes and recesses, citing a number of illnesses, and became a frequent visitor of the school nurse's office. For the next three math tests and two spelling tests, she was home sick with fevers. After speaking with Mr. Carver and hearing about her daughter's test avoidance behaviors at school, her mother was concerned that she was feigning illness, but when she started to take Marie's temperature on the days that Marie was not feeling well, the thermometer always verified a high temperature.

Upon her return to school, Marie would ask to stay in from recess or go to another classroom during quiet reading times to finish her work. As Marie missed more of the classes during which the material covered on the exams was taught, she began to pull B and C grades on her chapter tests. As her grades fell, her socialization increased, and on several occasions she was seen at recess laughing and playing with a large group of students. In class, she was less reserved and more talkative, even as her absences increased and her grades slipped lower and lower. After several months, she asked to be withdrawn from her pull-out enrichment program.

Joaquin

Joaquin, a bright fourth grader, hated studying. He believed that he should either know the information or not and that studying was too much work. When tests were announced in class, Joaquin would clutch his stomach and moan or put his head down on the desk and say that he was dizzy and that the lights were hurting his eyes. He would scarcely have been given the exam before he would begin to feel sick. He would turn his test over, walk up to the teacher's desk, and ask her, eyelids half closed and head bobbing slowly, if he could go to the nurse because he thought he was going to be ill. He would then go to the nurse and tell her that he had just thrown up in one of the boys' restrooms en route to her office. Joaquin would assure her that he felt better and ask to go back to class to finish his test, but of course the nurse would send him home.

Joaquin differed from Marie in that he would return to school the next day, immediately take the test he had missed or turn in the paper that had been due during his illness, and receive excellent grades on the work. Even though the work was late, he was never penalized for its tardiness due to the circumstances.

After several of these gastrointestinal episodes, Joaquin's parents brought him to the doctor, who recommended testing to rule out any disorder or food sensitivities. After that, Joaquin's stomach issues disappeared, but a series of fevers and headaches began, resulting in long stays in the nurse's office during exams. At home, Joaquin began to have trouble sleeping, and when he did sleep, he began to show signs of bruxism—grinding his teeth and clenching his jaw. His parents reported that his doctor recommended that he decrease his stress level.

You can probably guess the outcome of these stories. Marie eventually was caught manipulating the thermometer that her mother used, and Joaquin reported his behavior to me in the Safe Space. Both Marie and Joaquin were fabricating their illnesses and cheating to avoid completing their work in a timely and honest fashion. This type of cheating is so ubiquitous that it has a name: malingering. Malingering is defined as the conscious fabrication of physical or psychological symptoms and feigning illness in order to gain an obvious or tangible objective.[138] This form of deceit is hardly monopolized by clever students; it is perhaps one of the oldest and most well-known ways for children and adults alike to avoid unwanted tasks or consequences. The art of faking sickness is at least as old as Hippocrates, who suggested various categorizations of malingering in the early 19th century.[139] However, studies on patients who routinely assign themselves with fictitious symptoms or factitious disorders have shown that the individuals almost always possess above-average intelligence, and stories of clever children feigning illness in order to skip all or portions of school are common.[140] In fact, one of the archetypes in Dr. Rimm's list of underachieving bright students is known as "Sick Sam."[141]

Cheating behaviors often function as methods of avoidance, and malingering is a key example. What an individual seeks to avoid by feigning illness varies and can include anxiety, pressure over upcoming responsibilities, feelings of isolation, and boredom. For students like Joaquin, avoiding assignments by delaying tests and assignments offers the advantage of more study or work time. More than once, he also had the opportunity to see the exam before going home sick, so he had pre-knowledge of what was being tested if the teacher did not give him an alternate make-up exam. Some students, like Marie, seek to avoid social stigma. Marie did not cheat in order to obtain better grades or to make an unworthy assignment feel more challenging. She malingered in order to avoid being labeled as gifted, fearing the scorn of her peers if she achieved at a high level.

Gifted and talented students may cheat to avoid any number of labels regarding their intelligence. For some, this may be a fear of being *too* smart. For others, it may be the fear that they are not smart enough. Often, students with fixed mindsets fear that they will be seen as a failure if they do not get perfect grades, such as Joaquin. For students who have aligned their feelings of self-worth with their achievement, this can result in studying being replaced by cheating behaviors. This way, failure can be rationalized as not being their fault. It helps protect them from feelings of worthlessness.[142]

Malingering as Impression Management

Both Marie and Joaquin malingered as a form of impression management, or the deliberate effort to control others' perceptions of them as an individual. Joaquin maintained his high scores by feigning illness whenever he felt unsure about the outcome of a grade. Marie's desired identity, on the other hand, was that of a social, non-gifted girl, and she deliberately missed classes through malingering in order to maximize her social outcomes. All high-ability students, regardless of gender, can fall victim to negative feelings about their intelligence and other gifts, and this can result in avoidance behaviors such as cheating. In fact, at an elementary level, boys and girls seem to cheat at about the same rate.[143] The act of cheating through malingering is also not gender-specific, and it is seen in equal measure in both adolescent males and females. However, gifted girls are particularly susceptible to forms of cheating that allow them to deny their gifts to try to create an appearance of normalcy.

Although the cheating involved in Joaquin's case is more recognizable in the traditional sense of the word, Marie is just as guilty of manipulating her environment through deceptive means in order to change her grades. Marie might simply have refused to do as well on exams, but through systematic and frequent malingering she had actually manufactured an environment in which she had prevented herself from doing well. She knew that no one would believe her sudden low grades, and so she had created a scenario in which her underachievement would be understandable and her new identity as a B and C student believable to her peers. As her grades dropped, her feelings of social appropriateness rose.

Impression management is an issue faced by all high-ability students to some degree, regardless of whether or not they have been actively teased or isolated. One of the most common reasons for regulation and underachievement among talented youth—male or female—is the desire to fit in with peers.[144] They have this desire in common with their non-gifted classmates; in a study of over 5,000 third- to eighth-grade students, popularity was ranked highest in overall student concerns.[145] This need for acceptance begins as early as the pre-adolescent period, and we begin to see associated peer pressures, norms, and expectancies forming as early as fourth grade. As peer pressures mount and become more influential, students begin to recognize and describe feelings of being different from the group.[146]

Adolescence can be a particularly difficult time for high-ability children as they recognize these differences and fear that their accomplishments will be seen as threatening to their peers. Bright peers, when viewed through the lens of a competitive environment, may be viewed as unfair competition due to their substantial gifts and abilities. Middle school students in particular face an additional barrier, where working hard can make them look like a nerd, a category that they view as unpopular.[147]

Under these pressures, students feel compelled to underachieve in order to receive positive reinforcement from their peer group, turning in substandard work and curtailing their vocabulary and interests in order to be perceived as average. Bright children in this position often learn to avoid success and failure in equal measure, psychologically adapting to the norm of their peer groups.[148] According to one bright student: "So I think you maybe try to cover it up a little bit, or to show something else. I am really not that gifted, I am just like you guys."[149] This process is known as psychological adjustment, or the process of resourceful adaptation to one's environment, to include compromising and adjusting ability levels and values in order to cope or survive psychologically. Although psychological adjustment and impression management can accomplish student goals of feeling like an acceptable member of their peer group, they can also create serious consequences for the bright children who put too much pressure on themselves to create a popular or merely acceptable identity.

For some, regulation includes cheating behaviors as a way to avoid negative outcomes, rather than learning to cope with natural outcomes. Instead of being proud of her 100% math test grade and seeking to work on her relationships with her classmates in ways that did not compromise her ability level, Marie used malingering to avoid any future reoccurrences of the situation. In addition, her continued absences and poor study habits surrounding those absences resulted in skill deficiencies and lowered grades. Almost all underachieving gifted students, regardless of their ability, are at risk for these skill deficiencies as a result of their damaging coping mechanisms.[150] All Marie's effort and ability was being used not to develop her potential or meet her goals but to adjust herself in order to meet others' expectations, as gifted girls can sometimes be predisposed to do.[151]

The Effect on Gifted Girls

When gifted girls feel that their intelligence threatens their social relationships, the Horner Effect can come into play. In the Horner Effect, girls tend to purposefully under-reach their potential or hold back in order to please others.[152] This desire to avoid competition with peers in order to gain approval is not unique to gifted females, but it is more prevalent in that group than in non-gifted groups of either male or female, or in gifted males.[153] Paths of moral development in women may help explain this; a girl's personal ethics and compassion can directly oppose a classroom that is competitive in nature.[154] Gifted girls, who can be particularly emotionally sensitive to their environments, are more susceptible to the conflict that can arise if they feel that their competence and achievements make their peers feel inferior, and they may resort to downplaying or *regulating* their gifts through cheating behaviors. Girls and women commonly define themselves based on their relationships with others, and if students do not have ability-matched peers as well as high-ability role models, the amount of effort needed to regulate can undermine the development of talent.[155]

To an even greater degree, gifted girls who strive to identify with their age mates, as opposed to intellectual peers, may begin to believe that they are not really gifted. Though the effects of these kinds of attempts to blend in socially at the expense of nurturing one's gifts can peter out over time, unfortunately, it is not always the case. Kerr notes in a study of gifted women spanning over 20 years that some female subjects continued into adulthood believing that they were imposters and that they never were truly gifted.[156] Incredibly, many of these women attribute their identification to tester error and their consistent high achievements to luck. Even when individuals do come to accept their abilities, they may not be able to apply them to their lives in meaningful ways or to make up the time that they lost in failing to nurture their talents.

Though this loss of potential is not unique to gifted girls, they are particularly susceptible to prioritizing peer relationships over individual growth.[157] One study of over 600 children found that girls typically adapted to the ability level of their age-similar peers, and girls in third through ninth grade significantly chose to not join advanced classes if they would be required to leave their friends.[158] Avoidance-driven cheating behaviors can easily result when students feel like they do not have a choice or that they will disappoint others if they make "the wrong choice," such as deciding against advanced classes or enrichment opportunities. For Marie, this meant creating a feasible excuse as to why she was no longer gifted and no longer needed enrichment opportunities. Thankfully, Marie's teachers and parents were unwilling to accept her avoidance of her gifts and worked with her to help her identify positively with her achievements, but for many students, malingering and other avoidance behaviors can rob them of their chance to grow and experience all that their gifts have to offer.

Dangers of Continued Malingering

Practically everyone has "played hooky," called in sick, or gone home from school with a nonexistent ailment at least once in their lives. Malingering is so common that it may seem innocent in comparison to other cheats or lies that students could perpetrate. It is true that a single or small handful of malingering incidents are not necessarily indicative of a larger issue or even of the development of a cheating problem. However, malingering requires an individual to be knowingly deceptive for the purpose of gaining an objective. In addition, anyone who malingers seeks to avoid something or to gain something that they have not earned through legitimate means, which may result in students' unfair advantage over their classmates.

It is exceedingly common for parents to downplay the issue of malingering, if not as a whole, then certainly in relation to their own children. In the research for this book, over 90% of parents interviewed stated that their children—both those with and without a gifted label—did not lie. The truth is that almost all children experiment with lying as early as their fourth birthday; 80% of four-year-olds tested in a do-not-peek test cheated and then lied to researchers about their cheating behavior.[159] High-ability children may be even more susceptible to this, as they have been documented cheating and successfully lying as early as 2-3 years of age.[160] Even those parents who admitted that their children have attempted to play hooky or feign symptoms of an illness also asserted that they knew their children well enough to be able to determine whether or not they were being truthful, but again, research suggests otherwise. When parents and teachers are tested in relation to how well they can determine whether or not children are lying, they only score slightly higher than chance.[161]

Parents sometimes use evidence of their child's moral understanding as proof that they would not seek to deceive adults; however, there is a surprising lack of connection between how moral students are and whether or not they engage in lying. Even though most children serve harsher judgments to liars and are less forgiving of lies, regardless of purpose, it does not connect to whether or not they themselves engage in deception.

Another common misconception is that introverted, quieter students are more likely to engage in cheating and malingering, and some parents point to their children's excellent social skills and enthusiasm as evidence for their innocence. In fact, extroverted students often possess the confidence and social skills needed to make their lie more convincing. Lying requires not only advanced cognitive skills but also social ones, which makes it even more important for parents and teachers of bright children to recognize that their brilliant, excited young thinkers are hothouses for potential deceit. This realization is imperative not only for identification of malingering but also for the prevention of escalating physical or psychological issues.

The act of malingering is not in itself a mental disorder; however, it is linked to disorders such as Munchausen Syndrome, Munchausen by Proxy Syndrome, and Factitious Disorder Syndrome, which represent more serious and damaging forms of feigning illness. Individuals who present with these mental disorders often cite the more innocent malingering as something they did when they were young. There are no direct causal links established between feigning illness and later mental disorders; however, it is likely that a relationship exists. The simulation of illness can escalate if not caught and addressed at a young age. This escalation can begin to occur as soon as early adolescence. Malingering often begins with avoidance of negative outcomes, but as students continue to receive secondary, external rewards (the ability to stay home, extra sleep, attention, unsupervised time, etc.), they may continue to maintain their malingering far past the original intention.

One of the more dangerous escalations includes students physically harming themselves or inducing physical symptoms to support the credence of their claims, to manipulate the situation to receive sympathy or attention, and to escape the immediate situation. Casey, a bright seventh grader, was caught slamming her hand in her locker door repeatedly before a big test. She reported that she had been trying to break her fingers or at least create enough damage that she would be sent to the nurse with an excuse to avoid a final exam she did not feel confident that she could ace. Thankfully, she was caught before she had done any serious harm, but her dedication to injuring herself in the name of a grade serves as warning that some highly able children need help reestablishing their priorities.

Not only can unaddressed malingering escalate during childhood, but individuals who feign illness as children are more likely to continue their deceitfulness into adulthood. Adult malingering is often responsible for jeopardized relationships, careers, and poor coping skills for anxiety and stress. It also represents a drain on society as a whole. Illegitimate illnesses cost the U.S. around two billion dollars every year in erroneous medical charges, and this estimate has been reported as likely being conservative.[162]

Almost all people have malingered or will malinger during their lifetime. A single act of malingering or creating factitious symptoms is rarely cause for alarm; however, it should never be ignored. The ramifications for continued avoidance of school activities can include damaged academic, personal, and emotional growth, as well as the potential for dangerous escalation from feigned symptoms into manufactured ones. Parents and teachers should be on the lookout for potential development of these and other avoidance behaviors and seek out the possible underlying causes in order to prevent future occurrences of this or other cheating behaviors.

Malingering as Reported by Bright Students

What follows are common malingering ploys as reported by bright youth and adults. These are listed and described in order for parents and teachers to become aware of the patterns that may develop in order to help identify them in their own students. After each category of common symptoms and ploys are a few tips for prevention and detection, followed by general signs that your student may be falsifying their symptoms.

Fevers. In a 2000 review of 42 children with documented falsified illness, the most commonly represented symptom was fever.[163] In fact, fevers of unknown origin, or FUO, are one of the most commonly faked symptoms. This may be due to their often vague and unspecified nature; a fever can be elongated into other symptoms to perpetrate a multiple day illness, or it can be a singular incidence. There are many ways to fake a fever, as reported by clever students past and present:

"My Mother didn't ever check to see if we actually had a temperature. She'd just look to see if we were flushed and feel our heads with her hand. It's easy to get a good red blush and some heat on your skin just by taking your hands and rubbing them on your face for a few minutes." —Judy, 32

"You can fake a temperature by putting the thermometer in hot water." —Terrence, 16

"Drinking warm water right before your dad takes your temperature or holding some hot water in your mouth can give you a slight fever on a thermometer. Sometimes that's enough to make it seem like you should stay home, especially if you also are coughing or seem tired." —Aaron, 13

"Rub the thermometer really hard when Mom's not looking." —Anne, 10

"Some kids in my gifted class would skip class by putting the thermometer up to a light bulb for a few seconds." —E, 30

"We learned about niacin in sixth grade, and it stuck, how it could raise your temperature and flush you. Starting in about seventh grade, I would buy over the counter niacin vitamin supplements and take a big enough dose to make my skin red and hot and add one or two points on my temperature. Just enough to seem believable." —Roger, 26

To prevent these manipulations, parents and school nurses can maintain watch over students before their temperature is taken, not leaving them alone with the thermometer for any time. It is difficult to trick rapid-reading electronic brands, but most families own thermometers that are susceptible to tampering. Generally, it takes less than a minute for a thermometer to be manipulated in a way that can show a fever, so a student left alone even for a brief period of time has the potential to alter the results. Marie was later found to have manipulated her household thermometer with hot water in order to maintain the illusion of illness for her mother, who had become suspicious.

Parents in particular should stay with the student over a period of 5-15 minutes whenever possible while taking a child's temperature. This not only prevents tampering but also affords the opportunity for multiple data points as you repeat temperature readings. Consistent readings may also help give credence to students' claims as you watch to see if their skin quality improves or if their complexion continues to be flushed. Signs of fever can include flushed skin, sweat, heat, and rapid heart rate.

One of the more frightening claims was that of Roger, whose reported misuse of over-the-counter medication resulted in fevers that were real, albeit physically manipulated, without an underlying illness. Though Roger asserted that he had done research to make sure that he was taking an appropriate dose, it was clearly dangerous for an adolescent to abuse supplements in order to manufacture symptoms. Harmful reactions, unintentional overdoses, or prolonged damage with excessive use can occur when children create symptoms through pharmacology, and detection of this manner of deceit can be incredibly difficult. Incidents like this are thankfully rare, but it is important to remember that even the most brilliant and well-behaved child is susceptible to deception of that magnitude. If you suspect that your child's symptoms are false, even if they check out, do not hesitate in gently confronting them about your suspicions or seeking the opinion of a medical health professional.

Stomachaches. Stomachaches are another commonly reported falsified symptom by high-ability children. They are favored for their general, easy to fake symptoms. All children have experienced some manner of stomach upset in their life and are able to pull from the memories of their symptoms and parental response to act out their feigned discomfort. Stomachaches also have the benefit of being difficult to verify, unlike with fevers where the severity of which can be measured. However, for those students who fear being disbelieved for this reason, fake stomachaches are often followed by fake vomiting:

"It's easier for me to stay home sick than for my mom to let my sister. She is always cheating at games at home, and she's always asking not to go to school. I have to say that I don't want to stay home. I say I have [something] I need to do, please let me go to school, and pretend I don't feel well. And they tell me I have to stay. I'm more believable than she is." —Ollie, 11

"I would mix yogurt, chew on cereal... splash in some orange Kool-Aid for color and put it in the toilet and tell my mother that I was sick. Evidence!" —Jo, 25

"Stomachaches are among the easiest things to fake, but they don't always result in the most sympathy." —Paul, 25

"Hold your stomach a lot. I don't tell the teacher that I'm not feeling well, I wait for him to ask me if I'm okay, and then I just act really tired and say I feel gross. Sometimes I would ask to stay in for lunch or recess, and then they send me to the nurse's office." —Brandon, 10

"Tell the nurse you threw up. Tell the teacher. That's all you have to do, and you go home. Your Dad comes and gets you." —Monica, 9

The wide range of methods that students have to feign stomachaches are often detailed, complicated, and highly personal. Students who frequently create fake stomach disorders have a routine that they follow, so parents should watch for repeated patterns. Some students simply tell an adult they are ill or that they have thrown up out of ear- or eyeshot, but others rely on acting sick and waiting for others to question them. Some students report adding to this by making appropriate sound effects through a bathroom door when simulating vomit, and others even report creating a cocktail of fake vomit that is either left in a restroom for a parent or teacher to find—or even held in their mouths until the right moment. Most students outlined the importance of acting as if they are sick as a key component of the ruse.

One gifted adult in particular recounted his youthful malingered stomachaches, recalling that he would "set the stage" as early as the day or night before he planned on staying home, asking if he could skip dinner because he did not feel well. He said that he would then manufacture sickness the next morning—either feigned or manipulated. False reporting of vomiting may seem to many to be harmless, though disturbing, but be wary: Malingering has reached a dangerous point if students manipulate their gag reflex in order to induce actual regurgitation. This is always a risk when students feel that they will be excused from schoolwork as long as they produce some physical symptom of illness, and students should be monitored and questioned as to what they may be avoiding or missing by staying home. Parents should also take the time to teach their students about the dangers of forcing vomit when it is not a genuine bodily reaction. Many students may create symptoms without realizing the long-term harm they may be doing to their bodies.

Rashes. Rashes and other skin issues are another category of commonly falsified illness reported by bright children, though less so than fevers or stomach complaints. Since the symptoms of rashes are often physical and quite visual in nature, faking a rash usually requires students to manufacture some manner of physical manifestation of their "illness." False rashes are more commonly reported at school than at home, as it is rare for parents to hold students back from school for skin fluctuations, barring those that are contagious or the result of serious allergy complications. However, a student who presents a patch of red, purportedly itchy skin to the teacher will undoubtedly receive a timely nurse's visit. Below are some reported methods of rash fakery:

"Rub your skin for a few minutes and it will turn blotchy." — Ireland, 15

"I always had red bumps on the back of my arms. If I needed to get out of class for a few minutes, I scratch them a little to make the skin red and show the teacher. She never noticed I had them in the first place, so I would go to the nurse." —Eddie, 19

"Just tell your mom or dad that it itches everywhere. They think maybe you ate something that you're allergic to." —Alexandra, 9

"Makeup can work, but you can't let anyone touch you. Best couple that with a faux fever and you're good to go." —KT, 29

It can be particularly difficult to ascertain whether or not a physical symptom has been falsified or not. Often, the easiest way to determine legitimacy of rash claims is similar to stomachache claims—taking into account what the student might be seeking to avoid. What follows should be documentation not only of the nature of their symptoms but also the timing of their release from the classroom. Did their rash appear after a time when the student was left alone for a period of time, such as recess or a bathroom break? If they report that they received the rash outside of school, did they report their symptoms early in the school day or before an important test or homework assignment?

The illusion of a rash is sometimes created by cosmetics, and parents and school nurses can, without coming into skin-on-skin contact, carefully rub the area with a skin-safe, approved cleanser to determine if the area has been tampered with. Parents can also consult a physician to note which rashes are harmless or naturally occurring and learn to discount those as serious concerns. Students who have a heavy bout of crying or coughing, for instance, can experience facial petechiae—small, reddish or purplish spots caused by minor hemorrhage or broken capillaries in the face. They often appear around the eyes and are harmless in these incidences, healing within a few days even when the appearance may look severe.[164] For students with minor, explainable, or even irritation-based rashes, such as poison ivy rashes, that have healed, parents should be sure to alert either the teacher or the school nurse. This not only allays teacher concerns but also can prevent students from manipulating their way out of class under the pretense of a "mysterious rash," thus gaining a half hour in a nurse's office and out of an activity they seek to avoid.

Some students manipulate existing injuries either to exaggerate them or to prevent them from healing. Watch for students who pick, scratch, or rub foreign substances into wounds. Even a small sore, such as an insect bite or a pimple, can be dangerously manipulated into a larger, more serious infection. Another sign of falsified or manipulated rashes is location. Malingering students want others to see their injury, so these rashes often appear in areas visible to others, including the limbs and the face. If a rash is occurring in an area that is mostly hidden from view or out of reach of the student, such as the trunk of the body or the back, it is less likely to have been created or manipulated for the purpose of malingering.

As KT noted, sometimes students pair rashes with other symptoms in their false reporting. These can include fevers or reporting a sensation of burning or itching, but sometimes students report fewer appropriate symptoms as they seek to arouse adult concern. Younger high-ability students in particular often point to natural skin fluctuations and cite grandiose symptoms. A mole may be referenced as something that suddenly aches, or a dry patch of skin might be inexplicably cited as causing sharp pains or immobility in that limb.

The best way for teachers and parents to respond to rash-based symptoms is to address the reported claims with efficiency but little emotion. It is important not to discount student concerns, as a student who claims to be excessively itchy or experiencing difficulty breathing may be having an allergic reaction. Also, any open-skin wounds, whether the fault of an actual rash, student manipulation, or excessive scratching, need to be cleaned out and covered before the student comes into contact with other students or risks infection from foreign debris.

Student claims should be addressed but in a calm, non-emotional manner that leads the students to understand that they will be observed by a school nurse or other medical professional and that as soon as they are cleared, they will be returned to the classroom to continue with their school day. Let students know that they will, of course, make up what they missed when they were absent from the class. Tell frequent rash repeaters that they will also receive an alternate test or assignment if they seem to be seeking additional time or an advantage by leaving the room. Not only does this put students who may actually be injured and concerned at ease, but it also lets talented malingerers know that adults will not be manipulated and that the teacher or parent is not overly concerned by the reported symptoms.

Signs of Falsified Symptoms

Though there are commonalities and patterns that develop with some of the more favored faux illnesses such as fevers, stomach complaints, and rashes, it is important to specify that there are many other ways that talented children can and do malinger. It is impossible to create an exhaustive list of all the ways a child may seek to create false symptoms. However, here are 10 ways to help determine whether or not a student may be falsifying illness. This is also not an exhaustive list, and parents and teachers should recognize that there may be other reasons to explain why a student who is legitimately sick may show signs of falsifying their behaviors. Knowledge of students and their regular behavior can help parents and teachers make the determination of whether or not malingering may be present.

Students' reported symptoms are not consistent with their behavior.

For example, students claim they have a stomachache but are still hungry or asking for food. Students cite exhaustion but resist sleeping, or they describe pain in one area but then favor the other side or limb, etc.

Students' description of symptoms is vague or confusing.

If students are unable to explain what kind of pain they have or use only generic descriptions, they may be manufacturing symptoms. This often accompanies signs of inconsistent behavior and can represent a student who has not pre-planned to malinger. Vague symptoms, "I don't feel well," or "I feel sick," for example, when they are otherwise alert or functioning can represent a student who is seeking to avoid an unpleasant situation.

Students' description of symptoms is overly specific or grandiose.

Clever malingerers can often be discovered when they try to cover all their bases and report an illness that is overly specific or unlikely. These students have researched a particular disease and quote its symptoms, often without realizing that they have chosen a rare or unlikely disease. Students may also claim to have all of the symptoms possible for that illness. These students often use the Internet or textbooks to choose or describe a sickness and its features. Students who have a specific illness in mind also repeat points or symptoms in the same order if you ask them to tell you again how they feel or what hurts.

Students' symptoms "move."

This often happens when a student feels like he is not believed. A student with a stomachache that then becomes a headache, only to then report dizziness followed by pain in a limb, etc., is most likely looking to find a symptom that resonates with the adult he is trying to fool. If an adult begins to focus on one symptom or seems concerned about it, the other symptoms often drop or are no longer mentioned. The student has, in essence, "picked a horse."

Students' symptoms differ based on audience.

Sometimes, all it takes to distinguish legitimate symptoms from malingered ones is to change who the student believes is watching. Students who have legitimate symptoms should report the same symptoms and act the same regardless of who they are with: teacher, parent, nurse, friend, or sibling.

Student is resistant to treatment.

This note is often more appropriate for parents, as students who malinger in school generally desire to be sent to the nurse's office as a gateway for being sent home. Parents, on the other hand, who are approached by children who claim to be ill prior to school may find that they are resistant to proposed trips to the doctor or taking medication. If children resist to the point of suddenly feeling better and saying that they would rather go to school, it is more likely an indication of malingering. However, it is also important to note that this is a prime example of a time when past history is important. If the child has always been reluctant to take medication or visit health professionals, resistance to treatment is not an appropriate measure of manufactured symptoms.

The magnitude or duration of symptoms are inappropriate, inconsistent, or cannot be verified by medical professionals.

Students who claim excruciating pain from something that would not have caused that much distress—citing that they can't write because of a painful paper cut, for example, or saying that they cannot walk after stubbing their toe—are more likely exaggerating or manufacturing symptoms. Even bright children who have done research on possible symptoms are not medical professionals and often feign symptoms based on stereotypical ideas of an illness. Children who are often unsure of how illnesses truly affect the body may cite inconsistencies—for example, claiming to have double vision even when one eye is covered, or not reporting a loss of consciousness during full-body convulsions.[165]

Symptoms do not get better with treatment or get better and then worse again intermittently.

Students who are looking to avoid certain tasks may feel poorly during one class, then better again during recess or lunch, for example, only to feel poorly again afterward. They will want to come back from the nurse's office when the class is doing a fun activity, or they may stay home from school more than two days in a week that are not consecutive.

Students may be particularly uncommunicative, unwilling to discuss their emotional state or what is happening at school.

Students who are dreading or avoiding something at school or feel bored, isolated, or overly anxious often show symptoms of sadness or unpredictable emotional states that accompany their reported symptoms of illness. These can often predate the malingering by several days and, if unaddressed for long, can result in legitimate symptoms that develop from stress.

Symptoms appear suddenly or have little "build up" over a period of days.

Although we have already heard from some high-ability students who have noted that they "set the stage" by citing discomfort the day before they plan to avoid school, many students are not this prepared. Often, feigned illnesses can be determined by the length and lack of gradual appearance of reported symptoms. Though sudden onset of certain illnesses is possible, if a student wakes up with multiple strong symptoms—a heavy cough, stomachache, and fever, for example—that did not exist the night before, parents can suspect malingering.

What To Do If You Suspect Malingering

If you suspect that children are manufacturing their symptoms, one of the most important things to do is talk to them. Ask them, calmly and without judgment, how they are feeling and for details on their symptoms. Show that you are listening but not overly worried. After you have discussed symptoms, you may want to ask follow up questions or gather more information through taking their temperature, sitting with them, and other methods to verify symptoms. Ask children what they will be missing if they stay home, and after they respond, ask if they believe their teacher would verify that if you spoke to them personally.

If you still believe the illness to be falsified, do not set up your child to lie to you by asking them directly, "Are you pretending to be sick?" Instead, phrase your belief in a calm, non-judgmental way, and tell the child what you feel is happening and why. For example, you can tell a student, "I believe that you are pretending to be sick so that you can stay home from school. I think maybe you are avoiding something you do not want to do there, like a test, or someone you do not want to see today. We can talk about that if you want and look for something we can both do about it, but I do not feel comfortable letting you stay (or sending you) home from school with a fake illness. I am not upset with you for trying to stay home from school, but pretending does not solve the problem."

Open the door to communication in a way that children do not feel like they are going to be punished and that shows you are not disappointed or upset with them for the transgression of malingering. It is easy to get caught up in our emotions regarding lying and feel betrayed by a student we trust for deceiving us, but it is nonproductive. The first order of business should be to address what children are avoiding or seeking to gain and to help brainstorm ways that they can solve their problem without deceit. If, after the discussion, you still feel upset, you can bring up how important honesty is to you and address the emotions separately. Do not confuse the lying with the attempt to stay home. They are two separate issues and should be isolated from one another. For example, if a child had told you that he or she did not feel comfortable going to school one day because something or someone there was upsetting them, you would appreciate being told and would work with the child to help them solve the problem. Keep emotions tied to the issues to which they belong.

Likewise, if children become upset or emotional when they are accused of malingering, do not rise up to meet them emotionally. Stay calm and tell them that they should not be upset since your words came without any punishment or disappointment. You are only telling them how you feel based on what you have seen, and you are concerned about them and want to know what is really happening. Work through children's emotions before addressing yours and keep calm—both in order to soothe them and to let them know that you are not able to be manipulated.

Children who are kept or sent home from school after suspected malingering should have activities restricted in accordance with their purported illness. This should not be presented as a punishment but rather as a natural cause and effect. "You say that you feel like you have a stomachache, so today you are going to have bland foods that will not upset you more," or "You are tired and have a headache, so you are going to take some aspirin and lie down in your room quietly with the lights off so that you have a chance to feel better. You will not be watching television, playing games, or talking on the telephone until you feel better." Another note for parents is to ensure that you do not incentivize your child's illness with gifts. Although the causes of malingering are often to avoid something negative in one environment, incentives and secondary gains can reinforce the behavior and prolong it past even the initial avoidance behavior.

Parents who send a child to school after suspected malingering should be sure to let the school know about concerns so that the child can be monitored by the teacher and nurse both for the possibility of actual illness as well as for continued exaggerated or falsified symptoms. Likewise, teachers who suspect malingering should hold very similar conversations with children, though some teachers may feel more comfortable asking the school nurse to help with the conversation. Regardless, the parents should be called either before or after the conversation to let them know that their child is not in trouble, but that there is reason to believe that they are avoiding or seeking to gain something through malingering. Parents should be informed if there is evidence of which the parent would not be aware—reluctance in class, incidents of bullying or withdrawal from peers, or even the timing of the reported symptoms. Assure the parent that the child still has or had the opportunity to go to the nurse and receive treatment in a reasonable manner, regardless of your suspicions. Focus on concern for the student, as it may feel like an accusation for the student or the parent, and ask that conversations with the student continue at home.

More important, however, than identification of manipulated or imagined symptoms, is prevention through careful attention to possible underlying causes. Detection of malingering behaviors, without changes in the student's thinking and perception, will only prevent or slow the occurrence of that specific behavior in the future. Eventually, another negative behavior will take its place in lieu of a solution for the original problem, which still exists if only the symptoms have been targeted. It is up to parents and teachers to determine what may be causing malingering in students, but a good place to start is always to talk to the student, their teachers, or their parents about what they may be seeking to avoid.

In the case of Joaquin, who self-reported his cheating behaviors to me in the Safe Space, he was aware that he was afraid of not being good enough to achieve the grade he wanted without extra time or pre-knowledge of what would be on the exam. He was putting a great deal of stress on himself, as well as self-doubt, and was beginning to show actual stress-related illnesses, not too unlike the ones he had originally faked. Although the act of coming up with believable sicknesses was challenging by itself and Joaquin reported a certain amount of satisfaction in how well he had learned to manipulate symptoms to his advantage, the pleasure he felt in being able to cheat his way out of an exam did not make up for the overall stress that he felt.

Marie was less confident about what she sought to avoid, convincing herself even more than her teachers or parents, who eventually intervened on her behalf, that she was an average student that did not deserve the gifted label. Marie's malingering to camouflage her ability could only be overcome if she could identify more positively with her intelligence and perhaps find role models.

The next step, after identifying the possible underlying causes, is to help these students define what they are seeking to avoid, either by giving them alternate perspectives or by helping them develop more appropriate coping mechanisms to deal with their fear. Work with them to strengthen their confidence and self-esteem while simultaneously providing a safe environment for them where they can make mistakes during problem solving. If situations are larger than students can confidently deal with by themselves, such as an issue of bullying or abuse, then parents, teachers, or other authorities should intervene so that students are made to feel safe and supported. Although Marie's and Joaquin's interventions as detailed here represent two of the most common solutions for issues of malingering, other interventions from other chapters may be more appropriate for children's needs. Children may malinger in order to avoid boring assignments, for example, and may need help reevaluating their worth audit, or they may be experiencing emotional difficulties fitting in at school and may benefit from additional counseling services.

Give Bright Children Role Models

The main goal of Marie's intervention was to positively alter her perspective on what it meant to be smart. Her parents and teachers could have forced her to stay in school despite her protestations of illness; however, as with most cheating behaviors, the cause is more important than the symptom. An edict of "you will go to school no matter what" may result in children less prone to lying about the state of their health, but if they are still determined to regulate their gifts, they are still being dishonest with themselves. It is vital to gently confront students about their malingering and to create clear expectations regarding school attendance, but the true intervention should address children's emotional concerns and help them face what they have been avoiding in healthy and nondestructive ways.

For Marie, being smart meant isolation from her peers while she was involved in enrichment activities, teasing for getting high grades, and a feeling that she was letting her classmates down by ruining the curve. She had not yet begun to identify positively with her abilities. She saw them as being different and even dangerous to her classmates and friends, so she rejected them in favor of fitting in. Marie could not yet see the scope of her life and what being intelligent might mean for her and others. Although she had experienced some exposure to other high-ability children, she had not identified with them as her social group—quite likely because many of them were dealing with similar social issues. Marie was in need of a role model to portray intelligence in a positive light.

We connected Marie with a bright role model, a young woman from the community who had gone to the same elementary school as Marie several years before. At the time of her mentorship of Marie, she was finishing her undergraduate college program and pursuing her goal of becoming an engineer. Once a week for several months, Marie and Big Sister, as she called her, met and spent time together. During their meetings they discussed and practiced Marie's hobbies, such as her writing and music, and Big Sister shared her own excitement and passion about her own interests, including mathematical proofs. They also kept in contact through email, and, as a substitute for feigning illness, Marie was allowed to write brief emails to her mentor during school whenever she felt stressed and needed a 5-10 minute mini-break. Big Sister's involvement with Marie's schooling did not end there; twice she came to Marie's class to share one of the nature-related math projects they had been working on together. Together, Marie and Big Sister led the class in finding Fibonacci spirals in pineapples, pinecones, and shells, as well as going on a brief nature walk to identify naturally occurring mathematical patterns.

It was not long before Marie's grades came up as she caught up on her work. After two months of working with Big Sister, Marie asked to return to the enrichment classes. She no longer felt that being bright was undesirable, and she blossomed under the praise and encouragement of an older girl who showed Marie that being bright could be meaningful for her goals as well as her relationships. Not only did Marie's classmates accept Big Sister, but they enjoyed her confident, funny company and told Marie that they were jealous that they did not have a smart college girl for a friend. For Marie, it was a helpful realization that even if her classmates did not always appreciate or understand her abilities, they could still see the value in intelligence and confidence.

All high-ability children, girls and boys alike, benefit greatly from appropriate role models. Mentoring can be the crucial link between gifted children maintaining positive self-concepts into adulthood. Most high-ability girls face a sharp decline in self-concept between third and eighth grades as guidance and support wanes and girls are not challenged to pursue self-actualization. Even though Marie interacted with other bright children in her enrichment program, she had identified with her regular classroom peers in the absence of having a role model who supported and encouraged her to be proud of and to develop her abilities.

Role models do not need to be formally identified as gifted; they just need to personally identify openly as intelligent and be able to voice or show pride regarding their accomplishments. Although many high-ability children have intelligent adults in their lives in the form of parents, teachers, and other relatives, too many of them shy away from the role of an intelligent role model; they are not comfortable with openly showing their intelligence, apparently feeling that they should be self-deprecating about their abilities. Not only does this not help a bright student identify positively with their talents, but it can actively encourage them to *not* develop their abilities. More than once I have heard teachers jokingly tell students that they would never have been able to solve a challenging logic puzzle when they were the students' age, or that they would not be able to have written something as high quality. Even though the teachers intended to give the students compliments for a job well done, they inadvertently sent the message that they do not consider themselves smart; they do not value it as a part of their identity.

Parents who are in awe of their bright children's accomplishments can also risk sending this message when they tell their children, "Wow, you didn't get your math ability from me!" or "I don't know where you get that from!" Although it is meant as praise, it can suggest to students that their parents do not hold those qualities as important, nor do they possess them. Students use teachers and parents to model their concept of identity and self-acceptance. These admired role models hold a great deal of power and should actively show and tell students that being smart and having talents are acceptable and desirable traits.

All highly intelligent children need someone in their lives whom they respect and who wears intelligence with pride. Teachers can provide this, as can parents. Rather than telling children that you do not know where their intelligence came from or discounting your own good qualities, tell them what you are good at. Be proud of it: "I am a whiz at math. I find it fun. What are you really good at?" Humility is an important trait to model for bright students, but modesty should not go so far as to associate being smart with something that must be so bad that the adults in their lives firmly avoid the label.

To hear parents of bright children talk, you would think that all talented children are mysterious gifts from the stork, their intelligence and abilities errant mistakes that certainly did not come from anywhere in their family. It is a sad commentary on the number of gifted adults who grew up feeling the need to regulate, not unlike Marie, or to discount their abilities in order to feel like they belonged. Being intelligent is nothing to be ashamed of, and parents who are too humble or dismissive about their gifts risk teaching their smart children that there is something inherently different about them in a bad or wrong way. It is not enough to praise your children for their abilities; parents and teachers should be active role models in expressing personal pride and self-esteem without relying on external praise. Take the opportunity to tell your student about what you are good at. Be proud of your accomplishments, celebrate aloud what you value about yourself, and identify goals in order to encourage your students to do the same.

Sometimes teachers and parents can forget a very important component of a child's development when they focus too keenly on academic growth. The *self* of the child, which includes emotional and social well-being, self-image, and self-esteem, is an important element of a bright child's development. Though we sometimes focus heavily on grades and academic successes, remember that high-ability children are not defined solely by their grades, nor are their identities synonymous with their abilities. Remember the self, the inner spirit and personality, and support emotional needs as well as academic ones. Both Joaquin and Marie had fallen into a destructive pattern of fearing who they were, and they had begun to isolate qualities about themselves for either hyper-focus or avoidance. Parents and teachers can help students learn to recognize the dangers of this and encourage a focus on creating and celebrating a multi-faceted self-image. Neither Marie nor Joaquin should learn to define themselves only as intelligent, nor should they fear the label so much that they avoid it completely. Both students need help coming to terms with their multi-faceted identities and to develop positive self-images as well as non-avoidance-based coping mechanisms.

Supporting Joaquin

By the time Joaquin began to admit to his malingering ploys, he had already begun to experience stress-related ailments that were not fictionalized, such as bruxism, trouble sleeping, and a lack of energy. Joaquin had created a coping mechanism that led to a self-destructive pattern of cheating and achievement. His desire to have excellent grades led to his frequent delay of tests, papers, and other assignments through repeated malingering, which then created a pattern of believing that he needed to have extra time in order to succeed.

Prolonged exposure to a cycle like this not only prevents a student from understanding their authentic ability levels but also can put the body at risk. When students place too much pressure on themselves regarding the outcome of exams, their body creates a sort of escape mode: fight-or-flight, where chemicals are released in the brain as a response to fear. When the human body is excessively stressed, it produces an abundance of cortisol, a hormone with the primary purpose to break down bodily tissues in order to be used as an energy source. This can suppress the immune system, create memory problems, cause high blood pressure, and produce continued difficulties relieving stress as the body struggles to return to normal levels of the hormone. In addition, stress has been linked to the death of neurons.[166]

For students like Joaquin, this cycle can become extremely self-destructive, both academically and physically. It was important to discuss this with him so that he would understand how his feelings of stress and negative self-image were beginning to affect his brain. Exposing bright children to the *why*—the blueprints of how and why things work—often has a calming effect on them, and they value the additional information to help them make decisions and choices. Joaquin was aware that he had a problem, but he was unsure of how it began or how to overcome it. Metacognitive knowledge, or the ability to understand one's thought processes and why certain learning patterns occur, is extremely valuable for all students, not just those with high-ability.

One thing that Joaquin identified was his maladaptive perfectionist qualities, admitting that he was not often pleased with himself if he felt he "had to study," believing that it meant he was not as smart as others thought he was. While Joaquin never sought to procrastinate, he also never felt as if he had enough time to truly know the material, so he always felt ill-at-ease with his possible outcomes. He felt extremely competitive with others and judged himself harshly when others received better grades than he did. It was that sense of competition that drove him, in part, to malingering and cheating.

A main component of Joaquin's intervention was very similar to what Gus experienced. Like Gus, Joaquin struggled with a self-punishing, fixed mindset. He had convinced himself that working hard was tantamount to failure and that he had to fool others into believing he was as smart as they initially perceived him to be. Joaquin and his parents worked together to recondition his mind to support a perspective of growth and progress over fixed ability and outcomes. Simultaneously, Joaquin's teachers and parents used strategies to pull him away from his competitiveness and promote his growth and self-esteem relative to areas not related to graded academics. Here are some of those strategies.

Create Independence through Goal Setting

Although it would be inaccurate to call the formal identification of gifted and talented a totally negative thing, sometimes students and parents struggle with the label if the appropriate services and support are not in place for gifted children at the school level. Schools that identify gifted children should keep in mind that their social and emotional growth needs to be addressed as well as their academic progress, and that services should be in place for students to work with a variety of ability-matched peers and role models. Without support for the entire self of the child, formal identification can reinforce distorted self-concepts as children struggle to become what they think their identification label means or what they are expected to live up to.[167]

High-ability individuals typically respond to externally imposed values in one of four ways: one, they conform to the expectations; two, they withdraw from or avoid those expectations; three, they rebel against authority; or four, they assert their independence.[168] The goal is to help the student reach the most constructive of these, meaning to seek development of themselves and creation of their own goals through independent decision-making. Students who are independent tend to be resilient and face challenges with a problem-solving perspective that allows them to move past conflict in order to meet personal goals. Independent children do not work for praise, nor do they seek to please external expectations of who they are supposed to be. Their achievement is driven by internal motivation, as well as a growth mindset, and their self-worth does not depend on the approval of others.

Help students develop their sense of self-worth by asking them to focus on their interests, their talents, and their goals. Students can fall prey to hyper-focusing on those traits they have decided are indistinguishable from their identity—such as their intelligence, their looks, or how popular they are, for example—and can neglect other aspects of themselves that are equally important. Parents, teachers, and counselors often can support the self-actualization process by shifting the focus from academics and encouraging students to explore other activities and interests. By getting to know themselves better, including their inner sensitivities, likes, and dislikes, bright children can begin to feel a better balance between what they believe the world expects from them and what they expect from themselves.[169] This harmony of the needs, values, and inner constitution versus environmental expectations represents authentic development, or the process of a child growing on multiple levels in order to be true to oneself.[170]

Although intelligence is a quality that bright children should learn to embrace and celebrate, it is not enough to solve all problems, and if they rely on themselves as being "just the smart kid," they are bound to run into issues that their youth and inexperience have not prepared them for. By celebrating themselves as well-rounded, fully-realized individuals with feelings, talents, desires, and goals, children will be better prepared to be resilient when challenges occur.

This strategy of creating goals was used to help Joaquin create more appropriate coping mechanisms to deal with his fear of failure. These goals included personal interests, talent development, and academic growth. The only stipulation was that his goals were not to include any letter grades or percentages, so as to discourage him from returning to his previous obsessive behavior. Students should be encouraged to create goals that extend the curriculum as well as their interests. The goal is to offer alternatives for students' focus and energy that are healthier than trying to buy themselves more time through malingering or other forms of cheating.

Joaquin worked with his mother and teacher to create objectives for himself and met with his mother in biweekly goal meetings to discuss his progress and to receive help and feedback. Some of Joaquin's chosen goals included his desire to learn about tropical fish, to save enough money to buy a fish tank, to learn how to do tricks on his skateboard, and to work with his father on learning geometry. Through his goal meetings, his parents helped Joaquin refocus on the process rather than the product of his goals and supported him without solving his problems for him. Bright children with self-defeating defense mechanisms can benefit from this kind of individualized instruction, whether through independent-learning assignments or through supported work with an adult who does not serve to create competition between other students.

Success in goal-setting meetings should be measured by the student meeting or exceeding his or her own standards, rather than comparison to others or the act of assigning a letter grade to performance. When students are not forced to compete, they generally set reasonable and attainable goals. When grades are used, they should be implemented in a way that encourages continued risk-taking. Some of these measures can include grade replacement, as explained during Martin's intervention, individualized learning contracts, and the ability for students to contract for the grade they desire. When contracting for their own grade, students have more freedom and responsibility in choosing different elements of their assignments in order to earn a grade that they *choose*. Grade contracting is less applicable in regard to exams, so it was not used to a large extent with Joaquin, whose school anxiety was test-centric. However, grade contracting and other individualized learning contracts are often useful in the battle against a preoccupation with grades.

Joaquin's teachers and parents worked together to refocus his efforts on his personal goals and learning plan. They made resources, study time, and feedback openly available to him and encouraged his work ethic by praising his progress rather than the potential outcomes of his projects. This change brought a sense of clarity to Joaquin, who had been channeling so much of his intellect into trying to fit an imaginary ideal rather than utilizing it to focus on growth beyond the limited curriculum he had available to him. Despite Joaquin's growing negative self-concept, which increasingly denied his ability to get good grades without cheating, the truth was that he was limiting himself, and much of the work was not nearly challenging enough to stimulate him. Joaquin's expansions of the curriculum not only gave him an opportunity to stretch himself but also presented him with challenges that were both appropriate and personally valuable to him as an individual.

When the amount of competition is decreased, a decrease in the amount of stress often follows. Tailor interventions to students' individual needs, but a general rule of thumb is to help students pull away from competitiveness and encourage them to focus on improving their own performance. Competition can expose many student fears, including the fear of the unknown. Students who become obsessed with competition often exhibit perfectionist tendencies as they struggle to ascertain what teachers and parents want from them in order to be "the best." This ongoing and constant deciphering act can create significant stress as students put too much pressure on themselves to continue to achieve at high levels, or worse, to hide their abilities from others. Students with poor coping mechanisms to deal with the anxiety they feel over academic or social concerns can turn to malingering and other forms of avoidance behaviors. Left unchecked, this can lead to students developing negative self-images and skewed perceptions of their identity and abilities, as well as preventing meaningful learning from occurring.

Six
Ceedie

Ceedie's story is an unusual one, even thought represents another student whose cheating behaviors could be linked to perfectionist tendencies and a desire to manage the impressions that she made on others. Ceedie's journey is unlike the others highlighted in this text due to the unique nature of why she cheated, as well as the deep, emotional frustrations that were so connected to those behaviors. From an early point in her life, Ceedie felt both fundamentally different from her peers and separate from the adults in her life, and she concocted an elaborate method of deception she called "The Game" in order to better communicate with and understand those around her. In doing so, the greatest cheat that she accomplished was the systematic denial of her own gifts.

A highly talented little girl, Ceedie possessed strong emotional and physical sensitivities and experienced intense reactions to the world around her. Sometimes those emotional sensitivities manifested themselves in troubling and violent outbursts. For the longest time, no one could understand exactly what was happening to turn the petite, doe-eyed little girl into a self-destructive imp whose face would boil red with frustration until she would scratch deep tracks of anger into her face with her very short nails. She was not allowed to grow them; her mother said she had cut them every night since first grade, which was when the outbursts her mother referred to as "the fits" first appeared. As time went on, the episodes became more frequent and frightening, popping out at what seemed to be random intervals when nothing seemed to be amiss.

Ceedie's most common cheating behaviors centered on copying answers from other students' work. Unlike most students who copy from classmates, either during homework assignments or surreptitiously during tests, Ceedie was not looking to increase her grades. She wanted to ensure that her answers or scores were not so out of place in comparison to her classmates that she would be singled out for being strange. She was particularly afraid that her writing work would be read in front of the class because she felt isolated or ridiculed when she realized that her work was far superior to that of her classmates. She felt that they were judging her for it.

This process of reading other students' work over their shoulders, "borrowing" assignments from classmates' backpacks, and getting up out of her chair to ostensibly get drinks of water, sharpen her pencil, etc., went on for years as she tried to gauge the sophistication of her classmates work in order to regulate her own. She called this process "The Game," but in her mind it was increasingly serious that she felt out of place in her environment. Unbeknownst to the people in her life, she had been playing The Game since the second day of kindergarten. She cheated to try and stay abreast of the mind-bogglingly complex structure and rule base of this game she had created because she always felt that she ranked last on the "scoreboard." Ceedie continued to play, however, thinking this was the only way she would ever fit in with her peers. The only way to win The Game was to discover all of its unsaid rules and frameworks and to execute them perfectly, which translated to becoming a part of the friendship groups she felt isolated from. When Ceedie turned eight years old, the complicated lies she had been living started to unravel, and the secret she had been keeping for years came to light.

Ceedie spent a lot of time in the school psychologist's office. She had been having what could only be termed as severe emotional breakdowns at school. It is not atypical for highly intelligent children to be exceptionally sensitive to their environment and to have difficulty processing sensory information. For some, it manifests in a sensitivity to light, textures, foods, pressure, or sounds. One of my students will not eat anything with "noise" in it, and all foods have to be one solid color and texture. Forget breads with seeds in them or tapioca pudding. Others have the tags cut off of their clothing because the slight difference between the feeling of the shirt material and the tag causes them great distress. There are a variety of sensory integration disorders that commonly affect the gifted population, but it only becomes a problem for a student if it interferes with their ability to cope with the world around them, as Ceedie's did.

Explosion is not necessarily a term that refers only to an aggressive show of behavior; sometimes, like in Ceedie's case, an explosion can include anxious, sad, or repetitive expressions of inner turmoil.[171] Some of Ceedie's explosions would render her unresponsive to the people around her, almost comatose with rocking and chanting, while in other outbursts she would physically hurt herself. As the number of episodes increased, so did the regular appointments with the school psychologist, who understood that some, if not all, of Ceedie's breakdowns were rooted in social and emotional issues that sprung from her giftedness, particularly the marked asynchronous development and emotional sensitivities that were the underlying factors of the peculiar and mysterious Game.

The Fits

Ceedie's first involvement with the gifted education program in her school was a push-in model, which means that she received enrichment services and changes to the curriculum within her classroom setting, but subsequently she was in a pull-out program. Initially, she did not meet the qualifications for a pull-out program due to her behavioral outbursts, but the depth of her abilities led to an exception, and she was able to work with her academic-minded peers outside of the classroom. Once it was clear that she was not a danger to the other students and their learning processes, it seemed more damaging to keep her isolated from the enrichment group when it was so obvious that she was in dire need of something more. There was, additionally, the possibility that her behavior was a direct result of not feeling challenged enough in the regular classroom; holding her back because of emotional issues felt like a dangerous, cyclical event.

Her outbursts did not stop in the pull-out setting, but they were often different, and as a result of seeing her in both the regular classroom and a small group setting, I was able to see a range of the outbursts which her parents more commonly referred to as her fits. The outbursts were not loud. They were never screaming, hysterical sessions with kicking and attention-grabbing theatrics. If anything, the explosions were focused inward. To watch this little girl have one of her fits was to watch an internal combustion in slow motion, as perpetrated on the face of a child who had not yet found her niche in the world. Her parents warned the school to ignore the fits; they said that she was just looking for attention. But to see one of Ceedie's emotional outbursts was to watch a student who just wanted to disappear. She either shut the world out completely, as if it did not exist, or she tried to destroy herself.

Sometimes she blocked out all stimulation, rejecting anything that was not already a part of herself and the space she occupied. She would ball up with her knees to her chest, her arms pulled in tight or forced under her body so that she felt the pressure, the weight of herself and nothing else. Ceedie would often hum or chant a phrase so repetitively that the cadence of the syllables would lose their meaning and flow into a new shape, like a liquid conforming to the space it was given. You could speak to Ceedie when she was like that, or touch her, and you would be no more than air to her. She had trouble remembering anything that happened in that state and would even become frustrated if someone insisted that it had happened or attempted to question her after the fact. These episodes were infrequent, but they often seemed to come out of nowhere; she could go from perfectly responsive to blackout with little external warning.

The more dangerous of the episodes—and without question the more frightening—occurred after a certain amount of "amping up." When something frustrated her—often when she did not understand her classmates or her teacher's behavior, or when she felt like they did not understand her—she would become increasingly agitated until an episode ensued. Sometimes with comfort and reassurance that she was not wrong and that everything would be okay, she could be calmed back down before any danger occurred. However, it was not always possible to pull her away from the stressful situation and to reassure her since the source of her frustration often was not clear. Sometimes she would explain that someone on the playground had said something that hurt her feelings, or she thought that she had done something wrong. More often than not, however, there seemed to be no incident to inspire her agitation, and she refused to give details after the fact. Despite the best efforts of her teachers and other school personnel, it was not always possible to de-escalate the situation, and she would experience another one of the violent, full-on emotional explosions.

Ceedie would grit and grind her teeth so hard it was not uncommon for her to chip them, and her hands would become like those palsied— twitching, obeying only their own rules. She would use those twitching, taut fingers to twine up huge locks of hair at the sides of her face and rock back and forth. Sometimes she would scratch and push at her temples as if to forcibly will more understanding and peace into her skull. Her nose would run and she would scratch violently at it and her eyes, insisting that they itched and were terrible to put up with. Her face would burst red with the exertion she was putting onto it internally. The one time I tried to touch her during one of the outbursts, her skin was hot to the touch. I then tried not to touch Ceedie when she got that deep into the behavior because anywhere on her body that she felt pressure she would claw and scratch.

Over time, those around Ceedie understood about the events, such as to refrain from touching her or using any trigger phrases that might upset her. Her parents' instructions persisted: Ignore the outbursts and give Ceedie time out to cool down. For two years they insisted that she was faking, that it was not something she *had* to do but something that happened for the sake of her feeling unattended to. It took until the beginning of her fourth-grade year, only two weeks after Ceedie placed first in a district-wide math competition, for them to realize that something was genuinely wrong with Ceedie.

It was a normal day at school, and the fourth graders were out at recess. It was not a very hot day, still early in fall, and most of the students were taking advantage of the cool weather to play soccer and baseball in the adjoining fields. Only a few students were on the actual playground equipment, so no one was sure how long Ceedie had stayed crouched under the slide before a student finally noticed her.

No one knew how it started, but everything erupted at once when the classmate who found her ran to a teacher for help. The nurse was called while the teachers vacillated between trying to get her out from beneath the metal slide and holding back the rest of the students from their horror and curiosity. They had seen Ceedie erupt before, but never like that.

Ceedie was not trapped, but she had firmly wedged herself beneath the tiniest point of the slide where the slope met the earth. Every attempt to pull her free was met with violent swipes of her arms, and she began to bite herself wherever she could reach on her own body. She had scraped both of her arms on the bottom of the slide on the minutely sharp points where the metal was soldered to the slide's legs, and she was bleeding. She kept saying that it did not make sense and she did not understand. Finally, one of the gym teachers pulled her out and carried her, kicking and crying, into the building. In the aftermath, there was little gossip or discussion around the school about the incident. The eerie quiet that followed the event—even with the students who had witnessed it—seemed to speak to how frightening it had been for everyone and how little we understood what was happening to her.

When she calmed down enough to try explain what had happened, Ceedie said that she had "broken the connection" and that "it's like a lot of threads between people, between things, and you can't see it, and that's what makes it hard, but you can't break it." That was what she said over and over again—threads—but also that she wished they were really like a spider web because then at least she could *see* them. Apparently the threads were not visible, but if they were like a spider web she might be able to see it from another angle, like when the light hit it just right. Then she would be able to know.

The other students were not much more help in deciphering what had happened. Several students said that Ceedie had come out with them to recess but that she had stayed behind when the rest went to play soccer. A few students said they saw her there for a time, watching them, but then she was gone. No one had seen her go beneath the slide. No one could understand why she had gotten so upset, and we did not understand until two months later. After many visits to the school psychologist, Ceedie finally broke what was apparently her cardinal rule: She talked about The Game to her counselor.

"I don't want to play anymore," she had said, close to tears.

"Play what? Out on the playground with the other kids?"

"No. I don't want to play anymore. Just tell me what all the rules are. I give up. I try to be like them, but I can't. I'm so terrible at it, and it's just making everything worse."

"Making what worse, Ceedie?"

"Everything. My life. The Game."

And with that, she began to unwind the Gordian knot that was her world. But before we can explain the complexities of what The Game meant to Ceedie, it is important to see the unique way that she viewed her world through the double lens of asynchronous development and emotional intensity.

Asynchronous Development

The greatest issue that plagued Ceedie was her dramatically asynchronous abilities. Asynchronous development is a key component of the gifted identity, some say the defining factor in discovering whether or not a child is gifted. Children with advanced cognitive abilities may be many different ages simultaneously on a developmental standpoint.[172] Although Ceedie's chronological age was eight, her IQ score qualified her as highly gifted, with a score that put her in the 98th percentile for quantifiable intelligence. She read at a high school level, yet she had the fine motor skills of a first grader and the hand-eye coordination of a second or third grader. Tasks such as unbuttoning a collared shirt, tying her shoes, or dribbling a basketball were insurmountably frustrating for her, whereas reading and writing were effortless. Emotionally, Ceedie was the most difficult to place developmentally, since she vacillated widely between mature insight and emotional fits of rage and frustration. Ceedie was an amalgam of many intellectual, emotional, and physical developmental ages, a common feature of highly able children.[173]

Asynchronous development can occur in academic areas as well. Although some very bright children are strong in all academic areas, many others are far more talented in one area than in others. Even children who are academically balanced can be disregarded for gifted identification because they are not seen to possess emotional or social maturity. The picture of a bright child as perfect or even as a miniature adult leads many children to be overlooked for enrichment opportunities. The greater the asynchrony, as in the case of Ceedie, the more vulnerable a child is to being misunderstood.

Ceedie was brilliant, but she was still a child. Her parents had toyed with the idea of skipping her one or more grade levels, but it was only a matter of time—and an emotional outburst—that had them refusing the offer to accelerate. It can often be difficult for teachers to identify students as gifted when they have dramatic asynchrony in their development. In Ceedie's case, however, her abilities made it difficult to deny her gifts; there was never any doubt to anyone who encountered her that she was grade levels ahead of her peers academically. By the end of the second month of school she had read through all of her textbooks. By the end of the fourth month, she had read all of the books in the classroom library. She had the vocabulary and language comprehension of a high-school honors student; she wrote poems and stories that were sensitive, beautiful, and sometimes uncomfortably mature. She had the kind of soul that seemed to be merely borrowing a tiny body for a while. Nothing ever appeared to be difficult for her, but unbeknownst to the people around her, in Ceedie's exceptional mind, she was failing miserably. No matter how often she would cheat to try and understand and merge into the world of her classmates, whether it was hiding in the bathroom to take notes on what fellow classmates said, looking over their shoulders to read their papers, or even borrowing homework assignments from other students backpacks, it was clear to her peers that she was a high-ability learner. What is more, her emotional asynchronies and hyper-sensitivities often caused them to be uncomfortable around her. This often resulted in Ceedie feeling isolated and misunderstood, which led to the powerful fits that would rock her little body and cause her to scratch at her own face and hands.

Although the chronological age of a child may sometimes be the least defining factor of who he or she is as a learner, bright students are often held back to learn with their age-mate peers. But problems often arise. On the one hand, the student is bored and spends much time waiting for others to understand and learn what she already knows. On the other hand, the emotional and social abilities are much closer to the child's actual age, and when high-ability children misbehave or act immaturely, it can be difficult for adults to allow bright children to "act their own age," rather than their intellectual age, without reprimand. [174] Consideration for their actual age seems to disappear.

Adults who are aware of a child's unique and advanced abilities are often surprised when the student who can compose music or solve a complex equation cries because of missing the bus. Ceedie's parents were naturally very distressed by her emotional outbursts and her inability to cope with what were, to them, insignificant stimuli. They failed to take into account that beneath the academic developmental age she was still just eight years old and that, like all children, she could have abilities that were markedly less than her intellectual or even her chronological age. Though this can certainly account for emotional immaturity in bright children, Ceedie's emotional outbursts were also exacerbated by the extreme intensity that is another hallmark of gifted behavior.

Intensity and Sensitivity

Like asynchronous development, intensity is a trait that is commonly found among very bright children. Complex and intense reactions and the heightened awareness to stimulus, sensations, and emotions are lifelong attributes that cause high-ability children to not only think differently from their peers but also feel and perceive differently. [175] The distinction should also be made that it is not simply the *amount* of intensity and sensitivity that a gifted child possesses that is different from their peers, but also the quality:

> *One of the basic characteristics of the gifted is their intensity and an expanded field of their subjective experience. The intensity, in particular, must be understood as a qualitatively distinct characteristic. It is not a matter of degree but of a different quality of experiencing: vivid, absorbing, penetrating, encompassing, complex, commanding—a way of being quiveringly alive.*[176]

Emotional intensity, for example, is commonly found in high-ability children. Emotional intensity touches all experiences, from deepening a child's response to a happy event to creating explosive outbursts or severe anxiety during an unpleasant one. The higher the intelligence of a child, the more prone he or she is to social and emotional adjustment problems that result from an inability to integrate and adjust to the extremes of their emotions.[177] An emotional intensity can manifest itself, as it did in Ceedie's case, in more physical expressions and in extreme sensitivities.

Extreme sensitivities to different types of sensory input and stimulation are common in the gifted population.[178] Students who have difficulty processing the stimuli of the world around them and have trouble emotionally coping with failed attempts to assimilate and integrate that information may have a sensory-motor integration disorder.[179] The student who would not eat the noisy food or the one who could not bear the annoyance of the tag scratching in the back of her clothes are examples of students who had extreme sensitivity to various stimuli.

Ceedie was both extremely emotionally sensitive to the world around her and physically sensitive to specific stimuli, especially pressure. Ceedie had identified certain pressure points on her body, including her hands, arms, feet, calves, and temples that she would push on, sit on, or wedge between objects to satisfy a need for the sensation of equal pressure. She also responded very strongly to situations that she designated as wet or itchy. Being caught in the rain or forced to go without washing a sticky substance off of her hands would cause a severe emotional reaction. Her sensory input was heightened in explosive emotional states, the symptoms exacerbated to the extent that she would slam the back of her hands or fists on her pressure points until she could feel her blood pressure increase. Many students find relief through weighted stuffed animals, vests, or other pressure-inducing objects that help center or ground a student. Ceedie did feel some relief through large, weighted bean-bag animals that she would drape over her shoulders or hold in her lap, but the best way for Ceedie to calm down from her episodes were self-talk sessions in which she comforted herself with a nonsensical stream of words or repeated mantra. This relationship between the emotional intensities and her sensory sensitivities was not only causal but also deeply intertwined so that one might exacerbate the other or be used as a coping mechanism to help lessen the severity of the other.

What can be difficult to understand is that the problem does not stem from the sensory organs but exists within the way this information is integrated. The sensory organs collect the information and send it to the brain, which is responsible for taking the raw data received and translating it into something the body can use or store. More research is necessary to determine the cause, but somewhere between the sensory organ and integration, the information is either qualitatively or quantitatively damaged, and a child is left with what can be amplified or meaningless chunks of information.[180] When the child's brain has to work overtime to make logic out of seemingly nonsensical information, it can lead to a sensation of sensory overload. For parents who cannot see what is happening internally, these outbursts and shut-down behaviors can be particularly frightening and confusing. Through sensory integration therapy, Ceedie's outbursts became less violent, but they continued; her sensitivities were exacerbating the deep emotional issues she had internalized.

Complex Inner World: The Game

Ceedie knew she was different. She was aware that her hand was raised to answer every question while other students would hide their heads. She could not understand how her classmates could struggle with concepts that were so easy or get grades that were anything less than perfect. It did not make sense to her young brain. At that age, there is an extreme locus of self in the minds of the young. We are the center of our universe, and in our limited experience, *we* are all we know, all we can begin to understand, and we are safe in the thought that everyone is like us. We cannot imagine how someone else thinks and feels past our own experiences. Ceedie was brilliant enough to realize that something about this equation was amiss—but the estranged variable in her equation was her. Instead of realizing that she was naturally more intelligent than her classmates and that they might not answer a question correctly because they did not know, she filled the gap with an answer that did make sense to her; she could work to deny her abilities and become more like her classmates.

It was more complicated than just answers she gave on homework assignments or on tests. The Game was intended to answer all of the most difficult questions in her life. It gave her a chance to be like everyone else, and in her mind they were all playing a game together with secret and complicated social rules that she simply had to learn how to master. She struggled to learn these rules, such as when a student could let the teacher know you had the right answer, and when you were allowed, in a social sense, to raise your hand. What manner of vocabulary you could or could not use in class were also subject to scrutiny from Ceedie. The other students seemed so much better at this game, according to Ceedie, as they were calm and happy and had friends. When people liked her, smiled at her, and played with her at recess, she believed that she must be getting the rules of the game correct, but of course, no one could tell her because that was against the rules. When they made fun of her, called her "freak show" and "teacher's pet" and bullied her, or worse ignored her completely, that must mean that she had broken a rule. She had not understood the way these "threads" were connected.

All interactions between people were the threads, according to Ceedie. The way people spoke to each other, what they could say, and where, and how were all dictated by the threads between them. Actions were also a component: how they sat in a chair, where they stood, and who they could be near. Ceedie did not know why she did not have friends when, to her, she was doing everything the people around her were doing.

Ceedie could not see how complex she must have seemed to her classmates and how off-putting she was through her constant cheating and sneaking behaviors. She knew she was different, but she did not realize in which direction. For some reason, she could not bear to see herself as extraordinary, so she placed everyone else above her. Rather than accept that someone did not want to be her friend because they did not understand her, she reasoned that she must be breaking a rule in the elaborate system she had created. In that way, she had given herself some of the power and control. It was not that the other children were afraid of her or did not like her because of her intellect and her abilities, only that she had to learn when she could use them and when to modulate them like her classmates were so practiced at doing. Anything bad that happened to her at school did not feel as bad, in her mind, because she felt she had the power to fix it if she only acted differently. The result was the complicated, delicate Game.

Sometimes, though, it would overwhelm her as she tried to impose an order and internal consistency to what was not actually a giant game board, but rather an interlocked matrix of human interaction and individual players who did not even know they were playing. She would become frustrated when an action did not have the same reaction it had a previous time she had tried it. Using a large vocabulary with some students may not cause them to lash out with taunts and jeers, but the same words used with another, or at a different time or frequency, could be catastrophic. When this happened or when she forgot to play by a rule (raising her hand for every question when she was excited was a common rule break for her), her frustration point would boil over. She could not talk about the game because no one else ever did; she could not break that cardinal rule. Asking for rules or clarifications would be a terrible infraction, so she would seethe quietly within her own confusion and disappointment and increase the amount of referencing she did to classmates' work and actions.

The playground incident had not actually started there at all, but earlier that day in the classroom. Ceedie had observed another student the day before casually asking another what she wanted to do at recess. When the other student had calmly replied with a shrug and "Maybe the slides," the other had responded with a noncommittal "Yeah, maybe." Ceedie wrote down their conversation in her notebook and then followed them out to the playground to see what they actually ended up playing. She said she watched them all recess as they went up and down the slide together, sometimes one at a time while the other stood next to the slide and they talked. Sometimes they went down in twos, side by side and giggling like the best of friends. They even ran up the slide together. The next day, Ceedie followed the thread, picking a few girls in class and casually suggesting the slide without being too eager or suggestive about it. When more than one girl responded with a *maybe*, Ceedie was excited and barely ate her lunch waiting to get outside to play with her new friends.

When the students filed out to the playground, Ceedie continued in that easygoing vein, being careful not to break any of the rules, and made sure to stay well within sight of the four girls she had talked to so that they knew she was there, but not so close that they felt like she was following them—another thread she had observed in her classmates' behavior. When the majority of the class turned away from the slide and swings and ran down the field, the four girls went with them, and Ceedie stood in shock as their absence punctuated how much she had failed. She ran through all the threads in her mind, following them back and forth like a criss-cross grid between everyone involved. What had she not said or was it something she unwittingly added to the conversation? Had she spoken in the wrong tone or was it her body posture? Were you only allowed to ask one person to slide with you or could you only do it on Mondays? Were the girls the day before speaking in a code that Ceedie was not allowed to use because she had broken too many rules? Why was it soccer today? Could she join in or would that be the greatest rule break of all? Had they all tried to tell her something by leaving her behind? What if she just ignored it and went and joined in? Would they think she was stupid, then?

It was as if she short-circuited. There was too much information to process; she could not possibly make sense of everything in the world, no matter how much she tried to impose a sense of order on it. Ceedie had placed herself at the bottom of an invisible heap and had, over the course of four years, crippled herself beneath the weight of it all. Every action, every word, every accomplishment had been filtered through a complex and impossible set of cheats, rules, and standards. It was the price she had paid for wanting to be like everyone else above all else.

A Support Structure for Ceedie

Though Ceedie's is a unique and remarkable case of how a high-ability student misappropriated her abilities, it is not unique for children to systematically deny or repress their abilities in order to feel like they fit into their social group. Students with emotional sensitivities and overexcitabilities need the understanding of their teachers, parents, and counselors to learn how to manage their feelings. The first step is to accept that these behaviors are rarely acting-out behaviors; although Ceedie's parents assured the school that their daughter was merely seeking attention, the truth was far more complicated. Students who express themselves inappropriately or seem to react strongly to inconsequential stimuli can benefit from supportive counseling. In addition, offering creative and expressive forums where students can give an appropriate voice to their feelings can help. Work with students to help them alleviate their stress and to give them a safe space to express their frustrations and work through problems in a low-risk environment. Do not blame their reactions, but seek to calm the escalation of frustrations. Role-playing, creative play, and journaling are all examples of ways that students with emotional intensities can begin to work through their complicated feelings.

For Ceedie, the details of her cheating and her complicated game did not come to light all at once. She was in the care of a supportive and knowledgeable counselor, and gradually the details came to light. Her teachers were informed, and her parents began to look for groups that Ceedie could join after school that would mirror some of her interests and give her other social groups to experience. She started to go to a youth writing seminar that specialized in talented girls, and she met with a counselor after school. The main goal of these meetings was to gradually bring her to the realization that The Game had been fictitious and of Ceedie's own design, that there were no universal rules that governed how students should behave or how intelligent you could or could not be in order to have friends. They worked together to help her accept who she was and to work on managing her emotions and sensitivities.

Ceedie never had another severe emotional outburst in school after that, and she told her counselor that she had no need to cheat off of her classmates' papers any more. For several months, Ceedie also went largely silent during school. During this time, her teacher reported that she had ceased attempting to offer any questions in class, choosing to read at her desk or write in her journal until she was called upon. Then she would give the most detailed and well-thought out answers, as if she had been thinking of the response the whole time instead of devoting most of her attention to her own literary pursuits. She did not seem to care as much what anyone thought of her, simply answering fully and returning to her book, always writing. I asked her once in the resource room to tell me something about her writing. Ceedie had recently been so quiet, but I thought she might be more vocal about her writing. It was obviously important to her; she did so much of it. I do not think I saw any one book more than twice before a new one appeared.

My role in Ceedie's story is very small, but I will never forget the answer she gave me.

"I hate language."

To say I was surprised is an understatement. I struggled with a response; I did not know which tack to take, since I was not sure what she had intended by that brief yet powerful assertion.

I said, "I love your poems, and you're an excellent reader. Don't you feel like you're good at language?"

"Not the subject language," she responded, "Words and sentences kind of language."

"Is it people talking that you hate?"

"And writing. It's not so much because of what people say or don't say. Just that we do it at all. If there wasn't any kind of language, no one would ever know that they weren't exactly like everyone else inside. No one would know that the way they thought wasn't like everyone else. I wish no one could communicate with each other with language and we had to find other ways."

And then she left without waiting for a response. It was as honest and raw a picture of the inside of her mind as I had ever seen, and she did not fetter it with any of her rules on how to act when others were around, what to say, or how to say it. She simply spoke her mind and left with a composition book tucked under her arm, leaving me stunned that such a vast understanding could come from this sad and beautiful child. I was humbled by Ceedie's vision for the world.

Ceedie did not ask that everyone be the same. She did not wish that she were like them or they were like her, not even in her hypothetical perfect world. In Ceedie's utopia, people were free to be whomever they were inside, but everyone would love each other because they would be able to frame the world only from their own perspective. Everyone would be friends, brothers, and sisters, because they would believe that everyone thought and felt just as they did. Ceedie would have been blissful in the ignorance of her own lack of ignorance while her neighbors would be blissful in and of their ignorance, at least in comparison to Ceedie.

Over the next few months, Ceedie continued in her pull-out enrichment group, working with her counselor, and creating stories and poems in her young writers' group. Her "school voice" returned, and she began to excel at speaking her mind and working more often at her true potential level, using both her words and her actions as she liked, often independently of the group. She no longer downplayed her abilities or constantly monitored her actions and reactions to the extent that she overwhelmed herself and cheated herself out of what she wanted to do.

For one of our literature groups, we read *The Westing Game*, a book about a millionaire's complicated, multi-faceted game involving possible heirs, and Ceedie asked if she could read something different or do a report on it alone and then work with the group on something else. Beyond that, her only references to The Game were thinly veiled, and although school officials were still on alert to see what was going to happen with this emotionally sensitive child, Ceedie retained her talent for keeping much of what was going on inside her mind hidden. Externally, many of her teachers noted a great change in her; the outbursts ceased completely, her class work had improved (if not her participation), and the art teacher reported that she had started to make friends in her classroom, bonding over creative visions. She had even started to stay in during recess for extra projects with other art enrichment students.

Ceedie's parents worked with the school to ensure that there was consistent progress in both her school and home environments. One thing that came to light was that Ceedie had still truly believed that there really *was* a game and that the only thing she had wrong was to assume there were rules. Because she had created rules and they were impossible to live up to or to discover, she had turned to what she considered deceit and trickery, watching other students and deciphering their actions. She never saw anyone else studying the world like she did, so she had kept that hidden too, considering it to be a breach of the rules.

Ceedie threw away all of her old notebooks—the ones in which she had documented hours of conversations (courtesy of a shorthand she had designed herself), rules, and theories. She had replaced them with the composition notebooks in which she wrote her thoughts, journals, lists, ideas, and poems. She had started to draw and paint and make large collages; some of those she threw away, too, but only when she wanted to, not for any sense of self-punishment or reproach for a broken rule or misunderstood signal from a classmate or parent. She did not even want to punish herself for The Game; she simply realized that it was not fair to herself to have to discover all of life's complexities. The only person she had truly been cheating was herself.

Parents Need Courage

The challenges facing the parents of highly able students has never been more aptly described than in *A Parent's Guide to Gifted Children*: "Parents need courage—just as gifted children need courage—to continue to support their children's interests and intensities."[181] It is not easy being the parent of children who develop at such a different rate than their peers or who harbor such intense connections to the world around them. Trying to decipher complex behaviors like Ceedie's can lead parents to have very conflicted views about their children. It is common for parents to battle with how they see their own children: At one moment, they may be brilliant, high achievers with complex language and mature attitudes; the next, emotional, stressed, and maybe even out of control. Parents can feel powerless, even ineffectual, in how to support their children's intensities.[182]

Ceedie's parents mistook emotions and sensitivities for behaviors, or at least the lines had blurred. They saw the outbursts as attention-seeking behaviors. Only when The Game had come to light did they realize gradually that their daughter was simply overloaded with information; the symptom of her sensory overload had been the fits. Ceedie's actions were more like involuntary muscle contractions than decisive behaviors, and their existence was directly linked to the unexpressed emotions she had buried due to her self-imposed, no-communication rule regarding The Game. The outbursts could only be contained minimally without addressing the root of the issue. The adults in Ceedie's life needed to learn both how to validate her emotions and how to communicate with her in a way that delved into the complexities of her perceptions of the way the world interacted.

In the months following Ceedie's gradual unfolding of The Game, Ceedie continued to have counseling both in and outside of school, and for the first time, she started to visit a therapist outside of school with her parents. Even more positive was the fact that her counseling was focused on improving the way she could communicate with her parents and teachers rather than trying to lessen the extent of her intensities. The greater a child experiences the world, the less she feels welcomed by peers and teachers, particularly if those individuals do not understand that the child has a unique makeup that cannot be dampened.[183] Ceedie was the same person after disposing of The Game; she was still sensitive and imaginative and intellectual. The only difference was that both the internal pressures she had been creating and the external pressures caused by her cheating were alleviated. Just like Ceedie had developed a framework for dealing with the world, so did the people in her life have to reframe their understanding of her emotional and interpersonal needs.

By all appearances, Ceedie was a girl headed toward recovery and toward a more child-like life than she had ever allowed herself to live. Ceedie's parents had always had a difficult relationship with the concept of their daughter's fits, but her mother in particular turned a corner and embraced the need for ongoing communication and understanding of her daughter's sensitive and intuitive nature. Her mother spoke of her own upbringing, which had been devoid of gifted identification or services. She had always felt punished for being emotional and intelligent, and she described how she'd been called crazy as a child. Her response was to "wall up" her emotions and become outwardly stoic, a common response of children who are repeatedly exposed to damaging comments; they are likely to become distrustful of relationships and become guarded. She had made special efforts never to call her daughter names, but she was distressed to discover that Ceedie's sensitivities and careful examination of the relationships around her had already caused her to write in one of her journals that "everyone, even my parents, thinks I'm crazy."

Ceedie's mother had never intended to trivialize what her daughter was going through; she simply had not known how to address it. Though her daughter had inherited her fountain of intelligence, she had also received that equally deep well of emotion that Ceedie somehow had not learned to cap as well as her mother. Despite how awful they had seemed, the fits—and The Game, for that matter—were a bridge between two minds that were more alike than different. They had just never known how to communicate, and neither had realized how alone the other had felt.

One meeting, in particular, stood out. At the spring parent-teacher conferences, we ended up discussing The Game, and I mentioned how Ceedie had not discussed it in school ever again. Her mother admitted that she had not mentioned it at home, either, but that she thought it had been difficult for Ceedie to let go. She would catch her daughter staring at them, analyzing her family as if watching for patterns or threads, and seeming embarrassed when she was noticed. She continued in therapy, and it was helping her to realize that The Game was not real and that she had been the one to make it up, not the people around her.

"Does Ceedie miss it?" I asked.

"I think she does. Can you imagine?" She broke for a moment then, a crack in her strong exterior as her posture slumped and she came closer, her face tilted down to mine conspiratorially. "To come up with something like that... It went so deep. It touched everything in her life. I'm glad it's gone—or going away—but I wish I could have seen all of those webs that she saw. Did you know that she said she could imagine threads connecting everything? I almost wish it were real."

Ceedie's mother did not have her daughter's eyes, nor, I suppose, vice versa. Despite the differences in shape and the color, there was something uncannily similar about the expression they conveyed. There was so much hope there. She had been so terrified that her daughter was broken or weak, only to discover instead how strong she was. I think she admired what her daughter had created and felt humbled, as I had, by the breadth and scope of how her daughter had the courage to move past her negative coping mechanisms and embrace who she was. I wish the same for all of my bright children and their parents: understanding and courage.

Seven

PJ

I watched from across the table as the fourth-grade teacher rifled through a portfolio folder filled with student work. The portfolio belonged to a bright student that we shared: PJ, a precocious, sports-loving boy who had been identified as gifted in the second grade. His strength was writing; he had a unique and powerful writing voice and constructed deeply creative stories and journal entries, as well as making up adventure games for his friends to play at recess. I watched as his teacher selected several assignments and laid them on the table, turning them so I could see.

"So these are the ones that you could pick out?" I asked.

"These are a few that the parents could remember. There are more, but they couldn't be sure."

"This one?" I picked up a math assignment—marked 100%—and turned it to face the teacher.

"His father did that one," she supplied, and pointing to two others, added, "That one, and that one as well."

"What about the science journal?"

"That's mostly his mother."

I took it all in for a moment, thumbing through the composition book until I found a passage about the science fair, and remembered why the teacher had called the meeting with PJ's parents in the first place. PJ had dropped out of the school science fair at the eleventh hour, citing reasons that concerned his teacher enough to contact his parents.

"I'm assuming that PJ's story about his science materials was false?" I asked.

"Yes, his father was shocked. They did not know the science fair was coming up or that PJ had signed up to participate. He seemed appalled that we would think that they would not buy their son the materials he needed to complete his project. They never told him that he could not enter the fair."

"Did you tell him that's what PJ said to you?" I asked, curious as the details deepened.

"Kate, we talked about everything. That's only the beginning. He's been getting them to do his work for years."

The Power of Manipulation

Until now, we have sought to identify, understand, and prevent underlying causes of cheating behaviors, including boredom, fear, perfectionism, and the desire to fit in or to avoid unwanted circumstances. As we have explored these various methods of cheating—plagiarism, copying for and from other students, note passing, etc.—generally the *how* regarding cheating has been largely overshadowed by the *why*. The cheating strategies chosen by high-ability children can be quite impressive, but they vary widely from individual to individual. Beyond recognizing the signs of the behaviors, there is little good in dissecting the *how*s as a method of prevention, with a few notable exceptions.

One type of cheating that is commonly used by bright children is worth being explored independently of its underlying causes, as it can be greatly diminished with careful recognition and intervention, often regardless of the underlying cause. This method for cheating, known as manipulative behavior, can range from extremely subtle instances to cases such as PJ's, which are more overt.

PJ had made a history of lying to both his parents and his teachers. Some were small deceits, but others, such as telling his teacher that his parents would not allow him to enter the science fair as a way to explain his lack of a project, represented greater attempts at control. He had been lying to his teacher about his parents and lying to his parents about his teachers. In doing so, he had manipulated both sides into completing large portions of his work for him, excusing assignments, and allowing him extensions. The science fair incident was only the tip of the iceberg of PJ's control over his two main environments, and by all accounts, his behaviors had been occurring for several years. For many talented manipulators, this behavior can go on for years before it is discovered and if it is discovered, it is usually in the form of more subtle requests for help and lack of communication between home and school environments.

Although teachers and parents communicate in various ways—through telephone, email, letters home, and even in person—information regarding most day-to-day happenings is via the chief messenger: the children themselves. For news about the status of the daily home environment, a teacher relies on the input of the student, and for the general "how was school" mantra, parents generally ask their child rather than contacting the classroom teacher for basic information. At some point in his educational experience PJ had identified that he was the main source of communication between these two primary environments and that they relied on him, to a certain extent, to paint a picture of what was occurring. Once he realized this, he was able to use manipulation to play one against the other to exert his power over his environment.

The ability to control one's environment, whether through the careful understanding of protocol, methodology, or interpersonal skills, is an ability that uses many higher-order thinking skills. This is not to say that intelligent children are naturally predisposed to being dishonest or manipulative, only that those who attempt to challenge their environments and exert power over others generally possess substantial natural skill and cognitive ability that more easily allow them to do so. All students often look for—and find—ways to get their needs met by others without having to do some of the work themselves.[184] Bright children are no exception to this rule. In particular, underachieving bright children are highly susceptible to using manipulation, sometimes unconsciously, so much so that "Manipulative Maria" is one of the main subtypes of underachieving bright students, as named by Sylvia Rimm.[185] These children have the ability to talk their way into higher grades, easier assignments, or other benefits such as extended deadlines, through persuasion, omission of information, or outright lies.

A particularly common manipulation used by bright students is in obtaining excessive or unnecessary help completing school assignments. The difficulty lies in understanding what constitutes excess, especially since the behavior tends to escalate slowly over time until a pattern has developed. It often starts innocently enough. A student struggles with a school assignment. Maybe he or she did not hear or understand the instructions that a teacher gave or is unsure of where to begin in a research study. Having been taught to value the correct answer and to strive for an A grade, the student looks for help to ensure that he or she achieves these goals. Perhaps, rather than seeking perfection, a student's struggle with the assignment may not be related to the actual amount of difficulty but rather with the amount of worth he or she has assigned it. "This assignment is boring" can create a great deal of mental struggle for students who do not wish to complete something they view as irrelevant.

The student then shows frustration and either elicits help from an adult or is offered support when he exhibits signs of struggle. As time goes on, this can become an almost inevitable component of the problem-solving cycle. When work becomes difficult or students begin to show distress, they receive help. For many students, this process can become so ingrained that it is unconscious. Other students, like PJ, are aware of this cycle, and they learn to manipulate it to their advantage. They learn how to control their environments and their outcomes by knowing who and when to ask for help, and they can alter perceptions and influence outcomes by controlling information.

Gifted manipulation is, by its nature, largely a verbal art that uses the ability to compile, understand, and synthesize environmental cues and information in order to change or control the outcome of situations or settings. Students who are manipulative are often highly verbal with excellent reasoning skills (if not always logical ones) and an understanding of how to interpret and use nuances in verbal cues and expression. Although verbal manipulation is most common, manipulative behavior can also be physical in nature, including the body language of pouting, vocal temper tantrums, and crying. There are even instances in which bright students manipulate adults by refusing to physically leave or enter a space or by threatening harm to themselves or others if their will is not met. It is important to note here that threats of this nature should always be taken seriously, even if they are suspected as being more manipulative than truthful in nature. Students who threaten harm to themselves or others in any way should be in the care of a supportive counselor, therapist, or other mental health professional.

Why Bright Students Turn To Manipulation

There are many reasons why bright children may resort to manipulative behavior to solve their problems. For some, it begins as an extension of their own natural abilities and skills. When they use these skills and receive positive outcomes, their control is reinforced, and behavior patterns develop. The high sensitivity that is often characteristic of high-ability children can also help support manipulative behaviors. Sensitivity to one's environment creates strong perception and understanding of social cues and emotions, which result in a wealth of information to utilize. Highly able children often possess a sense of empathy, or understanding of others feelings, including the ability to sense emotional shifts in others. These students can intuitively sense when adults feel threatened or insecure, even when it is not vocalized or explained, which can lead to the ability to challenge their authority by manipulating their emotions, sometimes even in small ways.[186]

For some students, the process of subverting the authority of an adult comes from a sense of self-centeredness or a belief that their talents can change an adult-managed system. These students may feel like they are entitled to more power and freedom, not only over themselves but others as well. High-ability children's verbal precocity and logical reasoning are often more developed than their maturity and knowledge; however, remember that they are not equipped to wield such power over adults. Even when a child possesses the high level of verbal maturity that allows him to dominate in an argument, asynchronous development can lead to a lack of mature judgment to know how to appropriately wield this power. Just because children may know how to walk at a precocious age, for example, does not mean that they possess the understanding or knowledge of where to go or not go.[187] Intelligence is not the same thing as wisdom.

The ability to exert power over a situation can be a powerful coping mechanism to deal with one's inner fear of failure, lack of attention, and need for instant gratification. Some bright students are granted excessive power by their parents at an early age when parental investment eclipses into the realm of overindulgence and overprotectiveness. These students, aware of the intense investment that their parents have for them, learn to easily manipulate the adults in their lives; they often have a need for instant gratification, and this can play out as a need for constant and continued attention from adults.[188] Manipulators are often showmen to this end; they can put on different affects or moods to create certain outcomes, often through calculated emotional outbursts or even extreme flattery or mimicry of adults. Children who fear that they will not be given the attention they desire or that they are somehow unworthy of this attention (fear of failure) spend a great deal of time seeking praise, and they take criticism extremely personally.

Manipulation in children is not always just an attempt to gain positive outcomes through easier means. In some cases, manipulative behavior is driven by anger, frustration, or spite towards authority figures, and this can lead to some students engaging in direct combativeness and power struggles with adults. Students engaged in this form of manipulation seek power over adults in their lives, but they do not plan to use that power to gain the same benefits that most students who lie to adults do. Students may lie to, cheat, and otherwise manipulate the adults in their lives not to obtain positive outcomes but to mete out justice or punishment.

Students who do not learn to process anger in healthy ways can lash out at parents and teachers by manipulating their environment. This can often include a self-sacrificing or self-punishing aspect, as in the way that one student responded to the anger she had towards her classroom teacher. After being called out on negative behavior upon multiple occasions, Alicia began to retaliate with many seemingly pointless deceptions, distractions, and manipulations. She would proclaim that a classroom computer was malfunctioning or that she had spotted a mouse in the hallway, and she began to turn in all of her assignments without her name on them. Alicia's deceptions were designed in a way that she was almost always discovered, because her goal was not to avoid a task or gain an opportunity but to give her teacher additional work and for the teacher to realize that a student had "bested" her.

Parents and teachers often report frustration and even a sense of powerlessness when arguing with a clever student, as these students can be very adept at barraging a debate opponent with relentless logical and emotional opposition to satisfy their position. Arguing with a bright student can sometimes feel like coming to a battle unarmed; parents sometimes report feeling extremely inadequate in the face of their children's abilities.[189] High-ability students' detailed, adult-like rationalizations can so impress their parents and teachers that they can result in too much power for these children, who learn that dominance, aggressiveness, or manipulation are effective ways to avoid routine school or home tasks. These behaviors can cause gaps in a student's character or educational development as they frequently bypass skill development through their worth audit, judging assignments as irrelevant or worthless. Often, students who continue to skip developmental skill-building are able to continue for some time on their own verbal and mental precociousness, but eventually their existing skills will be deficient to meet more challenging experiences.

For PJ, his manipulation was used in part to avoid these unwanted tasks. PJ had gotten into the habit of telling his parents false due dates for assignments, citing dates that were days or even weeks past the actual deadline. He would also tell them that certain assignments were not being graded at all. To his teacher, PJ would then weave a story that he had been unable to finish his work because of a family emergency or because his parents would not buy him the supplies that he needed. He used these lies sparingly, realizing that overuse would prompt phone calls home. A more common ploy for PJ was to feign confusion over an assignment. He would take it to his father or mother, depending on the type of assignment, and ask for their help. While they were tutoring him on how to complete the work, they were more often than not unwittingly doing the work while their son watched and pretended to learn. Another avoidance technique reported by PJ's parents was the "school comes first" ploy. PJ would say that he did not have time to complete chores at home due to a large school project that was imminently due, or simply that he needed to stay up past his lights-out time because he still had assigned chapters to read. If his parents questioned why he did not do it earlier, he would say that the chapters were only assigned that day (or recently enough to support his need for urgency). PJ's parents never had cause to not believe him; like many bright children, his reputation for excellent behavior and performance caused his audiences to believe him.

Another reason that students manipulate their environment through lies is to gain specific positive outcomes or advantages. For example, PJ would often inform his family that larger, more creative projects were not being graded and that he was doing the projects on his own for fun. He would then encourage one or more family members to get involved in helping. Once, PJ brought in a model that his sister had made because he told her that it was not for a grade, but that he simply wanted to demonstrate her work for show and tell.

Sometimes high-ability students seek to gain benefits other than improved grades through the use of lies. One sixth-grade boy told his parents about a current class project about growth cycles and that he had a special assignment to complete. He regaled them with tales of a local farmer who had come to school and dropped off a number of eggs. He reported that the class had watched over the eggs in their classroom until they hatched in their incubator and that they had then been assigned to individually raise baby chicks to adulthood in order to journal their growth in detail. The parents allowed the student to bring the baby chick home. The student did keep a journal and excitedly watched and recorded the progress of the chick, but when the baby grew into a full-grown, loud, crowing rooster, the parents contacted the teacher to see when the farmer was going to come take the animals back. Both the parents and the teacher were baffled to discover that the chick had actually come from a friend of the student who raised birds; there had never been a class incubator, a lesson on growth cycles, or any school assignment.

This form of lying or elaborate story telling is often seen as a more innocent form of manipulation and is commonly reported by parents of bright children. Stories such as these seem to hold less of a stigma than the use of lying to influence grades and school performance. One gifted adult reported a story of how she had lied to her parents when she was in first grade about needing to complete a series of reports: one on dinosaur teeth, another on dinosaur feet, tails, etc. As this was long before the advent of the Internet and because the information was oddly specific, her parents had to take her to a series of libraries in order for her to find enough data to write her reports. Only when the teacher contacted her parents, pleading for them to go easy on their daughter and stop having her write so many extra assignments, did her manipulation become apparent. She had been telling her teacher the same lie that she told her parents, only changing the assigner of the work. The extra reports had not been for a grade or an actual assignment. The girl had only wanted more information and either had been afraid that she would not be allowed to go to the library without a school reason or had been curious as to how much power she had over her two environments.

This is not to say that the parents and teachers of bright children should naturally be suspicious and distrust what their student is telling them about what is happening at home or at school. The key for parents is to realize that the possibility exists in all individuals to have a tendency to manipulate the truth when they fear getting in trouble, seek to avoid something unwanted, or wish to gain something. PJ wanted an easier way to complete his work; he was able to manipulate his family to help him with his assignments. It is easy to fall into the trap of thinking of PJ as just a bad kid, one predisposed to lying and cheating, but the truth is that the discovery of his falsehoods came, as most tales of high-ability cheating often do, at the complete shock of his parents and his teachers. PJ was a student who had never had a grade other than an A on his report cards and was extremely well-spoken and well-behaved. He had never gotten a referral for misbehaving at school and he seemed well-adjusted with friends. That is not to say that all talented manipulators are so well-adjusted. Some are aggressive and nonconformist and can find it difficult to make appropriate friendships due to passive-aggressive behavior, low self-esteem, and social difficulties that relate to their need to control their relationships.[190] We all want to think that we have an idea of who a cheater is, but the truth is that all children, regardless of their background, upbringing, and intelligence level, can cheat, lie, and manipulate.

It is important to accept that your bright children are not perfect. Everyone has the potential to make the mistake of lying, either by total fabrication, exaggerating the truth, or by omitting key details. We never like to admit that our children, particularly those who are so remarkable, might be engaging in dishonest behaviors. We fear that it reflects poorly on us as parents or teachers. Unfortunately, it is that same fear that can allow us to turn a blind eye to even the possibility of dishonesty. We do a disservice to our children by not accepting that they are children first and need to be taught and corrected when they make mistakes. The vast majority of adults willingly report times when they were dishonest as youth, either to their parents, teachers, or friends, yet it is rare to find parents who are willing to admit that their children also may have been dishonest. It is that avoidance that prevents us from supporting our students in growing and learning from their mistakes. The choice to ignore students' mistakes is what truly reflects poorly on us as parents and teachers, not the mistakes themselves.

Allow for Struggle

Being a parent of a bright child can be a role fraught with difficulties, misunderstandings, and complicated choices. High-ability children frequently face difficulties as they work in a school structure that was not designed with them in mind, and parents often feel helpless when it comes to supporting their child's unique needs.[191] A great deal of advocacy is often required to be the parent of a precocious child, both in the school environment and in personal and home environments. Parents of high-ability children may be called upon to explain to relatives or friends who have difficulty understanding the emotional vulnerabilities, intensities, and other unique characteristics of highly able children. Sometimes it can feel like this advocacy is a full-time job. The lack of understanding by others can cause the parental protective reach to overextend into all arenas of a child's experience, sometimes to the detriment of the child's growth. All parents want to see their children succeed and be happily fulfilled, but sometimes this can lead to a preoccupation with providing children with ideal circumstances at all times. Some overly permissive parenting styles can rob students of self-esteem and self-respect by insisting upon only positive experiences. These parents cannot view their child except through the lens of "But he's just a kid"—helpless and deserving only easy experiences.[192] Unfortunately, this often has the unwanted side effect of removing authentic struggle and unpredictability from childhood experiences. The act of seeking out the path of least resistance for a student can consequently subvert actual growth, which is brought about by self-efficacy and problem solving.[193]

The best way to prevent this subversion of meaningful growth is to avoid doing a child's work, even if the intention is not to complete their work but only to help them through difficult portions or to re-teach concepts. This note is not exclusive to parents; teachers can fall to the mercy of the same good intentions. Teachers and parents should serve as facilitators, not as direct aids for completing work. Even if a bright child is not actively attempting to manipulate completion of their work, a parent's actions can unconsciously support a child's development of "learned helplessness," or the psychological state in which students feel powerless to help themselves. Without the chance to prove to themselves that they can work through challenging situations, students may begin to falsely believe in their own inability to solve problems. This trait is often found in, though not mutually exclusive to, students with perfectionist tendencies.[194]

Some parents may be unwilling to stop helping their children with their homework or projects, citing that they trust their children and do not believe them to be engaging in cheating behavior when they ask for assistance. Although parents who feel this way may very well be justified in the trust they have for their children, they should probably stop anyway. Preventing manipulative cheating is a nice side effect of no longer completing some or all of your student's work, but it is not the most compelling reason to avoid the practice. Regardless of whether or not a child may be engaging in manipulative behavior by seeking parental help, parents risk increasing dependence, preventing their children from developing coping mechanisms to deal with struggle, and increasing the phenomenon of learned helplessness, even if they complete only portions of a student's work for them.

The psychology of control can create an almost cyclical, if somewhat contradictory pattern in this way. In this pattern, students attempt to manipulate outcomes by having others complete their work for them. That act of control can, if repeated over time, lead to feelings of learned helplessness, which is marked by a decisive *lack* of feeling like one is in control. Many cases of learned helplessness are caused by a student's negative reaction to failure, which over time can result in the incorrect belief that they have no control over what happens to them based on their inability to produce positive outcomes. For some students, however, failure is not a prerequisite. Students can infer that they are helpless from the context, that is, students can gather from the environment that they would be unable to control positive outcomes through their actions. Allowing someone else to take over a job previously done by the student, having someone complete their homework for them or with them on a consistent basis, or other signals that suggest to the child that they are incapable of independence can become implications to the student over time that the aid of others is vital to their success. This is known as self-induced dependence.

In studies in which different groups of individuals are randomly labeled as "independent problem solvers," "group problem solvers," or "boss and assistant," those with the dependent labels not only produced consistently poorer work but also rated themselves as being less competent at problem-solving tasks.[195] The negative effects of loss of control in its early stages are feelings anxiety and stress. As these feelings progress, students exhibit increasingly more manipulative behavior in order to restore the loss of power.[196] Eventually, this can result in chronic learned helplessness.[197] Thus, the simple act of seeking control can often lead students to feel less productive, less accomplished, and increasingly helpless.

Parents and teachers can learn to accept a certain amount of "positive failure" rather than seeing every mistake or low grade as a harbinger of a future of challenges. When children are pushed to succeed and begin to associate failure as something to avoid at all costs, they are inadvertently also shielded from character growth. When students do not have a chance to experience struggle, they can easily become uncomfortable whenever any difficulty is presented to them.[198] Allow students to experience struggle (and failure) and to attempt to solve their own personal challenges of childhood so that they can develop resilience and coping mechanisms to combat later difficulties. In order to succeed, students have to first learn how to fail.

Some parents find it difficult to transition from helping their children to telling them that they must complete their work solo, and it is important to recognize that there can be a continuum of types of support. When, for example, is it acceptable to help a student problem solve or brainstorm? We want to allow students to run through their full problem-solving process whenever possible. Students should have the opportunity to brainstorm, struggle, try solutions, and see the natural cause-and-effect consequences of their actions. Ask students to try a problem from multiple angles and with many attempts before you describe a concept or give them supporting details of another way they can find the answer.

It is not harsh to allow a student to explore all avenues to solve tricky problems, especially if your language is supportive. Rather than telling a student, "You are so smart, you should be able to do this on your own," which represents a fixed mindset, express to them that "it is less important to me if you get the answer correct. What is important is that you are working through a hard problem, and I am proud of your work effort. Don't give up." Sometimes, of course, a parent can remind a student of an equation if he or she is struggling to find it and asks for a reminder, or a teacher can tell the first few letters of a word to look up in a dictionary, but too many parents and teachers fall victim to their own desire to help a student avoid struggle and unconsciously subvert the natural problem-solving process of discovery, attempt, and, yes, even inevitable error.

Another way to help children without removing the all-important personal struggle from the situation is to help them with the structural components that are not being directly tested but which can affect the outcome of their success. For example, students with poor organizational skills, difficulties setting study schedules or goals, or other non-subject related deficiencies can be given specific help in these areas. By helping students with guidelines and structure for studying and work, parents can support their students in persevering through difficult challenges. Creating contracts or independent study plans as well as reward or incentive charts also help some students who struggle with completing tasks on their own.[199]

To parents who hate to watch their children experience the pain of feeling like they are not doing well on an assignment, realize that their frustration—and maybe even your own—indicates fixation on the end result of their work rather on the learning process. Your desire to help them with their homework, even if only to check it for completion and correctness, can help cement that fixed mindset. Ask yourself: What is the worst thing that can happen if I do not help my child with his or her homework? Answer: He or she might not understand it, might become frustrated, experience emotional turmoil, and even get a poor grade as a result. As frightening as the progression seems, remember that these things are all elements of the beginning of a cycle of learning. If your child brings home a low grade on an assignment, you can sit down and go over teacher feedback, encourage the child to ask questions (rather than offering immediate hints and suggestions), and discuss what could be done differently next time. There is no punishment for the low grade; the grade itself represents its own natural consequence of student's actions (or lack thereof).

When discussing a low-grade, address the child's emotions calmly and without judgment. You can ask why getting the low grade (or not understanding the concept) has distressed him or her so, and use strategies to encourage growth-mindset thinking. Be patient and show the student that you are not distressed with the *grade* but focused on the *process*. Do not allow students to apply excuses to the low grade such as "I didn't have time," "The teacher doesn't like me," or "I didn't understand the assignment." These are manipulative statements designed to convince both you *and* the students themselves that they are not responsible for their failure. Parents and teachers can remove the stigma associated with low grades by modeling and explaining how mistakes fuel our progress. Mistakes should not embarrass or humiliate a student, but neither should they be taken lightly or dismissed through manipulation.

Do not be afraid of a low grade, or even two or three: The elementary level is an ideal, safe forum for students to learn the meaning of failing forward and for modeling how not to dwell on false notions of what a grade means. Remember from the chapter about Martin that children who have an understanding of 95% of a math concept are not "A Students" or even "Straight A Math Students," as if the letter representation of their current curricular understanding has somehow become tied up in their identity.

There is no shame in not understanding all of the available information on a topic or in being told that they still have a way to go to hit what the school system requires for complete mastery (if that is their goal). In addition, you should expect a comfortable pattern of both growth and regression in your bright child; it is perfectly natural, and one should not expect a child to be constantly productive.[200] When children are given space to regress and grow naturally, they are better prepared to accept and learn from their mistakes. This balance between success and failure, when allowed, can show children that their parents trust them to take risks, to try to solve their own problems, and to take their own path. Students who are accepting and productive about failure are far less likely to feel that they must succeed at all costs—a mindset that often leads to dishonest behavior such as manipulation.

It is important to note here also that all children, including bright ones, have deficits in some areas, and particular consideration is needed for students who are twice exceptional—those who are identified as gifted but also have a learning disability. For these students, it can be difficult to ascertain whether or not their desire for help with assignments stems from dependency or from true disability. Although all students, including those with learning disabilities, can benefit from appropriate struggle and independent work, it is not helpful to deny students access to learning strategies and supports when they are appropriate. Table 7.1 can help you distinguish between the two.

Table 7.1. Ways to Discriminate between Dependence and Disability

Dependence	Disability
1. Child asks for explanations regularly, despite differences in subject matter.	1. Child asks for explanations in particular subjects that are difficult.
2. Child asks for explanations of instructions regardless of style used, either auditory or visual.	2. Child asks for explanations of instructions only when given in one instruction style, either auditory or visual, but not both.
3. Child's questions are not specific to material but appear to be mainly to gain adult attention.	3. Child's questions are specific to material, and once process is explained, child works efficiently.
4. Child is disorganized or slow in assignments but becomes much more efficient when a meaningful reward is presented as motivation.	4. Child's disorganization or slow pace continues despite motivating rewards.
5. Child works only when an adult is nearby at school and/or at home.	5. Child works independently once process is clearly explained.

6. Individually administered measures of ability indicate that the child is capable of learning the material. Individual tests improve with tester encouragement and support. Group measures may not indicate good abilities or skills.	6. Both individual and group measures indicate lack of specific abilities or skills. Tester encouragement has little or no significant effect on scores.
7. Child exhibits "poor me" body language (tears, helplessness, pouting, copying) regularly when new work is presented. Teacher or adult attention eases the symptoms.	7. Child exhibits "poor me" body language only with instructions or assignments in specific disability areas and accepts challenges in areas of strength.
8. Parents report whining, complaining, attention getting, temper tantrums, and poor sportsmanship at home.	8. Although parents may find similar symptoms at home, they tend to be more sporadic than regular, particularly the whining and complaining.
9. Child's "poor me" behavior appears only with one parent and not with the other, only with some teachers and not with others. With some teachers or with the other parent, the child functions fairly well independently.	9. Although the child's "poor me" behaviors may appear only with one parent or with solicitous teachers, performance is not adequate even when behavior is acceptable.
10. Child learns only when given one-to-one instruction but will not learn in groups, even when the instructional mode is varied.	10. Although the child may learn more quickly in a one-to-one setting, he/she will also learn efficiently in a group setting, provided that the child's disability is taken into consideration when instructions are given.

Some children who are truly disabled also become dependent. They key to distinguishing between disability and dependence is the children's response to adult support. If the children perform only with adult support when new material is presented, they are too dependent, whether or not there is also a disability.

Adapted from: Rimm, S. B. (2008), *Why Bright Kids Get Poor Grades and What you Can Do about It*, Scottsdale, AZ: Great Potential Press.

Parents often feel that their child's gifts are an awesome responsibility. According to James Borland, former director of the Columbia University Center for the Study of Education of the Gifted, "They don't want to squander their child's chance for success. Giftedness is not something you pin down easily and it's not going to disappear if you make one mistake."[201] Just as it is acceptable for a gifted child to stumble on the path of their education, parents should not be too hard on themselves as they overcome their own challenges on the journey of guiding a bright child. Teachers, too, should understand that finding the right amount of challenge for a bright child is a process. You will not become an expert on supporting struggle and challenge in your bright students right away, and the process will likely feel frustrating at first to both child and teacher. Forgive yourself when you come upon stumbling blocks and learn to view your struggle through the same lens that we encourage bright students to use.

A New View on Struggling

Some of the work to help combat PJ's manipulation was not only focused on increasing his parents' tolerance for his frustration and struggle but also on his teacher's perception of her student's needs. PJ's teacher was like many of her colleagues in that she hated to see struggle in her students and was afraid that they would feel less intelligent or capable if they did not experience full closure at the end of each lesson. To her, and to others whose fears follow this path, realize that it is okay— even optimal—for students to experience some frustration with their learning. Learning is like working out a muscle. If the weights are too small or the exercises are too repetitive, the workout is far too easy and no progress is made. If the challenge is too great, you can do damage by overextending or stressing the muscle, and that can prevent further growth. Instead, make your workout one that challenges you just enough, with interesting and different opportunities for growth so that you can build up your tolerance and ability. Students need to be frustrated just enough to propel them forward. For teachers, that might mean that the traditional "all-lessons-have-closure" mantra can be extended beyond a single class period.

One technique is for teachers to challenge their students to open-ended games and problem-solving opportunities that do not allow for immediate closure. Mrs. English a gifted education teacher who worked with second-grade students, used to have her students line up all the chairs in the room, most of which had been collected over many years and were of all different shapes and sizes, from shortest to tallest. Only after the chairs were lined up were students then to line themselves up tallest to shortest and sit in the opposite chair, meaning that the shortest student would be in the tallest chair, etc. After these few instructions, Mrs. English would allow the students to begin. No leaders were chosen and no other rules were given as the teacher sat back to observe the class's problem-solving skills.

The first time I witnessed the chair challenge, the room instantly erupted into chaos after the instructions were given. Several students began to shout over one another, vying for the opportunity to lead the others with their strategies. Other students, unwilling to listen, took their own chairs and moved them into a line that was decidedly *not* correctly graduated by height as the shouting students still held their chairs hostage. Other students, uncomfortable with the chaos, sought comfort from the teacher by asking for additional rules and clarifications, but she would only instruct them to return to their problem solving. This went on for 10 minutes before she instructed them to put their chairs back under their desks. "We'll try this again in a few days," she explained, and she then moved the students on to another activity.

This was the second attempt of the chair activity with that particular group. Although I had been surprised that Mrs. English did not offer guidance during the process or instruct loud students to stop screaming over their classmates, she later explained that the students who were calling out and attempting to be leaders were simply working through their own problem-solving strategies, as were the students who tried to solve the problem without anyone else's help. Both failed, she explained, and the one thing that every student had in common was that they did not need her, as the teacher, to tell them that their strategies had not worked. The next time they attempted the challenge, she said, students would try different strategies. They would likely go through a phase of believing that their strategies were correct even when they did not produce workable results and would blame others not following them as the reason for failure. Eventually, she explained to me, as patiently as she had allowed the students to work through their own challenges, they will come to a solution on their own. Some of her groups were able to complete the challenge in two or three tries. Others required most of the year to cycle through their difficulties and find ways to work together to solve their problems. And how, I asked, did the students feel when they did finally solve it?

She smiled. "Elated. They are more proud of their accomplishments when they have to work out the answer."

This strategy is not only useful for problem-solving games and strategies on how to use teamwork. Teachers and students alike can learn to accept ongoing learning and struggle with their schoolwork. Give bright students fewer yet more challenging problems. Engage their thinking by having them answer questions with no one right answer, and send them home to think about challenging questions before allowing them to check their work against an answer sheet. Parents and teachers who are uncomfortable with the students' inadequate responses or lack of immediate completion should resist giving answers too quickly. Students who become fixated on instant gratification with their work are much more susceptible to seeking quick ways to achieve a high grade. These quick fixes are not always dishonest in nature but certainly may include any number of cheating behaviors. Students who enjoy the process of problem solving more than the end result are far less likely to manipulate others into supplying them with an instantly gratifying answer.

Allowing a certain amount of disorder, whether the struggle of a student sitting at home at the dining room table bemoaning that he or she "will never get this" or the chaos of a classroom with merging strategies and problem-solving tactics, is one of the most difficult elements of being a teacher or parent of a bright child. The reason it poses so great a challenge is because our desire to offer our students peace and understanding comes out of our love for them. We want the best for our students and often do not realize when our desire for them to excel deprives them of authentic struggle and the ability to cope with unpredictability. By striving to provide only the most advantageous circumstances, we inadvertently destroy the development of a threshold for how much challenge and difficulty a child can tolerate, effectively robbing them of a vital coping mechanism they will need throughout their lives. If you want your children to succeed, you must first understand that they need to learn how to fail.[202]

The vast majority of parents are well-intentioned in their desire to help their children with school assignments, as are teachers who assist students before they have experienced true struggle. This desire to support the bright children in your life is less misguided than misdirected. Parents and teachers are not always aware what other roles they can play as partners in the education of their highly able children. One of the single most helpful things that a teacher or parent can do to support bright children is to improve the quality of communication regarding their education. Not only does this greatly decrease the likelihood of one environment being manipulated against the other, but it also sets a foundation for meaningful goals for students.

Improve Parent-Teacher Communication

Productive communication between home and school is the foundation for establishing a collaborative working relationship to support bright students. Both the quality and the quantity of communication between the parents and teachers of bright students are important. Both set the tone for a mutual expectation of honest and authentic student success. In addition, remember that, even for the most controlling child, it is not realistic to overlook the students themselves as middlemen or to exclude them from the communication process. In fact, involving the student as a member of the team, when appropriate during the exchange of ideas, can help prevent further student manipulation of their environment. Good communication that involves clever children can positively affect how academically and socially adjusted they are, as well as how they view achievement as a whole. By establishing open and clear discussions, parents and teachers must be willing to start "from scratch," even if students may be actively omitting or fabricating key details of their school or home experience to the other party in ways that may make parents or teachers uncomfortable. Student-relayed information is always susceptible to being colored by students' personal perceptions and may not represent an accurate picture of a situation.

Some parents can feel frustrated and overwhelmed that their child's enrichment needs are not being met, and communication can suffer as a result of not knowing where to start. They rely on what they hear from their child. Common roadblocks at the school may include inadequate funding or support for enrichment programs, inconsistent or inappropriate gifted identification, and a lack of understanding about gifted education law, pedagogy, or best practice in the schools. Parents and teachers alike can feel overwhelmed and underprepared in the face of what is best for bright children and may even have differing opinions regarding the status of the children. Parents and teachers can slog through this quagmire of challenges until ongoing communication is unproductive, halted, or even hostile. Add the problem of students who may be mis-communicating information between home and school, and the prospects for meaningful dialogue seem very unlikely.

Parents and teachers should not worry too much if they find themselves facing some or all of these difficulties. Even in ideal circumstances, parent-teacher communication may begin on the wrong path, but it can be righted and collaboration can be achieved. Although the quality (or existence) of the school's gifted education program is important, as are the attitudes and background knowledge of parents and teachers, meaningful communication does not necessarily hinge on these factors alone. In fact, improving communication and encouraging honesty in students can be achieved even in less-than-ideal circumstances. The key is to start to disassemble some of the most common communication glitches that occur, not only between parents and teachers but also between the bright children and the adults themselves.

Talented manipulators can become aware, even unconsciously, of these common gaps in understanding and learn how to exploit or use them to their own means. Communication glitches often start off as real difficulties for students. As students see the effect that certain statements have on teachers or parents, they begin to use them in more manipulative ways in order to obtain key outcomes. Parents and teachers should keep that in mind and always address issues at their root rather than looking to place blame. For example, when a student or parent comes to me with a concern such as "My parents won't buy me science supplies," I assume that any duplicity that is created by students saying one thing and meaning another is unintentional or unconscious, and I seek to involve the parents to address the situation head on. We will look at how to translate the possible meanings behind what students tell their parents or teachers, but often the best way to solve issues is to not let them become serious glitches or impediments to communication.

A communication glitch is a statement by a student to either a parent or a teacher, often about the other environment, that can cause dissent due to misunderstanding or disagreement. Each side looks for causes and explanations from the other side, or worse, they rely strictly on the experience and input of the student to base their decision on cause and effect. Like a computer glitch that can cause errors and flaws in overall performance of the machine and its processes, a communication glitch can create ripples of distrust and misunderstanding in a parent-teacher relationship, even when parties sit down to amicably discover the source of the confusion. Below is a list of red flag statements that may cause communication glitches.

Table 7.2. Common Red Flag Communication "Glitches"

Things Said to Parents	Things Said to Teachers
I'm bored.	I'm bored.
I hate school.	My parents never help me with my homework.
No one likes me.	I couldn't do my work because we're busy/sick at home.
My teacher hates me.	My parents will be mad at me if I don't get this right.

Let's explore, for example, a common communication glitch between home and school where the student says, "I'm bored," and by extension, "I hate school." I lump them together because they do often come on the heels of one another and are generally said to parents in the home environment. Naturally, when parents hear these phrases communicated by their children they are troubled, terrified at the thought of their students sitting in a classroom day after day, bored and miserable. They contact their child's teacher, relay what has been said, and are often met with disbelief and sometimes open disagreement. It is one of the most common glitches in home-school communication regarding high-ability students, as well as one of the single most frustrating ones that causes great distress for both parents and teachers.

Why are parents so often met with disbelief when they tell their child's teacher about the student's boredom or other woes? The simple answer is that, in a majority of cases, the child may be exhibiting no symptoms of these feelings at school. The teachers see the child as a well-behaved, enthusiastic learner who has never said that they are unhappy.

Teachers, though, generally do not see the same child that gets off of the bus at the end of the day. There are several reasons for this. Some students are very good at internalizing their feelings, particularly negative ones, feeling that they should cope with their emotions without help from outside sources. School is often directly associated with obedience, which can further impress upon students the belief that they cannot express displeasure with what is happening around them.

Also, some bright students dwell on and amplify emotional moments and can be hyper-sensitive to seemingly small details that matter greatly to them. An otherwise normal day can be recounted to a parent as "the worst day ever," thanks to what might have been a single, seemingly minor incident. The student may have experienced a low grade on an assignment, a playground disagreement, or an embarrassment (real or imagined), but as the event is replayed in their minds through the end of the day, it may end up being seen through a maximizing telescopic lens as terrible and all-consuming. When students attempt to cope with these emotions on their own, a single stimulus—even one unrelated to the original incident—can trigger emotional outbursts or feelings of sadness and "hating school."

It is often at the end of the day, when the student feels safe at home in a neutral environment, that these emotions and expressions occur. It is not that students are necessarily lying about their feelings or even that they are wrong to feel the way that they do, but parents should realize that they might be seeing the "sum of the parts" at the end of the day—the final compression of the individual emotions and events that the student experienced, rather than a fully accurate portrait of their child's school experience. Manipulation may be a factor, but even if it is not, students may still portray an inaccurate version of the truth.

Orson, a profoundly bright young man, used to meet his mother as he got off of the bus every day and immediately begin to cry. When questioned about what was wrong, he would exclaim that he hated school, no one liked him, and the work was boring. He would continue most of the night terrorizing his younger sister and alternating between anger and sadness. When his mother contacted the school, she was dismayed to find that his teachers did not see the same behavior. He was a model student, respectful, and creative. Moreover, he had never spoken to his teachers about his negative feelings. His mother felt that he must have expressed his unhappy feelings at school and that his teachers were lying about his model behavior, simply unwilling to help, or not looking hard enough to find the signs of his despair.

What both sides needed to realize was that their perspectives were correct insofar as their experience with the student. Neither side was lying about its experience with Orson. It is not only entirely plausible but extremely common for a child to present few to no outward signs of distress in one environment only to carry it over into the other. It is not always one-directional; some students experience emotional outbursts, tantrums, or challenges at school and then are calm and appropriately expressive in their home environment. Although some are inclined to assign blame to the individuals in charge of those arenas—namely, the parents or the teachers—it is important to realize that finger pointing can halt the progress of improving and identifying the underlying issues. Just because a child is calm in one environment and shows his or her stress in another does directly correlate to cause and effect. Again, even though a student's actions may be done in an intentionally manipulative way in an attempt to establish control, the parents and teachers should still meet and seek underlying causes and possible solutions. In other words, open and honest communication between parents and teachers can help solve the issue regardless of whether or not it is manipulative in nature; so distinguishing between the two is not immediately important, though it can play a part in the underlying-cause discussion.

First, approach all communication regarding your bright students, even and especially if there is a problem to be solved, with a positive and flexible outlook, including the shared assumption that both parties—school and home—share the same primary goal of helping the student. Too often, the first goal of parent-teacher communication regarding bright students is the venting of frustration and the assigning of blame. This is rarely productive because it usually puts individuals on the defensive. Whether the parent assumes that the teacher is not doing enough to combat the child's boredom or the teacher assumes that the child is only stressed at home because of the pressure that the parent is placing on them, the creation of a cause-and-effect relationship between blame and a student's emotions is a draining and thoroughly unrewarding endeavor.

Second, parents and teachers should avoid turning the conversation into the game of who knows the student best. Students can capitalize on this by telling differing stories or showing different affects at home versus at school, creating dissension when the two sides argue over the truth in student contradictions. Actively respect and accept that both parties have unique information regarding the behavior and action of the student, even if only a differing perspective based on environment. As long as both parties believe that the other has the best interest of the child in mind and that they do not share identical perspectives based on the information they have gathered, neither can assume that the other was intending to cause the child harm, and the conversation can begin from a point of mutual understanding and problem solving.

In Orson's case, for example, his mother met with the classroom teacher and the principal several times, and the meetings were generally unproductive. The majority of these meetings consisted of each side arguing on the defensive, feeling that the other party was accusing them of either exaggerating or downplaying Orson's struggles. The teacher would calmly explain and use evidence that showed that Orson was doing well in school but not so well that he needed extension work, and that he was presenting himself as a well-adjusted, happy child. The parent spent the meeting recounting the misery that her child was exhibiting at home and explaining her frustration and anger that no one believed her. The meeting would have been much more effective if both parties had asserted at the beginning that they both wanted what was best for Orson, that they respected the information given by the other side as being true insofar as their perspective, and then begun problem solving without pointing fingers. Rather than saying, "My child is bored in your class and hates school," which immediately can put a teacher who has no firsthand evidence of this on the defensive, a parent can make a world of difference by approaching it from a place of giving and gathering information.

Both parties should then explore the possible causes of a student's unhappiness or other problems and the resulting behaviors in the two environments. Orson may have been troubled about something in particular and only playing the happy student at school to cover his negative emotions. He might have been truly happy at school until negative moments occurred, when an all-or-nothing, black-or-white mentality took over, causing him to exaggerate stressful emotions at the end of the day when he reached his safe environment. He could have been seeking some particular outcome by making his teacher believe that he was content or by making his mother believe that he was unhappy. Whether or not the reality of a child's dislike for school is appropriately gauged, the jumping-off point should be to realize that both parties need to see the other half of the coin before leaping to solutions, especially before they discredit the other side for causing or exacerbating the problem. Keeping a productive and positive relationship between teachers and parents is vital. If you believe your child's woes are being seen yet ignored, that partnership will inevitably decline without trust and realization that both sides are working towards a common goal. Table 7.3 gives a few more examples of the possible meaning behind what students say to their teachers.

Table 7.3. What Do Children Really Mean?

Examine the information you have about students before responding to their expressions of feelings. There are many possibilities for the true meanings of what they say. Listen to their words and interpret them with adult wisdom. When children communicate to you about their home lives, here are some possible interpretations of what they may mean.

What Children Say	What Children May Mean
My parents make me work all the time.	The child may have too many chores, or...
	*The child may be required to do one chore a day and argues about that.
	*The child may never have had chores before and is being required to do something for the first time.
My parents never help me with my homework	The parents may not help, even when the child has an appropriate need, or...
	*The parents may have helped regularly and are now trying to encourage independence.
	*The parents may have been out and could not help last night.

Adapted from: Rimm, S. B. (2008). *Why Bright Kids Get Poor Grades: And What You Can Do About It*. Scottsdale, AZ: Great Potential Press.

Next Steps: Approach the Problem

The next step, once possible underlying causes have been discussed, is to approach the most likely problem or cause by addressing it directly. Language is vital here. Neither side should feel like it is going to be put on the defensive. This "approach the problem" language should also be used to look at underlying causes of an issue even if a meeting did not take place. You may have discussed with your child a possible problem, or have a good idea behind what is happening, and want to suggest a possible course of action with the teacher, for example. Approach-the-problem language is quite useful in these circumstances.

If the issue is that a student dislikes school and likely needs additional support, parents should avoid statements like, "My child hates school and needs more/different school experiences." Instead, a positive replacement might be to say, "I wanted to tell you something that Orson has been telling me at home about how he feels about school. I want to know what your experience has been with him. He told me last night that he hates school. Has he said anything to you? Can we meet to share thoughts and figure out where this is coming from?" This follows the meeting guidelines of immediately finding common ground: helping the child, as well as establishing respect for both viewpoints. E.g., "You have information about and experiences with my child that I do not. I validate that, and I value your input. Let's work on solving the problem together."

For teachers, instead of responding with "Your child is happy at school and does not need any extra work," a positive replacement, for example, would be, "From what I have seen, Orson is still playing with his friends during indoor recess, still working well with his partners, finishing his work appropriately, and has not shared any negative feelings. It sounds like he is telling us two different things. Let's see what we can do about that." It could seem like negative finger-pointing to place the onus of responsibility on the child, but there are no blame statements in the way the teacher has responded. The teacher simply is stating what she has seen and is validating that she believes the parent sees something different at home. The first teacher statement risks contradicting the parent in a way that says "I don't believe you." The second seeks collaboration toward a solution.

Similarly, instead of a statement such as "My child is bored and needs more challenging work," a positive replacement statement would be "Orson is saying that he's bored at school. If this is so, I wonder if it might help if he had some more challenging assignments. I understand that he may not be working in a way at school that would show you that he needs this. Can we get together and talk about how he has been behaving at school as well as his work habits so that we can look at this as a possibility?"

And finally, instead of a teacher responding that "Your child does not need/cannot handle enrichment work," it is far more productive and validating to say, "We can definitely discuss enrichment work as well as what characteristics a child typically shows that make me feel that giving them more challenging work is appropriate. Right now, Orson is completing his work in a way that has not shown me that he is ready for enrichment, but we can look at what he is showing you at home and what may be causing the discrepancy at school. It may help to talk about something called his worth audit. If he is as ready for enrichment work as you say, we may need to address the way he looks at his assignments first."

Involve Students in the Process

It is important that students are involved in the process when communicating with a teacher about how to ensure that your child is making the most of the day at school, rather than expending his energy and problem-solving ability with finding ways *around* work. Children can be more than messengers. Asking them to present their work for the teacher-parent meetings is a good start and can be integral in keeping the meeting focused and positive. The overall goal should be to have the student understand why the meetings are taking place and to involve them in the problem-solving process. Parents and teachers have the best of intentions when they suggest alternate work for their bright student, but they may overlook the vital step of having the student participate in selecting and understanding the enrichment work. Being involved in the meeting is an opportunity to facilitate greater learning for the student who can then help design the process or the product. Clever students often find learning on their own more rewarding than the work that they avoid in school, and we can use these fertile minds to help broaden their school experience.[203] For students who have focused their creativity and problem-solving skills towards making more interesting, "teacher-proof" cheating behaviors, this can be a particularly positive way to focus their creative energy and ideas. These students are already planning their day, choosing what work they will complete and what they will outsource to others. Teachers and parents can reclaim that energy and channel it towards more honest choices.

Another positive side-effect of students feeling like a part of the planning process for educational modification is that students make fewer stress-related choices about their work. When students feel stressed about their deadlines, the quality of their work, or even their ability to complete a challenging assignment, the stress can lead to cheating behaviors. In fact, several of the top reasons cited for high-ability cheating are based on stressors—e.g., students feeling that they have been assigned too much work to complete in the time allotted, that they are being pressured, and that they have to maintain their high grades.[204]

When students are a part of the process of deciding what enrichment work they will complete, they become intimately aware of the components of what, why, and how. They understand why they are completing that particular assignment and what standards it fulfills as well as what their criteria for evaluation will be. This way, bright children not only know why they are getting a certain grade but also have the information available to determine whether or not they agree with that grade. Although this seems to open up an area rife for manipulation, remember that manipulation is quite often a desire for power and a grab for control where an individual feels like none exists. When a creative child seeks to manipulate an adult, it often represents a coping mechanism to deal with their fear of lack of control rather than a true desire to make others helpless or exert power over them. By allowing students to be a part of the planning from the beginning and by answering all their questions about why they are being tasked to complete a particular assignment, they are more confident that they understand its overall purpose. This can give students a sense of choice and possession over the project, which results in a lessened need to manipulate the situation. By giving students more focused responsibilities, you decrease the amount that they exert their desire to control in other, more negative ways.

When students are bored in school or concerned that they will not be able to get the grade that they desire, we have seen how they can turn to dishonest coping mechanisms to achieve their goals as well as to avoid negative outcomes. Students who crave control, such as PJ, are particularly adept at this creative manipulation. What is unfortunate is that these students often do not realize that there are perfectly acceptable and even excellent ways for them to use their creativity to solve these problems. They either do not believe that they will be allowed to do so or mistakenly believe that questioning teachers and parents about the work they do in school is not permissible.

It seems odd, even laughable that a little girl would lie to her teacher and parents in order to work on her dinosaur reports, but how was a first grader to know that any educator would be happy to let her work on an interest project? She had never been told that she was allowed to work on assignments that were of her own choosing. All modeling up to that point regarding learning had been that of an adult authority figure—either a parent or a teacher—assigning her specific work. It is impossible to expect a student to be able to formulate acceptable alternatives and solutions to challenging problems without understanding the scope of the system in which they work; we cannot assume that students can ignore what modeling that they have received in order to simply know something else may be appropriate. In fact, most forms of questioning the authority of the educational system or seeking to understand its boundaries are seen as taboo by a majority of students with understandable reasons as to why. Most students are never told in their educational careers that they have the right to question a decision made by a teacher or to ask why they are being required to do something. When students do question decisions—or throw out the inevitable "Why are we doing this?"—they do not know how to do so in the best way to get results, or in a way that is not seen as disrespectful or willful. You have to teach students that arguments and discussions can be incredibly positive, even and especially when had with authority figures, but they also need modeling and structure to support *how* to disagree and why.

One problem bright children often share with their parents is how unprepared they feel to tactfully approach teachers without offending them.[205] Just as communication between parents and teachers must start from a point of respect and common goals, children should be taught that when they approach an adult with a question or challenge, neither party should feel on the defensive. This can be achieved by modeling effective communication skills and problem solving for your child and by working with them to learn how to replace arguments and power struggles with appropriate and productive disagreements.

The goal of education and parenting is not to completely prevent children from challenging adults. It is true that talented manipulators often use a range of arguments—from logical to emotional—to control the outcome of a situation, and this can lead to a student who is unafraid to lie in order to win a point. For this reason, it might seem that a suitable alternative is to disallow students from arguing with adults in order to prevent this manipulative behavior. However, this can often have the opposite effect. If students who are afraid that they will not be in control are completely prevented from arguing their points, they may turn to increasingly more manipulative tactics, including emotional blackmail and increased incidences of lying and cheating—often covert—in order to continue controlling their surroundings. The best way to curb these behaviors is to set guidelines and boundaries for the students for what behavior is acceptable. Provide students with positive forums in which to express themselves that do not prevent them from feeling like they have lost control. Often, this means allowing positive arguing in the home with siblings and parents, provided that the student has been "taught" how to argue appropriately.

How to Teach a Student to Argue

It is unreasonable to expect that a child will never disagree with her parents or teachers. In fact, arguing can even bring about increased deductive-reasoning skills, problem solving, and better overall communication. Students who are taught how to reasonably disagree and to argue their points rationally have been shown to be more confident, to be less likely to be persuaded to do drugs or alcohol in their teens, and to interact better with their peers.[206] The key is to teach your students how to argue and negotiate rather than fight. An argument is the process of bringing an audience to your point of view or to find a reasonable compromise based on mutual understanding of one another's points of view. A fight is a process by which you seek to dominate your opponent and to win at all costs. When most talented manipulators are disagreeing with their parents or teachers, they are not actually arguing; they are fighting. They are not seeking to convince the other side of their point of view or to understand other perspectives; their main goal is to control the situation.

The three types of arguments, rooted in ancient Greek rhetoric, are ethos, pathos, and logos.[207] Talented debaters may use one or all types within the same discussion, tailoring and shifting their arguments as they become ineffective. Logos is an argument based on logic. For example, children who tell their parent that they cannot complete their homework because they forgot their book at school or that the due date is not for another few weeks and they want more time to research are both logos based arguments. Pathos is an argument based on emotion. Students who cry while completing their work or have a temper tantrum to get their own way are using pathos. Ethos is an argument based on reputation and character. This is often a far more subtle type of argument, though it can be vocalized by students. Students questioned by their teacher over why they did not turn in their homework might bank on their reputation by saying, "I promise my homework is done. I've never forgotten my homework before, and I always turn it in. I think I must have lost it."

One way to encourage honesty in students is to make use of the concept of ethos. Jay Heinrichs teaches children that lying is not only wrong but that it is unpersuasive.[208] Those students who thrive on showmanship are those who are keenly aware of their adult audience and can understand better than anyone that they risk alienating their audience by ruining their trustworthiness. By teaching students the different forms of rhetorical discourse, you can capitalize on the concept of ethos and how it can be used to their advantage. Students who embrace the challenge of productive arguing realize that their reputation is the foundation of persuasive ethos and seek to protect it. They cannot use ethos as a bartering chip if there is no credit in that bank.

One way to tell the difference between productive arguments and manipulative ones lies in the structure of the argument. If a student switches rapidly between logos-, pathos-, and ethos-based arguments, or if you feel caught off guard by how quickly the argument has changed direction, it is likely that their end goal is to win at all costs. Catching an opponent off guard is a way to trap them into making an irrational response, often based purely on emotion. Those irrational responses then become further ammunition for the student to say that he will not follow the adult's instruction or that the adult is not being fair (a pathos-based argument).

For example:

Sid: *Mom, may I go over to Archie's house?*

Mom: *Not until you finish your homework.*

Sid: *But it's not due until Monday. I still have two days to complete it. (Logos)*

Mom: *If you finish it now, then you can go to your friend's house.*

Sid: *I've never lied to you before! I always get my homework done; I promise I'll do it Sunday afternoon if you let me go now. (Ethos)*

Mom: *No.*

Sid: *It's not fair! You never trust me! You think I'm bad; you think I'm lying! (Pathos)*

Mom: *Sid, why are you getting so upset?*

Sid: *(Crying) If you don't let me do my homework on Sunday even though I've promised you that I can do it, it means you don't trust me. Making me do it right now makes no sense unless you don't trust me. (Logos & Pathos)*

This argument between Sid and his mother is an example of a manipulative exchange. Sid's goal (to go to his friend's house instead of completing his homework) is all-important to him. The fact that he is switching rapidly between argument types suggests manipulation; if he truly believed that his position was a valid one, he would have more support for his argument within one of the argument types. If he had a legitimate reason to go to his friend's house based in logic, for example, he would have supporting details and continue to argue his position based on that tenet.

It is common to use more than one argument type in a discussion but more as support for the original point, not, as Sid used it here, as a way to trap his mother into agreeing to his desires. Sid did not use logos, ethos, and pathos to appeal to his mother's argument styles as they shifted throughout the discussion but rather as ways to manipulate her into feeling like she had upset him and that she now had to allow him to do what he wanted in order to prove that she trusted him. In his exchange, even if Sid's mother did not allow him to go to Archie's house, Sid still probably has the upper hand because he has rattled his mother. She may seek other ways to show Sid that she trusts him, offering him other rewards in order to make him feel better.

Encourage discussions and arguments with your students that are positive and effective, and quickly and without emotion shut down arguments that are not productive. Point out what is inappropriate about the argument, and let students know you will address it with them at another time when they are better able to argue productively. It may seem counterintuitive, but the best way to have a productive disagreement is to teach students *how* to argue effectively, not simply to discourage or forbid arguments altogether. One study through the University of Washington of the argument pattern of hundreds of married couples over a period of nine years showed that the couples who were successful over time did not argue less than non-successful couples. They did, however, argue differently. Both the unhappy couples and those who divorced fought, attacking one another in order to win the argument. Successful couples were seen to argue in order to air out problems and disputes, and then look for outcomes.[209]

It is not enough to simply discourage fighting in your students. Students will not automatically agree with others because fighting is not allowed. By exerting dominance over students in a way that makes them feel powerless, parents and teachers can unwittingly cause in their students feelings of resentment, continued lying, and other subversive behaviors. It is possible to allow students to have their own sense of power while maintaining your own as the authority figure. As the authority figure, you can teach students how to be open to other points of view, how to be reasonable, and how to properly use the tools of expressing differing opinions in a positive way.

Parents should teach students to approach teachers, for example, with problems that they have with their work. It helps if you confirm this with teachers early on in the school year in the presence of the student. A great time to accomplish this is during the first meet and greet with your child's teacher, perhaps an open house early in the year. As we said before, most students have no previous experience or modeling with how to express discontent or request for change to a teacher, so they avoid it completely. A positive exchange that establishes the guidelines for this procedure can help establish a new perspective for a student who may need to call on the teacher to help them change an inappropriate assignment. For an example of this exchange:

> Parent: *Mrs. Brown, we have a rule in our house that Connor can say when he has a different opinion than we do, as long as he approaches us respectfully, tells us what bothers him and why, and offers a solution based on either logic or emotion. We agree to listen, take the time to think about it, and give him a decision about it.*

> Mrs. Brown: *I think that's a good rule.*

> Parent: *He's very good at doing it at home, but sometimes he has trouble with it at school. Sometimes an assignment will be too easy for him, for example, but he is afraid he's not allowed to say anything. Sometimes he just doesn't know that he can ask why he's being asked to do a certain task. How would you say he should approach you if he has a question like that?*

> Mrs. Brown: *Connor, you can always come up to me and tell me when you think something is too easy or if you have a question or a suggestion for something else you want to do. I will always help you know why I want you to do something. I like the rule you have at home, and you can always use it here, too.*

Form an ALLIANCE

Even when students fight with you, it is important to still show them that you are listening to what they have to say. Acknowledge what they are feeling and do not be afraid to tell the student that you need time to think about your response. You can tell the student that you "will take it under consideration and give him your response at the next meeting (or tomorrow)." By removing yourself from the altercation and not answering right away to a student request or complaint, you can prevent emotional responses. You can also avoid being trapped by inadvertently contradicting yourself or being caught by the student in a flawed argument. Give yourself time to come up with a response. You can tell the student that you will confer with his or her other parent or teacher. This not only gives you the benefit of being sure of your response, but it also solidifies to the student that your answer is final, which it should be. If students are able to manipulate you into reconsidering decisions, then the cycle begins again. In Figure 7.1, suggestions are offered for how to create an "ALLIANCE" with students. For more great ALLIANCE acrostics to help bolster communication between parents, teachers, and students, see Sylvia Rimm's excellent resource, *Why Bright Kids Get Poor Grades and What You Can Do About It.*[210]

Table 7.4. Parent Anti-Arguing ALLIANCE. Reprinted with permission.

Ally with a positive statement of interest.

Listen to what the child says.

Learn about what the child is thinking.

Inquire to determine if there are other issues missed.

Answer wisely only after taking time to think about the request.

Name two or three reasons for your response.

Consequence if the child reinitiates arguing.

End. Absolutely do not re-engage in the argument.

EIGHT
Victor & Arthur

We have discussed the need to identify the underlying causes of cheating behaviors in bright children as a method of prevention, and we have explored many possible causes in the children we have profiled so far. But what about Arthur, the longtime forger we met in the Introduction? Which underlying cause gives meaning to his seemingly inexplicable cheating behavior?

Though boredom is an ideal place to start when looking for the cause of high-ability cheating, in Arthur's case it may not be appropriate. Consider the limited and very specific cheating behavior in which he engaged and how it did not seem to suggest frustration with the curriculum or its pace. In contrast was Terry, our terminally bored fifth grader, for whom frequent dishonesty served to quell her feeling of frustration. She was not loyal to one method of cheating, nor did she limit her academic dishonesty to specific subjects. Though it's likely that Arthur did experience some degree of boredom in his school career, his forgery—which represented an isolated type behavior that was infrequently used—would not have presented him with consistent relief from monotony.

It is also clear that Arthur did not seek to manage how others thought of him through impression management, like Amy or Marie, as he never told anyone about his cheating behaviors, nor did his efforts improve his social standing in any way. His forgery did not represent, as it did for Gus, avoidance as a side effect of perfectionism. He did not need to hide his grades from his parents or his teachers, and he did not display any other signs of maladaptive perfectionism. Perhaps Arthur's crime has the most in common with PJ's since a certain amount of manipulation was involved in the way he avoided being discovered. However, there is a clear distinction; PJ's manipulative ploys both prevented him from needing to complete all of his work and afforded him certain advantages over his classmates such as additional time or support, whereas Arthur did not receive any benefit from his unethical behavior. Or did he?

When questioned as to his motives, you may remember Arthur said that he did it "just to see if he could." It was a creative challenge, an opportunity to recognize flaws in an existing system and to test his own hypothesis. Arthur's cheating behavior represents the final underlying cause—the reaction that bright children have when they are deprived of an appropriate forum or medium for their creative ability and how that can evolve into a wide range of detailed and often highly imaginative cheating behaviors. Students who cheat for these reasons often derive great pleasure from the trick itself, often more so than what (if anything) they seek to obtain through their dishonesty. In some cases, such as Arthur's, there may not even be a recognizable goal for the behavior. For these clever students, cheating is seen as a sort of game that allows them creative expression and discovery, somewhat like a prank that is harmless except in the sense of causing consternation. The act of cheating alone, or at least the sense of accomplishment at solving a puzzle and winning a self-created game, represents the reward for these types of students.

Though this "con artist" trope of the brilliant ne'er-do-well who cheats simply for the sake of cheating is often the one displayed in media and print, it is one of the rarest forms of high-ability cheating that I have encountered—at least in its purest form—both in my practice as an educator and in my research on dishonesty among this talented population. It can be difficult to detect, for although the underlying goal is to explore new creative outlets, the creative cheating may also be driven by additional contributing factors, including but not limited to boredom, impression management, perfectionism, or social and emotional needs.

In this chapter, we will explore the creative cheating type, as well as strategies for teachers and parents to support these students in meeting their goals without relying on dishonest behavior. We will revisit the story of Arthur, the clever boy who had discovered a novel approach to circumvent a school-wide rule, and we will meet Victor, a multi-talented, very imaginative student whose world was driven by creative cheating expression.

Victor

Victor was a sixth grader when I met him, though he could recall cheating as early as second grade. His was another case of self-reporting following a resource room cheating discussion with peers. As always, the students were more talkative when the discussion began small; they described note passing and sharing ways they had supposedly heard of other students or friends doing it. Only after they became more comfortable that they were not the only ones did the students begin to claim personal responsibility for cheating methods. In that group of fifth and sixth graders—a total collection of about eight students—the discussion then turned to forgery, mainly on how a (hypothetical, of course) faux parent note could excuse late assignments, excuse one from class early, and allow one to ride home on a friend's bus. The subject of forgery evolved into questions and then into research on famous forgeries throughout history until finally their time was up.

Victor, a short, spectacled boy, stayed behind. He was not in the half of the group that was heading to lunch, but he had taken his lunch bag out of his backpack anyway and placed it on my desk.

"I have something to show you, Ms. Maupin. Is it okay?"

"Lay it on me, kiddo. What do you have?" I assumed he had done something creative to his lunch bag and was looking for my opinion on the quality of his work.

From the bag, he procured what looked like a small, laminated square. The typed text across its face read "Hall Pass," as well as the smiling face of one of the Special Subject teachers. (Special Subjects were classes that all students had on a weekly basis, such as Library or Gym.)

"What did you want to tell me about this?" I asked cautiously, not wanting to accuse him of stealing the pass before I understood why he was showing it to me.

"I made it," he exclaimed, proud of his work yet wary to hear my reaction. Then he handed it to me, and I delayed responding as I examined it.

On closer inspection, it was evident that the pass was not actually laminated. Victor had simulated that look by taping over the cardstock square with two large pieces of packing tape. Since there were only two pieces of tape, they did not create the small, overlapping lines that Scotch tape would have. The tape halo was cut down to about a centimeter around the cardstock square, giving it the perfect lamination appearance on the quick look. The card itself had been printed, but the picture of the teacher was an actual photograph, slightly raised up from the page— something else I did not realize until closer inspection.

"How did you get the picture?"

"I cut it out of my yearbook. She didn't use that same picture for the pass, but she's facing the same direction in the picture as she was in last year's yearbook picture. They're close enough. The hardest part was finding the right font to look right. But it looks good."

He was right. I would not have suspected that the pass was fake even if I had asked to see it in the hallway. For a sixth-grade student, this was a quality forgery.

"Well, Victor, I can see the thought that you put into making this. It's got a lot of problem solving in it, and I appreciate the level of detail that you challenged yourself to do. I'm impressed by those things. I wish you had picked something more honest to show your creativity with, though. I think you know I can't let you keep the pass, but because this is a Safe Space, I will keep it and not give it to anyone else."

"It's okay. I can't really use it, anyway."

My confusion led to his explanation of how the pass process worked. The Special Subject teacher in question had two passes on a table near the front door of her class. When someone asked to leave the room, they were to take the pass and place it on their desk before they left the classroom. When they returned they would put the pass back on the table so another student could use it. Victor's pass was all but useless. Even if he brought it into the specials room, he was still required to ask to leave the room and the pass would remain on his desk. It was far from a get-out-of-class-free card.

"Why did you make it?"

"Because she had her picture on them. And they were laminated. I think she only made them that nice so that if a kid forgot and took it to the bathroom or something, it would still get back to her looking nice. Or so someone could return the pass. But still."

"I don't understand, Victor."

"They're still the hardest hall passes in the school to make. It's like a challenge, like 'See, I made one that you can't fake.' So I figured out how to do it."

Holding that pass in my hand and listening to Victor's explanation, I found myself remembering Arthur. The parallels made it difficult not to. Not only did they share the same crime—forgery—but their reasoning mirrored one another. They gave purpose to their actions by expressing their desire for challenge. They reveled in their ability to conquer something that had been set before them as unconquerable. It had been several years, and two schools prior, since Arthur's confession, yet he was fresh on my mind. I had always regretted not becoming more involved in the aftermath of that discovery. Even though I had suspected what Arthur had intended through his crime, I never really knew for sure, nor had I explored it with him the few times we saw each other post-confession. Through Victor, I saw a second chance to explore this seemingly unexplainable form of cheating and to help him and others find better outlets for their thirst for challenge and creativity.

I kept both the hall pass and my word to Victor. Initially, I offered it back to him under the stipulation that he give it to the teacher who had the originals. He would not have to say that he had done it as a forgery but only as a present. Victor considered, and seemed intrigued at the thought of another adult seeing his work, but ultimately decided against it. He said that it was enough that one person knew what he could do. It was important for his skills to be recognized, even if only by one person. It is amazing, particularly to parents and teachers of bright individuals, how often their students will risk implicating themselves as long as the possibility exists for them to be listened to and understood, but for high-ability children struggling with a school experience, there are worse things than cheating-specific punishments. To that end, I asked Victor to meet with me again and share more of what he had done or could do. Even with the reminder that he should, per Safe Space rules, expect a response from me, he agreed, and we had our first "tricks of the trade" meeting over lunch in the resource room shortly after.

Victor's first meeting admission was no less than a forthcoming implication of one of his accomplices. Imagine my surprise when that person turned out to be none other than *me*! I was hardly a co-conspirator, but Victor explained how I had been persuaded into inadvertently providing him with creative cheat sheets—and on more than one occasion.

Cheat sheets, also known as crib notes, are any type of concealed information that aid someone in remembering information. They range from downright cheating, such as having a concealed slip of paper or writing in an unobtrusive place during a test, to merely questionable, such as someone having notes to help them during a public speech or presentation. Crib notes are ubiquitous in cheating and are one of the most common methods students use, though the sophistication of the method of writing and concealing these cheat sheets varies depending on the age and education of the student.

Though the most common variety of cheat sheet is very likely the traditional, palm-sized square of paper with information painstakingly copied in small print, teachers should take note: There are myriad ways a clever student can hide a cheating aid:

- ✔ Written directly onto skin, clothing, accessories, casts, bandages, or shoes

- ✔ Written or carved into a desk

- ✔ Copied onto a gum wrapper or water bottle wrapper (and reaffixed to the bottle)

- ✔ Hidden inside of a pen or written on a writing utensil

- ✔ Hidden in the sheath of a calculator or written beneath the cover

- ✔ Written on a book cover or other personal items that can be left in the aisle without seeming out of place

- ✔ Written onto scratch paper

- ✔ Programmed into a graphing calculator

- ✔ Stored in a cell phone or handheld device

- ✔ The "Reverse Cheat Sheet" —if students have more than one class period to finish an exam, they may write notes or questions on scratch paper and remove it from the room to study or ask for help before returning with the answers on a more traditional cheat sheet.

Teachers should not only remind students of the cheating policy or honor code prior to testing but also vary their habits in checking for prohibited material. Students who are apt to cheat tend to pay close attention to a teacher's checking ritual and will create cheating methods that reflect that. It is impossible to create a cheat-proof environment; there will always be methods of creating and hiding cheat sheets that teachers cannot or will not be able to check for. A teacher's best defense is to make his or her routine unpredictable.

Before some exams, tell students to leave their backpack and all books in the hallway, or instruct them to switch seats. One fourth-grade teacher who led her students in relaxation stretches and poses prior to testing recalls the time a cheat sheet dislodged from a student's sleeve during a surprise jumping activity. Start a "row check," giving special attention to any material that students have on their desk prior to a test, and make note of changes in their clothing and demeanor. It may seem harsh to go to such lengths to check against elementary-aged students, but it does not have to be framed as an inquisition, simply as a reminder for students to act according to their moral education.

On at least four or five occasions in the past year, Victor had come to me during open resource room time with papers that he would ask for my help in copying or altering. They were always school related—sometimes a list of spelling words, a labeled map, or even his math notes. He would then ask for Xeroxed copies. The unusual part of the request was that he wanted them reduced in size, usually around 50-60% smaller. Victor's explanation was that he pasted them into his notebook, two or three a page, and used them to study. It was his mother's solution, he said, for his forgetfulness; if he could keep his regular papers at home to study but also had a backup at school, he would be less likely to forget his work and would have a backup if he did misplace one or leave it behind.

As a teacher, I'm always looking for novel approaches to help students remember their work and to use creative solutions to solve their own problems, so I was happy to help. Despite my eagerness, I hadn't been Victor's first "mark."[211] Originally he had asked a teacher in the copier room for aid, telling her that the copied pages were for his teacher. What he did not anticipate was that the shrunken papers would then be delivered to his teacher's copier room mailbox rather than returned to him. Victor realized he would have to find someone who would not be suspicious that the papers were for his own use. I did not ask him why I was chosen as a target. Not only do I make no secret that I am a big sucker for problem solving, but students are more likely to be able to manipulate those individuals who they feel are easy to persuade or are particularly helpful. As harsh as it may seem, manipulators often target the individuals they know and trust the most.

But how did Victor conceive of his cheating plan in the first place? Apparently, it came out of where he sat in his classroom—the back row— and the amount of time he spent in his classroom staring at the back of the chair of the student in front of him. The back of the chair, like many school desk/chair combinations, had a loop of metal piping that formed a sort of long rectangle on the back before becoming the legs of the chair and the base of the desk. In that loop was a more receded flat area of blue plastic (the front of which comprised the back rest) just large enough, Victor realized, for a small square of paper. It would not be visible from the front of the chair or even directly from the side, thanks to the metal loop, but only from a narrow angle of space where Victor sat and a few feet to his left and right.

After Victor obtained the shrunken cheat sheets, he brought them to class with tape affixed to the paper. When neither his teachers nor neighbors were looking, he would quickly attach it to the back of the desk in front of him. When the test began, he literally had all of the answers right in front of him. Even if his teacher walked up and down the aisles looking for cheating behaviors, which Victor said she was apt to do, she never thought to look in such an obvious place. At the end of the test, Victor would discreetly remove the half sheet and pocket it. Victor delighted in hiding his cheat sheet in plain sight.

Creative Cheaters

Many are familiar with the well-known 1986 movie *Ferris Bueller's Day Off* and its titular character, a charming and clever high-school senior who cons his way out of school and into a day of fun with two of his friends. In the film, Ferris uses clever misdirection, malingering, and manipulation to full advantage, ending up on a parade float in the middle of Chicago, gaining a seat at a reservation-only restaurant, and deleting evidence of his truancy from the school's computers, among other things. Although the work is purely fiction, there is something about the lengths that Ferris would go to in order to have a good time that speaks to the motives of bright, bored children who can put more effort into avoiding work than actually doing it.

Even though it is unlikely that you will find your bright student skipping school in order to ride on a parade float, it is not unknown for clever children to seek challenge by turning the mundane activities in their day into something more extraordinary. Some students accomplish this through creative expression; for others, deception and con artistry may serve to whet their appetite for the exciting or simply serve as a release from feelings of monotony. Leta Hollingworth, mentioned in the first chapter as an early expert on the education of the gifted, called these ploys and deceptive acts "benign chicanery" and once commented that she believed them to be absolutely necessary to children of high intelligence. Gifted children may be strongly attracted to these acts by how difficult it can be for them to navigate through mass education.[212]

Brilliant young con artists do not exist solely in fiction; real life is filled with clever youth who have learned how to beat the system, often for the sole (or primary) purpose of the challenge factor. Kevin, a gifted young man who tested in the top percentile for mathematics and spelling, would spend his weekends and summers volunteering with his local Red Cross chapter and the Special Olympics. He seems like the last student you would expect to cheat. Yet, by 12 years of age, Kevin discovered a way to ride any bus in his home town of Los Angeles for free. After telling a bus driver that he wanted to get a transfer punch for a school project, he found out where to obtain one and purchased one for himself. He then watched to see where the buses stopped for cleaning at the end of their runs and checked the dumpsters until he found a partially used book of transfers. For the cost of the $15 hole punch and some problem-solving ingenuity, Kevin had a free pass to anywhere in the city. However, it seems that the end goal was not the free ride after all, as he told both of his parents what he was doing; many bus drivers knew as well. Kevin had done it for the thrill, the excitement of beating the system.

Our young Kevin is none other than Kevin Mitnick, whose skills led to a brief yet illustrious career as one of the world's greatest—and most wanted—computer hackers and, later, a renowned securities expert. Mitnick began hacking computers and phreaking phone lines in his early teenage years. Phreaking, a slang term that is a portmanteau of phone and freak, is the art of breaking into or manipulating the security of telecommunication systems such as telephone lines or networks. Both Steve Jobs and Steve Wozniak were noted phreakers before their entrepreneurial successes. By the age of 16, Mitnick had gained access into some of the nation's largest and ostensibly most secure companies' files, including Digital Equipment Corporation, Motorola, Nokia, and Sun MicroSystems. Mitnick gained access to highly private information, including source code, new product specifications, and employee and customer databases. However, his actions were not driven by money. Despite having access to over 20,000 credit card numbers and other sensitive customer information, evidence suggests that Mitnick never used any of the information. During legal proceedings, when questioned why this was, Mitnick stated that he only wanted the trophy of the database itself; using the cards would be wrong. He likened it to a game of chess, strategically acting in order to outsmart your opponent and feeling the satisfaction after winning a game of skill. He never sought to profit from his actions, at least not monetarily. He did it for the sense of fun, the fascination of being an explorer.[213]

Another example of this creative cheating is one of the most prolific con artists of all time: Frank Abagnale, Jr., who famously impersonated an airline pilot, a doctor, and a lawyer, as well as passing millions of dollars in fraudulent checks, all before he had graduated from high school. Abagnale, whose life story was fictionalized in the popular movie *Catch Me if You Can*, was fascinated by the way things worked and learned early how to circumvent rules. At age 15, he became excited by a challenge he dreamed up: how to get over $3,000 in two months through fraudulent trading from a credit line for a local gas station. Unlike Mitnick, Abagnale *did* profit from his cheating but continued to choose cons based on both their difficulty and their opportunity for learning. He used his gifts for problem solving and observation by identifying loopholes, both in how the banks' procedures were established and carried out and in personal arenas, noticing that certain professions or personas were perceived as more trustworthy and valued than others. When he impersonated various professions, he was not seeking financial gain so much as to see if he could pull it off; it represented a great challenge.[214]

Like both Abagnale and Mitnick, high-ability, creatively bright students often have little attention or motivation for classroom environments, particularly when the challenges they have set up in the form of deceptions provide so much more stimulation.[215] Students with this creative profile put themselves through a series of graduated challenges, escalating as their skills improve. The end goal is to successfully trick others and to find loopholes and strategies around existing rule structures. The greater the challenge, the greater the thrill. Frank Abagnale once said that it was all done for the thrill of the scam. Children are at risk of being corrupted by the powerful pull to circumvent the system, to get from point A to point B as quickly as they can. For these otherwise decent students, their actions often seem harmless.[216]

When Giftedness Is Clouded

Bored, gifted and talented students such as Arthur and Victor (and even Terry, to some extent) who are exposed to prolonged periods of unchallenging material often turn to creatively entertaining themselves.[217] These imaginative escapes run the gamut from daydreaming to literal escape from their classrooms. Gifted children, especially those who come into the classroom already knowing upwards of 60-75% of the material that will be taught that year, often learn through experience as well as inference that they will be left to their own means. Never is this truer than for the gifted students who are not properly identified or served.

Although many of the children we have discussed were identified as gifted through a formal process and often at a young age, Victor was not formally identified until quite late in his elementary career, partially due to a diagnosis of ADHD, which clouded many of the symptoms of his giftedness. For some students, the prolonged wait for—or complete absence of—appropriate enrichment services can enhance the need for these students to fill in the gaps themselves. Studies have suggested that many gifted children are never formally identified or served. There are many reasons why children might fall through the cracks, including a lack of a service model or formal procedures for identification on a district level, conflicting score profiles or asynchronous development, the distractions caused by poverty or dysfunctional families, or even lack of knowledge of what a gifted child looks like. This unobserved population of high-ability learners is particularly susceptible to creative forms of cheating, particularly if they have become adept at entertaining themselves.

Teachers and parents should remember that a variety of data should be used to support identification and service of gifted students. Though it is never wise or prudent to move students along a challenge continuum before they can prove their capabilities, as this may risk the child developing gaps, parents can advocate for their children using different methods of assessment. Identification of giftedness should never rely on one data point. Teachers should also be aware that many negative characteristics that can preclude students from service may actually be *caused* by that lack of service, such as boredom with routine tasks, refusal to complete work, stubbornness, and defiance. Other negative features may be directly related to a child's giftedness itself, such as messy work, criticism of self, emotional sensitivity, nonconformity, and impatience with failure.[218]

No gifted child is perfect, and most gifted and talented students do not fall into a recognizable or archetypal package. In the biographical accounts of 400 20th-century gifted, eminent adults, more than half had difficulties in the classroom.[219] By holding Victor back from enrichment and acceleration services due to issues with inattention- and

ADHD-related noncompliance, the school inadvertently created a greater incentive for him to entertain himself; his challenge of choice was deception.

Just as there is never a perfect gifted student, the ever-elusive perfect fit is also imaginary. Each student should be assessed for his or her ability level and readiness using a variety of different collaborative and data-driven measures. Parents and teachers should remember, however, that no student, gifted or otherwise, should be seen as "one label per customer" and excluded from programming because of special needs that are created by or in opposition to his or her gifts. If the level of service begins at a student's deficits, and gifts are not recognized or supported, the likelihood for expression through creative cheating increases.

How to Recognize a Creative Cheater

Creative cheaters share common traits as well as similar methods of deception and manipulation, and parents and teachers can look for these traits to learn how to avoid some of the more common ploys. Most traits prevalent in creative cheaters, however, are also present in those bright children that do not engage in deceptive behaviors, so it is important to keep an open mind when identifying which of the following qualities your children may possess.

In addition, the traits themselves do not point to automatic wrongdoing. However, the degree or focus to which students use these often positive skills can help teachers and parents identify their intentions and actions. Just as it is important to not assume that children cheat simply because they have outgoing personalities, it is vital not to see your child as being above cheating. As you read and as you interact with high-ability students, remember that what these students seek to do is often seen by them as a game of skill. Though some adults may fear that by labeling what these children do as skillful, we risk glorifying deceptive actions, it should be noted that the ability to lie convincingly represents an advanced cognitive skill. As Frank Abagnale acknowledges, awareness is 99% of solving the problem. The first step in preventing fraud is to admit that it is not only possible but also often easy to accomplish.[220] This is exceedingly the case for our multi-talented bright students.

They fish for information. Creative children love to know how things work. They crave detailed understanding about their interests and the world around them and, as any parent or teacher of a bright child knows, the quest for the *why* never ends. These characteristics often lead to intensive questioning and information gathering on the part of the gifted child. Though questioning is present in all bright children to some extent, some students use specific questioning to gather information intended to deceive. This level of information gathering is known as social engineering and often accompanies creative cheating.

Social engineering is the act of using deception and influence to manipulate others. Although some social engineers manipulate others in order for personal gain or advantage, just as often the primary goal is the information itself. Many students simply get a thrill from possessing secret knowledge; they are "data seekers."[221]

Parents and teachers should not be wary of bright children's questions just because they are asked, nor should they refrain from sharing information due to suspicion. However, adults should get in the practice of asking students what they intend to do with information and watch to see if a pattern is developing. Does a child's questioning seem to follow a trend or circle around a central point? Does he or she ever use previously learned information in later arguments, particularly to illuminate contradiction?

Teachers, watch for these types of questions: "What would you do if…," "Would a person get in trouble if…," or "Could someone do this on the assignment?" Creative children love to look for loopholes in assignments, projects, and even daily routines. They often test their theories in a hypothetical setting before exploiting them in real life. Very bright children know how to use to full advantage every piece of information they have. Another note for teachers is to be cautious about the amount of personal information you give students. That information is a coveted prize for data seekers. Even if they do not seek to exploit the information, they prize knowing what other students do not.[222] It may seem harmless, but data-seeking for the sake of gaining power over others should be curtailed.

They word their questions and requests carefully. When being questioned or given information by a clever student, be less mindful of what they say versus in what *order* the information is given. The important nugget is usually in the middle. People are generally the most attentive at the beginning of a spoken series of data, and they are more apt to respond to the last piece of data. The information sandwiched between is the least likely to receive attention. For Victor, this presented itself as a sort of formula that he used to escape his classroom and roam the hallways.

He would start by telling the teacher that he was expected in the resource room, the office, or the cafeteria—anywhere that was reasonable. He said his trick was not to ask but to tell his teacher very casually and confidently that he needed to be a certain place at a certain time and should he do his assignment before he left or after? Or in Victor's own words:

> *If you tell Mrs. Paul that you have to go to the gym, she asks you why and sometimes even calls the gym teacher to double check. But if you say I just came back from the bathroom, now I have to be at gym, do you want me to do the homework assignment before I leave or after, she only answers your question. She doesn't care about the other thing you said before that, and you can leave.*
> –Victor, 6th grade

Victor's trick was in "burying" his information. Buried information is surrounded by data that may be unrelated or are easy to skip over. Buried information often ends with a question or a request. The guile is usually obvious when students ask for sensitive facts; teachers and parents are more likely to be suspicious, so some students will instead gradually escalate using the bury method.

Another common speech pattern in these students is the careful omission or wording of their requests or responses. Despite the seeming incongruity, many bright cheaters do not enjoy direct lying and will avoid it whenever possible so as not to feel immoral. Teachers and parents should question short or seemingly clipped answers. Ask for specific explanations rather than filling in the blanks yourself. When a student says, "I didn't do my homework. Our power went out," don't be afraid to ask for more information. The statements are likely true considering how clipped they are; however, the insinuation—the student could not do his homework because his power was out—is implied rather than explicit. The power outage may not have lasted long enough to cause any delay in homework, and it even could have happened on a different day. It is often easier for individuals to justify the morality of omissive lies. Statements such as these allow listeners to draw their own conclusions since they have been set up in a way to naturally suggest cause, and they are often believed.

They bank on their credibility and personality. While in prison for his crimes of fraud, Frank Abagnale's review committee once chastised him for his perfect behavior while incarcerated, accusing him of conning the prison system. He was a criminal, so of course he must act like a criminal, right? In actuality, after a two-year study by a criminologist-psychiatrist during his final prison sentence, Frank Abagnale was told that, psychologically, he had no business being a criminal in the first place as his criminal threshold tested extremely low.[223] The truth is that many masters of deception are extremely poised, well-spoken individuals. Moreover, it is not completely an act; many of these "resourceful offenders" are often the sort of people with whom you would want to be friends. They are excellent listeners, have remarkable memory for details, are empathetic, and are usually extremely resourceful.

I once asked Victor what he would do after his escape-from-class act. Where would he go? He said he would wander aimlessly around school until he decided to return to his classroom. And what would Victor say when he was asked by someone why he was wandering the hallway between classes? He did not have an answer for me, and the reason was surprising. In all his years of avoiding class, not one individual—teacher or student—had ever stopped Victor in the hallway to ask him where he was going or where he should be. It reminded me of a student from my first year of teaching, an affable little girl who would wander into my office to decompress at all hours of the day. Sometimes she would come to ask a question or to discuss something that was on her mind, but just as often she would wander in and end up in a corner with her book or notepad and stay for five or 10 minutes before wandering off again. Even when I would get calls from her teacher looking for her, I never got the impression that she was in trouble; the teacher simply assumed the little girl must have had some good reason or authority to be wherever she was. A certain amount of trust is often afforded to high-ability students, partially due to the reputations they have built for excellence and trustworthiness and partially thanks to the amount of experience that teachers know bright children have with working independently.

Personally, I never found Victor wandering the halls, and he rarely came to my room during his jaunts out and about, but one day I found him sitting outside his classroom. He was engrossed in a book, his back against the wall. I was there to meet with several groups of my students in their classrooms to model the meeting process with their teachers. Each meeting took anywhere from 10 to 30 minutes. After I left each class in that hallway and went to another, I noted one common factor:

Victor. One, two, three, classrooms later, Victor was still there, reading. After my fourth and final group, I went over to him.

"So you've been out here the whole time," I said, making sure to not set him up to feel the need to lie to me. Victor would either correct me or acknowledge my suggestion.

He put a thumb in his book and looked up, considering. "Mrs. Paul forgot I was out here."

"Why were you out here in the first place?"

"One of the things you can buy with reward points is to read in the hall during silent-reading period."

"I think you know what I'm going to say, kiddo."

"I should go back inside."

"Bingo. You could be missing something important. Besides, teachers really need to know where our kids are at all times."

Victor shrugged. "Okay. I'll just tell her that I lost track of time." Unfazed, Victor stretched, put a bookmark in the page he had been on, and went back into his classroom. I learned later, when discussing the incident with his teacher, that Victor had not gotten in trouble. He had not even needed to provide an excuse; his reputation as a responsible young man who was the type to get lost in a book had been enough proof for her that he had not intended to manipulate her. During that conversation, by the way, I also learned that the hallway reading reward had been one that Victor had suggested for the list in the first place.

Creativity and Links to Deception

Unequivocally, the single most prevalent trait possessed by creative cheaters is their abundant and unique creativity. Of course, many bright children are highly creative, possessing a vivid imagination, unique language skills, and a deep curiosity about the world around them and how it works. Bright children often possess a passion for understanding their world through creativity, and the value of creativity in our students is clear. The creation of new ideas, divergent thinking, and re-imagined boundaries set the stage for advancements in technology, art, music, engineering, science, and social structures. Creativity, when focused appropriately, is responsible for our improved lives and should be regarded as a valuable commodity.[224] Both children and adults benefit not only from the products that are obtained through positive creative expression but also from the personal characteristics that are related to creativity, such as a positive ego, a sense of autonomy, and a tolerance for ambiguity.[225]

Creative individuals possess a wealth of transferrable skills; however, the outlets to which these skills are applied are extremely important. While creativity itself is not inherently negative or positive, it can be channeled into creating negative or positive products. Some students, like Arthur and Victor, may experience a lack of opportunity to express themselves creatively in positive ways. Rather than using their abilities to invent constructive products, these two used divergent thinking to find ways around the status quo and to subvert existing rules.

Creativity often begins with dissatisfaction with what already exists. If students are not given the permission to be creative problem solvers or are not provided with parental or teacher support when they try something unusual, their solutions may often be seen as defiant, disruptive, or attention seeking. They may become increasingly dissatisfied as a result. Some of the negative qualities and characteristics related to creativity are antisocial behaviors, lack of social concern, defiance, and ego. In addition, strong mood fluctuations, ranging from overly excitable to depressive states, are more common in creative individuals.[226] When creative individuals, who see their world as an open realm of possibilities for change and improvement, are stifled to conform to what they see as arbitrary rules and expectations, they may channel their creativity into less positive means such as deceit. When perceptions of injustice exist, such as high-ability students who feel like they are being unnecessarily punished for being bright, or even that they are being stifled, the risk increases that they will be creative toward harmful or negative goals.[227] However, when authority figures are seen to give individuals more respect, power, and control, the creativity that is produced is positive in nature.[228]

We need to encourage creativity in our students and to allow them the freedom to express their divergent thinking in suitable ways. Creativity that is stifled does not lead to rule following. Suppressed creativity is more likely to lead to negative products than a complete moratorium on novel expression. Though some have argued that creativity itself is neither good nor evil, it is indisputable that creativity can be used for ill gains. On a small scale, students like Arthur and Victor may use their skills to engage in cheating. On a larger scale, think of the creative, manipulative advertising to which we are subjected on a daily basis that may promote products that are unhealthy, or the damaging effects of global con artists such as Mitnick and Abagnale.

The driving force behind any advancement in our society—for good or for evil—comes from countless creative individuals who use their ability to reject typical systematic approaches and instead use diverse options for solving problems. It is easy to think of these individuals as careless or destructive. However, negative creativity is not commonly the result of deliberately evil intentions but rather of unexplored fascination, a lack of awareness of negative consequences, and deception or coercion by external factors.[229] Boredom, or a general lack of appropriate stimulation appropriate to a student's ability level, often becomes that force of unexplored fascination for students that directs them to negative, nonconforming activities.[230]

Without the availability of positive outcomes, students may find their own avenues of expression regardless of the long-term or negative consequences. We must remember that whenever a student deviates from the norm, it not only leads to creative ideas and expression, but it can also lead to crime. Gascon and Kaufman, in fact, defined deviance as the meeting place between creativity and crime.[231] Take for instance the true story of one Rhode Island man who retired from his work as a custom jewelry maker and was later arrested for one of the largest casino-token frauds of our time. Bored in his retirement, this man came into possession of a detailed hundred-dollar slot-machine token and was intrigued. After admiring the craftsmanship and art of it, he wondered if he had the skills to counterfeit the token. He worked for more than a year on the challenge, finally perfecting a token that would fool not only the eye but also the electronic coin comparators inside the slot machines. Though he did use these forgeries illegally, his crime had not started with the intention of wrongdoing, but rather with the promise of a creative challenge.[232]

The connection between creativity and unethical behavior has been well documented. In Amy's chapter, we began to explore this link through the research of Dan Ariely, an expert on dishonest behaviors. His research revealed that all individuals cheat to a certain degree but that creative individuals are often the most prolific cheaters. How frequently individuals cheat is often directly related to their ability to justify their own behavior. Humans want to see themselves as honest and will attempt to distance themselves from their deceitful behavior or to downplay it as reasonable or expected. Those who are less able to justify shady behavior are less likely to engage in it, whereas those who can creatively explain or "tell themselves better stories" can continue think of themselves as being moral even as they engage in cheating behaviors. Therefore, the more creative the individual, the more skills they possess to envision unique ways to circumvent rules.[233] With intelligence and enhanced motivation to be creative comes greater ability to justify their behaviors, which can lead to bright children who are able to disassociate from their dishonesty as well as the possible negative consequences of their actions.

Channel Creativity

What should happen, then, when a child is caught cheating simply to test the rules or to see whether they can pull a scam over on a parent, teacher, or friend? Our first instinct is often punishment, to remind the students of the rules of conduct and reprimand them accordingly. Another common response is to make it more difficult for the child to cheat through increasingly restrictive policies and procedures. To some extent, there is a place for both of these reactions. However, too many individuals use punishment and restriction as the entirety of the intervention and are surprised to find that they have not only failed to curb creative cheating but may have forced the cheater further "underground" or simply posed a greater and more appealing challenge. Another possible side effect is that these students may begin to associate creativity with punishment or wrongdoing.

The best prevention and response for creative cheating is to help the student channel his or her talents into positive outcomes both proactively and reactively to the face of cheating. In truth, the fact is that there is often far too little opportunity for creative expression in the classroom, particularly in the area of high-level thinking. Frankly, many teachers not only struggle with implementing creativity in the curriculum but also may discourage it inadvertently.

Few teachers would say that they oppose creative expression, and I have never seen a teacher disparage a student's drawings or criticize a musical piece that was shared during show and tell. However, many teachers do not realize that creativity exists outside of the traditional artist mediums. By limiting their understanding of what constitutes creativity, teachers may be doing many small things throughout the course of the school day to discourage students from playing with their divergent thinking processes. For example, Arthur's mother recalled an instance from Arthur's school career. His class was learning about basic shapes. In the assignment, a simple in-class task, students were instructed to create some of their favorite shapes out of different materials—noodles, pencil drawings, beads, pipe cleaners, and other media—on large pieces of construction paper. When Arthur's teacher saw him drawing dots—single-point, small dots—on his paper using only a pencil and no other materials, she repeated the assignment to him.

When Arthur explained that he was drawing the shapes from very high up like a bird would see them, his teacher responded by telling Arthur to start over. She said he had to draw the shapes large enough for her to see them, and he had to use a variety of different materials just as the other kids were doing.

The teacher's reactions are understandable. The point of the exercise was that it would serve as informal assessment for the teacher to measure which shapes her students were able to comfortably create from memory without help. The tactile nature of the materials was to add fun to the experience and to make it easier for those students still struggling with the fine-motor skills needed to manipulate their pencils. Arthur's rendition did not give her an idea of his current understanding of the material. It is unlikely that she was attempting to discourage his creativity; it is also doubtful that she even recognized his actions as creative. She may have seen the work as defiant, disruptive, or even something as harmless as attention seeking. By asking him to redo the assignment, her likely goal was to ascertain his ability to recall and reproduce shapes.

What Arthur's teacher did not recognize was that Arthur, who had already mastered the material being taught, was not attempting to defy the assignment but only to add an additional element to it. Arthur had made the assignment more interesting and challenging by reimagining it from the eyes of a bird flying far above the shapes. When she rejected Arthur's approach to the assignment without explaining why or giving him other options for creativity, the teacher had inadvertently discouraged his creative expression.

Arthur's mother was able to remember the story because she could never forget the forlorn look on her son's face when he came home and told her that he had gotten "in trouble" for not being like the other kids. Thankfully, Arthur's mother recognized the emotional snowball effect that her son had experienced as he magnified the incident and knew that her son had not actually been punished by his teacher. She did, however, express to me how much of a difference it would have made for her son to be allowed some leeway in those small, creative ways.

That is not to say that it is easy for a teacher or a parent to recognize when to allow children to make their own rules and when to hold them fast to existing instructions. The teacher in this instance was not being cruel, nor did she have any problem with creative expression. If Arthur had created a shape that was multi-colored or linked up with other shapes on the page, she would have likely praised his vision and creativity, even if it differed from the pictures of his classmates. She would have recognized his ideas as novel and responded accordingly. Additionally, even if she had correctly identified Arthur's approach, it did not change the fact that she still required evidence that Arthur understood the shapes that had been taught. If she allowed Arthur to create an alternate assignment that did not fulfill her instructions just because she knew he could do it, how would she explain that divergence if his seatmate—whom the teacher knew needed the practice—tried something similar? Few teachers would be comfortable with telling a student that there are different rules for different students based on their ability levels. The issue is a complex and multi-layered one.

This incident is a primary example of why it can be so difficult to parent or teach a creative child. Even when something is done with best intentions, outcomes are often impossible to predict. The assignment was not one that precluded creativity; in fact, it was open-ended enough to encourage a variety of different expressive answers and ideas. Arthur managed to find something that was extremely creative, but because it did not fulfill the objectives of the assignment, the teacher was required to redirect his efforts. She did not intend for Arthur to go home sad and confused; she only sought to assess his knowledge in order to teach him more effectively.

Even teachers who struggle to differentiate all of their assignments and to create a multi-layered curriculum can become overwhelmed with the added complication that a creative mind can provide. It is impossible to predict all of the divergent ideas, perspectives, and even loopholes that bright creative minds can discover. The goal, then, should not be to try to define and contain all of these possibilities but simply to let students know the objectives or the intent of an assignment when it is given to them. If Arthur had been told that the object of the assignment was to inform the teacher's understanding of what shapes they could create without help, he would have been able to channel his creativity in that direction. If after this explanation, he still creates his bird's-eye-view, he could be further prompted to use the objectives to transform his creativity into something that will tell the teacher what he knows. Whenever a child creates something that seems oppositional, treat it as a creative product, praise its originality and flexible thinking, and then instruct the student to transform it according to what you are assessing.

For example, Arthur could have been praised for his original viewpoint and how unique it was, isolating the creativity itself as positive. Then the teacher could have explained that the objective of the assignment was for her to know how many shapes he could create from memory. As creative as his bird's eye view was, it did not help her understand his knowledge. He could have been asked to hang up his creative drawing first and then start again, or he could have even drawn a magnifying glass and accompanying bigger pictures around his dots to show the teacher what the bird would see magnified.

In a way, the dilemma Arthur's teacher faced is not much different than that of Victor's, especially if Victor had been aware of his actions. Though Arthur's assignment does not represent an example of cheating, both students presented work that did not help the teacher know how much they had learned. Their creativity (both positive and negative varieties) clouded the main objective, which was for the teacher to assess student understanding and their own teaching practice. The first step for addressing creative cheating, then, is similar to how Arthur's teacher could have addressed his unique approach to the assignment: Separate the creative expression from the unwanted action, praise the type of creativity, correct the unwanted action, and then redirect the creativity to a more positive outlet. Perhaps Arthur would not have moved on to feel challenged by forgery if his creativity had been appropriately recognized and supported from a young age. We will explore specific examples of ways to redirect creativity later in the chapter. The first step is a teacher's or parent's ability to recognize creativity in the student.

Recognize Creativity

Teachers and parents may think that they are capable of recognizing multiple forms of creativity in their students, yet history is filled with instances of highly creative individuals who were misunderstood or unidentified at an early age. Louisa May Alcott was told by her editors that she would never write anything that would sell. Louis Pasteur was rated as being a mediocre chemistry student, Walt Disney was fired from an early job due to his "lack of good ideas," and Thomas Edison was considered too stupid to learn.[234] All of these individuals are now regarded as eminent and highly creative in their fields, but at the time, others in positions of authority were unable or unwilling to see their divergent ideas and novel expression as valuable.

Aesthetic expression may be the most commonly understood form of creative ability; however, students do not need to paint a picture or be able to appreciate the beauty in a piece of music or dance in order to be labeled a creative individual. Creativity takes many forms, and individuals with that uniquely divergent way of processing information may exhibit any number of creative characteristics, including:

- ✔ Independence
- ✔ High energy
- ✔ Attraction for the unknown, thirst for answers
- ✔ Idealism
- ✔ Sense of humor
- ✔ Curiosity
- ✔ Tolerance for ambiguity, open-ended problems
- ✔ Deductive reasoning
- ✔ Keen visualization of problems and information gathering related to problems
- ✔ Intuitive thinking, or the ability to bridge information gaps with ideas and little information
- ✔ Focus
- ✔ Flexible thinking
- ✔ Fluent thinking, or the ability to produce a number of workable solutions
- ✔ Originality
- ✔ Elaborative or detail-oriented embellishments on an original thought

Creative, bright children are often aware of their own creativity, and they value how original they are. They are not afraid to take risks to try something new, and they are often willing to cope with hostility in the name of their ideas.[235] Though flexible thought processes may be seen by adults as being disrespectful or disruptive, enforcing rigid standards of conformity is never a good response, as it can lead to rebellious or authority-avoidance behaviors. However, teachers and parents should also be wary of allowing students the power to make decisions about which rules are flexible and which are not. Allowing flexibility and unique thought around a main, rigid concept is far more productive for students than teaching students that they are exempt from following rules. Cheating is a perfect example. Students should not be allowed to use their ability to create or manipulate loopholes to gain an unfair advantage over other students; however, they should still be encouraged to take risks in appropriate areas. Imagine the rules and requirements of school or home life as the frame of the house—rigid, strong, and designed to work together to hold up the structure. The rest of the house—the interior layout, the furnishings, and the exterior appearance—are for students to decide using creativity to carry out their vision. A house made completely of decoration would never stand, just as the framework alone is not worth living in. Ideally, concepts and creativity should support and complement one another in a balanced relationship.

Various strategies are helpful for parents and teachers in fostering the development of creativity in bright youth. Resourceful cheaters benefit from increasing the amount of creativity in their environment. Outlets such as creative games, open-ended assignments, flexibility and choice with assignments, or innovative problem-solving assignments that do not allow for cheating can decrease or even halt a student's need to seek other challenges. Several methods, including the "video-game" method, the "hire-the-hacker" strategy, and using mnemonics and metacognition strategies to help students "cheat their own brain," are described below. Teachers and parents can create their own similar strategies, keeping in mind that the underlying goal is to isolate the creative elements of an assignment and allow students to build their creativity around a central framework of ethical behavior. By channeling student energy into constructive activities, we can help them feel good about their accomplishments without relying on the empty reward that comes from manipulation. Creative cheaters feel that their maneuvering is instantly gratifying, and they will not turn to the more long-term beneficial interactions without help and support.[236]

Video-Game Method

As was mentioned previously, creative cheaters treat academic dishonesty as a game. Kevin Mitnick described his hacking behaviors in terms of video-game play, and every new accomplishment felt like achieving higher and higher levels of a video game. He felt the thrill of both advancement and improvement. The appeal of having accomplished something both incrementally and in a way that seemed purposeful—all video game players understand that Level 1 must be completed prior to Level 10—is a great incentive for many individuals. Video games encourage players to achieve complete mastery at each level and then to build on that while simultaneously starting anew from the next, more challenging level. This forces the player not only to adapt but also to evolve his or her play and learning. This rarely happens in schools, where students are either "good at doing school" or not. They may not have the opportunity to enjoy their mastery yet continue to be challenged further.[237]

The structure of playing video games, with their different mastery levels and achievements that build upon one another, must be appealing; otherwise, individuals would not spend so many hours focused on conquering them. In addition, the way video games are created often negates the need or desire to cheat. One study has shown that bright students do not waste time cheating on activities or pursuits that cannot be *won* by cheating, and video games were listed as an example. If a game was not seen as being able to be manipulated, students followed the rules faithfully without attempting to circumvent them. Students do not usually waste time manipulating rules that cannot be broken, so if a rule or a game has complete consistency, students will follow the imposed (or natural) structure.[238]

Teachers and parents can use the same strong pull students feel to faithfully complete video games to their own means both at home and in the classroom. Treat learning as a series of levels. Teach students how things connect and how one piece of knowledge attaches to another. As video games do, celebrate whenever a student makes a meaningful connection. Provide assignments or activities that must be authentically performed rather than tests that assess only recalled information. The video game analogy may be applied even directly. Teachers can inform a class excitedly that they will "Level Up" when they finish an introductory unit and will be able to do greater things and have more challenges in the next level of learning. Each lesson or unit objective is a certain skill or point to be gained. Once students show mastery or can complete a unit of study to a certain degree, they have earned the point and may move on. Give students power to add objectives or "bonuses" to extend their knowledge breadth and depth. Constantly give students concrete examples of how their previous learning created a foundation for what they are now working on. It can be difficult for all students, even bright children, to remember and appreciate the building blocks of knowledge. Treat an easy lesson or an introductory review as a "Level One." Many students understand the analogy of a video game and can accept that they must prove their skill on the easier challenges before they are able to skip to higher levels. Just like video games, however, where experts are able to complete a level on "fast forward," allow your clever children to prove themselves at a quicker rate whenever possible.

The goal is to teach students to value perseverance and to model how important the independent components of introduction and practice can be, even for highly able children. In the world of gifted education, practice is often seen as a dirty word. It can be synonymous for boredom or redundancy and is often abandoned as unnecessary during a worth audit. It is true that practice, in the sense of continuing to work on something previously mastered, often can be boring. However, what students should be taught is that practice is invaluable to the cognitive process of information becoming automatic. There are other cognitive, long-term benefits to diligent practice. In a study of prominent scientists, the most remarkable discovery was that these eminent individuals had in common not exceptional brilliance as measured by standard IQ tests but incredible persistence and a high threshold for mental exhaustion. Their willingness to persevere through problems was what had set them apart and made them great.[239]

Make students aware that all practice can be beneficial. Although it is easier for an individual to persevere through challenges that are appealing, studies have even shown there is benefit in the ability to persist through even menial tasks. In a decades-long study, Carmit Segal, then a Harvard postdoctoral student and now a professor at a Zurich university, tested how personality and incentive interacted by giving individuals a basic clerical coding test. The test included comparing meaningless lists of words and numbers and decoding answers with a given bank of letters and numbers. The task was easy but extremely repetitive. Though there is little distinct need for students to be capable of comparing meaningless lists of words and numbers, and it is true that the students who did better on the coding test may not actually possess greater coding skills, their scores reflected two things. The first is that they tried harder, even though the original task was more or less meaningless. The second is extremely meaningful; the students who scored highest on this coding skills test were more successful and earned more money over time than low-scorers. The coding skills test was actually a more reliable predictor of success than intelligence. This may be due to the values of the labor market, which places a high stock on the kind of internal motivation required to try hard on a test even when there was no external reward for doing well. Perseverance is a vital skill.

By teaching your students to persevere through activities, you help them develop more advanced skills by making the easier concepts automatic. Automaticity takes a great deal of practice, not only over time but also over a variety of activities, and there are varying degrees of comprehension.[240] Although bright children have the ability to pick up information quickly, if they are unable to commit to meaningful practice, they are far more likely to have picked up only shallow knowledge. They need to be able to automatically transfer their knowledge outside of the classroom and be able to recognize a newer version of an older problem they have already solved. The goal is not to simply experience activities but to practice them. Bright children deserve the right to improve their performances and to see themselves as active learners rather than shallow absorbers. Our clever children pick up information so effortlessly that we can sometimes forget that they can benefit from a deeper understanding of the curriculum.

"Hire the Hacker"[241]

There were happy endings to the stories of Kevin and Frank. Though their exploration of creative abilities led to immoral and illegal activities, their skills themselves were never wholly negative. Both were eventually offered positive outlets for their abilities and flourished as a result, abandoning their lives of crime for meaningful and honest professions. They did not require the illegal activities so much as they craved a challenging and stimulating outlet for personal expression and personal achievement. Teachers and parents can provide similarly for their students by recognizing students' skills and helping them find positive outlets for them.

After Kevin Mitnick's prison sentence for his computer and phone crimes, he used his skills as the world's most wanted hacker, though his focus was greatly shifted. As a securities expert, he found a satisfying purpose helping companies prevent and catch security breaches. Given a challenging and stimulating outlet for personal expression, individuals who cheat creatively are far less likely to resort to deceptive practices. Kevin's story is not unique. Many "resourceful offenders" have turned their lives around by becoming consultants, turning their creativity into a marketable, ethical resource by consulting on matters of security for companies and even law enforcement agencies.[242]

Frank Abagnale went on to work with the U.S. Government in preventing fraud and parlayed his skills into the creation of a very successful anti-fraud consulting company. He suggests that he is still a con artist with the difference that he now focuses on positive rather than negative outcomes.[243]

Despite the lack of a market for young clever children to create their own anti-fraud companies or to work with the government to catch computer thieves, the principle of the hire-the-hacker strategy is the same. Offer creative children the opportunity to help you solve problems in the school. Creative cheaters are very adept at the structure of a problem. They are able to dissect an issue and use the loopholes and flaws present to their advantage. Refocus their talents toward helping with issues like tardiness, late homework, locker theft—even the issue of students cheating! Pick any problem that hits close to home; it will give them the chance to healthily exercise their creative problem-solving skills.

There is a reason Frank Abagnale made such a talented consultant on crime and forgery; he had the ability to look at a system and find its flaws and loopholes for exploitation. He began using his power for good, and your students can do the same. He refers to this redirection as "putting down a positive con," applying the same passion and attention to detail that allowed him to get away with some spectacular deceptions to the equally challenging art of catching and stopping fraud instead. By using his creativity for positive outcomes he was able to reclaim his talent.[244]

Employ reverse brainstorming. Teach students to turn the problem around, even as you do the same by employing students' to help in preventing note passing, school vandalism, etc. Mitnick described it as finding the difference between ethical hacking versus unethical or the catchy "darkside" of hacking. One of Mitnick's teachers, who recognized his talents and saw how dangerous they could be, allowed him to write security programs for the school's IBM minicomputers instead of expelling him from the class. He took the challenge as a compliment and graduated with honors on the completion of his work. After graduation, he briefly had a job that he felt used all of his skills fully and thus no longer felt the need to hack.

Use Mnemonics & Loopholes to "Cheat the Brain"

Bright children are particularly drawn to loopholes, shortcuts, and plans, in part because they may engage in divergent thinking more often than their classmates. The cognitive flexibility, which bright children are capable of, allows them to question consistently, to search for truth, and to value ideas and theoretical analysis. As a result, creative children often experience preoccupation with certain problems.[245] The human brain loves to find shortcuts, easier pathways in memory or perception. Parents of a bright and talented child know how frustrating it can be to feel like they are losing an argument with their own child because the child has thought of a logical loophole to sidestep a rule. In her book cataloguing different gifted experiences and behaviors, Deborah Ruf recalls Ross, an elementary-aged boy who used a loophole in a school rule to his own advantage. During winter months, students were not permitted to go outside for recess if they were not wearing snow pants. Ross created a pattern that allowed him to stay inside on his own schedule; he only wore his snow pants on Mondays, Wednesdays, and every other Friday.[246] He had found a loophole that allowed him to have some variety at recess time; he stayed indoors on Tuesdays, Thursdays, and every other Friday by coming to school without his snow pants.

This tendency to look for and find loopholes can lead to cheating behaviors if the means to a shortcut is apparent to a student or if a plan he or she might hatch seems more stimulating than studying or creating honestly. It seems contradictory, but the high-ability mind loves complexity and ease in equal measure. Why not use this to your advantage as the parent or teacher of a bright child? The use of the right mnemonic device as a code to assist one's memory can simultaneously appeal to a child's love of a plan and a shortcut, while providing a stimulating accomplishment to achieve without resorting to deception. Mnemonic devices or puzzles are not a substitute for providing adequately challenging work for bright students, but they can provide an honest distraction when a more appropriate assignment is not an option. (For example, on a mandated performance assessment or a pre-test designed to assess ability, requiring an accurate and honest read.) Do not forget, as well, that many high-ability children may have lost, or never learned, the ability to adequately assess an assignment's worth. In the retraining process, in which children learn how to more accurately audit the worth of assignments, mnemonics can help them focus on the task at hand without resorting, or reverting, to less honest behaviors.

Help your students deconstruct something other than the test or the essay, the goal being to refocus their abilities by using their own desire to strategize in a positive way. Have mental games planned for those high-ability students you fear are not attending to important information because they have mentally checked out or decided an assignment is not worthwhile or meaningful to them. These challenges can be as simple as asking a child to keep track of the number of times you say a certain word or "hiding" a secret code word in your lesson and letting students know that their job is to listen close enough to make a certain signal when they hear it. The challenge can be concrete as well. Some students do well multi-tasking with a simple maze or puzzle while they are attending to a verbal lesson. There is a basket in my classroom filled with knots that students have tied out of lengths of different types of string. For students who require small activities to help them refocus their desire to strategize, these knots can be picked up any time and quietly tackled at their seats while they listen to lessons or work on assignments. The mental energy needed to identify the way the knot was created and how to undo it is often great enough to refocus students but not so great that they cannot also attend to what is being said in the classroom. Once they are able to untie the knot, they are to tie another, more challenging knot to leave for the next student. Memory games can also be an effective way to challenge your students.

Memory is quite selective. As far as anyone knows, humans only have a finite amount of working memory, and what we know about memory suggests that we cannot create or build more of it, only manipulate and make the most of what we have.[247] Tricking our memories into holding more and working for us is something that very much appeals to bright children, particularly for those who are looking to find ways around conventional rules or to conquer the conventional. What is better—or more challenging—to "cheat" than your own mind? Parents and teachers alike can inspire their students to tame their own minds. Start by telling them that they will forget 80% of what they will learn that day. It will help them understand why you are asking them to do certain things or why you expect both depth of understanding and practice work from them. It also helps your students understand that there is a cognitive difference between information that is understood and information that is able to be recalled for synthesis and evaluation.

The first way to cheat the limited size of your own working memory is through the integration of actual knowledge. Make the processes that manipulate information in working memory more efficient. This means listening to information carefully, thinking about it, and practicing it. This process moves information from working memory to long-term memory. Neither the simple desire to learn it nor repetition alone will create memory.[248] The key is to engage students in the tricks of how their memory works; thinking carefully about information is tedious enough for the brain that it does not want to repeat the process over and over again. Instead, the brain will save itself time by storing that knowledge for later use.

Your memory is less a product of what you want to remember than what you spend time on. Roger Von Oech recommends individuals make metaphors out of what they are learning as a deep-thinking strategy.[249] Have students compare what they are learning to a car, a working community, a doctor's office, or a playground game. Pull random objects or relationships and have students debate: Is the Revolutionary War more like the relationship between a father and a son or the rules of a soccer game? Why or why not? The brain enjoys novelty and pays attention to it.[250] By adding these and other interesting elements to lessons, or to activities for children at home, students' brains engage to remember more information.

The goal is to let students in on these "secrets of the brain," many of which are described by neurologist Judy Willis in her book *Inspiring Middle School Minds: Gifted, Creative, and Challenging*.[251] Teach children how stubborn the human brain is, how lazy it can be when it comes to actual thinking, and that its goal is often to get by with as little information recalled as possible. The brain is an automaton in many ways, and even elementary-aged students can be challenged to understand both how their minds prefer work and how to conquer the limitations of their finite memories. Before introducing a memory-hack strategy, remind students how their brain "wants to" think and how they can trick it into thinking differently. Whenever possible, give students a directorial role and ask them to create their own rules for how they will learn a piece of information. When students create their own rules for how they learn and how they will act or behave, there is a neurobiological response that results as they enlist the prefrontal cortex to challenge the more automated functions of their brains. This not only helps students divert their focus from tempting stimuli, but it also prepares them for future encounters with persevering through difficult information.

There are many mnemonic techniques that parents and teachers can use with their students. Remember the one that goes "*I* before *e* except after *c*," or the one to help remember days of the months, "30 days hath September, April, June, and November; all the rest have 31 except February, which has 28." A good mnemonic creates a bridge. Below is a list of more common mnemonics that appeal to high-ability students.

Peg system. In a peg system mnemonic, numbered lists are attached to "peg points" that are easy for students to recall. Often they are in order and represent body parts from head to toe (one is forehead, two is eyes, three is nose, etc.), the order of colors in the rainbow, parts of a book, etc. After learning this easy list, students create a paragraph or verbal explanation of each word or idea they need to remember. Though it seems like students would have to remember twice the information, the peg list is easy to memorize and the amount of recall for these paired lists or short stories is incredible for students even days or weeks later. Peg systems are excellent for facilitating recall of a list of vocabulary words, instructions, or even as independent challenges for your high-ability students. Peg systems can also be rhyming (one is bun, two is shoe, etc.) or personalized by students in your class. A can be Abby, B is Brandon, and so on. If you were trying to have students recall their homework assignments for the night (Table 8.1), you could have a student tell a peg story:

Table 8.1. Mnemonics as Used to Remember Homework Assignments.

On her way home, Abby was attacked by a monster who wanted to eat her math workbook. He had only eaten pages 12-14 and was starting to choke on an improper fraction when Brandon came and lured it away with the promise that he could eat his storybook. But the monster did not like the "The Pumpkin Patch" story, and they thought they were doomed until Catie came up whistling, practicing tempo. She scared away the music-hating beast.

Mnemonic	Homework Assignment
Abby	Math pages 12-14
Brandon	Storybook: Read "The Pumpkin Patch"
Catie	Music: Practice tempo

Method of Loci. The students use a place that is very familiar to them, such as their room, classroom, or even their soccer tournament field. They walk the place in their mind starting from the entrance, and then walk left around the edges of the space in a circle until they arrive back at the entrance. On this mental journey, students associate common objects that they know are in their room with whatever they are trying to remember. The trick is to make the association large and crazy. If students are remembering the parts of a flower, do not encourage them to associate a petal with a light switch, have it *become* the light switch, or encourage them to imagine that they walk in and switch the light on, but instead of light they are showered with petals. Each new station of their walk represents a different association.

The bonus of the Method of Loci is that it can be done in under 10 minutes—less after students have an established "walk room" with stations. Tell the students that the reason it must be a familiar room is because you know your brain has already put that into long term memory, and we want to sneak or cheat additional information into that existing memory. Students not only love the idea of sneakily hiding wanted data, but they are also impressed with how quickly and for how long they can hold onto material. I have had students come back to visit years later and recite their first loci lists from the original loci lesson.

Create an acronym. We commonly use acronyms and acrostics as ways to remember information. Have students create funny and unique acronyms for themselves that not only help them remember information but also gives them a laugh. Using first letters as cues can also help when you give instructions. Give students a list of four instructions for a task or an assignment, and then ask them to share possible acronyms. The best or funniest one can be written down on the board, their assignment books, or even across the top of the assignment.

Create a song. There are two ways to use this method. The first capitalizes on piggybacking new information on previously remembered facts or information, such as the Method of Loci. You can instruct students to use the tune of a song they already know to help them remember even large chunks of information. More than one student has learned the state capitals and the periodic table of elements thanks to this mnemonic type.

The second option is to have students create the song themselves. It does not need to be complicated; even simple songs that use repetitive notes can help students remember. In order to create a song from scratch, students must think about the material more closely, which triggers the transfer into long term memory.

Build in loopholes. One excellent way to use students' love of loopholes is to build one into every assignment you give to clever children, and allow students to exploit it if they are able to successfully identify it to you. (Note for parents: This is also usable for home chores, extracurricular activities, etc.) Not only is this an excellent way to have students deeply study what they are being asked to do, but also it tells you how good your student already is at finding the *what if* in a given task. These built-in loopholes can be small and may reference deadlines, numbers of resources or components required, or even how many students can work together under which circumstances. Teachers or parents who struggle with building or identifying appropriate loopholes can simply offer their high-ability children the option to bring up when *they* have found a loophole. If it is one that the teacher or parent sees as needing to be closed, the student's reward will be to exploit it that one time before the assignment is changed. This also veers into the hire-the-hacker strategy of encouraging students to make their information known.

Another way to give the whole class a loophole is to give students one "all-cheats-allowed" test each marking period. Use it as an experiment to have students exploit all of the deceptive practices that they can imagine. Encourage their creativity as well as their post-test share. Though many would argue that it is not truly cheating if the student is allowed to bring notes, books, or cheat sheets, or to copy off of a friend, it can still give both parents and teachers an insight into how students think as well as excite students to feel like they are beating the system.

Memory works on the basis of cues. These cues may be kinetic, visual, or verbal in nature. The best mnemonics either make sense of the material in an orderly fashion so that the cues naturally follow one another for easy retrieval, or they inspire connections with other cues by attaching them to more vivid elements of recall. Exploit episodic memory by using one color of paper for all the assignments and handouts related to one unit so that you can easily ask them to recall "the blue sheet" or "the yellow assignment."[252] Another strategy is to teach certain subjects or ideas from different areas of the room, asking students to make note of your location as you point out specific pieces of information. Remember, let students into the secret of the mnemonic device and how it works on a cognitive level whenever possible. Not only does this fascinate students but also helps connect the moment that they learned a piece of information to the point that they are asked to recall it.

Some of the techniques are based on physical actions. Recent studies have shown that activating even basic motor functions can improve mental performance. Individuals tend to test higher on mental acuity tests when they are engaged in basic motor skills prior to an assessment, outscoring those individuals who sit quietly prior to being tested.[253] The action taken does not need to be related to what is being tested; students can manipulate a ball, tie and untie knots, or even play cat's cradle. A sizable portion of the human brain is dedicated to hand-related tasks. This is largely due to the way human hands developed as we evolved and how the brain had to respond to keep up with all the myriad of functions of which the human hand became capable. As human hands became more complex and their capabilities became greater, the brain developed new ways to make sense of what the hand was doing.[254] Because of this natural and substantial connection between the mind and the hand, students can take advantage of greater mental acuity through even simple motor functions.

The goal is to include students in the process, to consistently tell them *how* the memory trick works, and to encourage them to practice their new skills.

Victor, Arthur, and Your Children

Victor's secret weapon turned out to be not too dissimilar from that of the famous con artists we discussed in this chapter; he was so willing to divulge his knowledge of how to cheat to adults that he was a perfect candidate for the hire-the-hacker strategy. He continued to work with me, first in identifying his own ploys and then by transitioning to looking for new ways to prevent further cheating in the school environment. He even helped make a checklist teachers could use before beginning a test to look for cheating behaviors, and he enthusiastically agreed to help write an honor code for students to sign before working on a long-term project that could involve plagiarism. Once Victor found an appropriate way to not only share his skill set but also to find ways to challenge himself, he no longer felt compelled to cheat. He went on to be a middle-school role model and has told me on subsequent visits back to the school that he plans to become a judge.

I wish I knew what happened to Arthur. I hope that in the years since we last saw one another, he has been surrounded by both support and structure for his creative abilities. His sense of curiosity about how things work would not have been quelled. I hope his parents and teachers began to plan activities that supplied him with positive outlets for his creativity. I hope his teachers knew that many bright youth may not have developed a sense of perseverance and need modeling to see the value in the levels of instruction. I hope that they helped teach him that practice is not a dirty word. Talented children such as Arthur deserve the opportunity to achieve mastery and not just shallow knowledge, especially as creative cheating is often rooted in a student's desire to personally accomplish a seemingly insurmountable challenge.

And your own children? They may not be like Arthur or Victor, but whether or not you suspect your children of academic dishonesty, they can almost certainly benefit from the strategies outlined in this chapter, particularly if they are highly creative. Use proactive strategies such as the video-game method, mnemonic training, and the hire-the-hacker strategy to supply students with a repertoire of ethical solutions for their boredom. Let students in on the secret: Offer them knowledge about why they have been asked to complete a certain task and use their desire to understand the structure of their minds to focus their actions. High-ability cheaters are excellent at deconstructing what happens in the classroom; they can be brought to an understanding of how to deconstruct lessons in a positive way. Put their cheating behavior skills to a more appropriate use, rather than associating their skills with negativity. It is *how* they use these skills that should be abolished, not the talents themselves. Leta Hollingworth did not speak about ridding students of that benign chicanery, only that adults should help students channel their desires meaningfully. If a student is caught or self-reports creative cheating behaviors, separate the cheating behavior from the creative act itself and treat each accordingly. If these elements are not isolated, teachers and parents risk either punishing the creativity or praising the negative behavior.

Walter in High School

Up until now, this book has focused primarily on elementary-aged bright children for two main reasons. The first is my familiarity with that level of education; I have taught high-ability children in grades K-8, and the stories of young cheaters came directly from those schools. The second and perhaps more important reason not to broaden the conversation of high-ability academic dishonesty has been to attempt to identify and prevent it at its root. Bright students begin as early as elementary school to build negative coping mechanisms to deal with difficulties. Too often, cheating is only looked at within the context of upper secondary grades, college, or graduate school—long after habits and patterns of dishonesty have developed among students. Although it is not impossible to alleviate both the symptoms and causes of cheating at these higher levels, the problem becomes exponentially more challenging and the stakes become higher as students begin to prepare for careers and lives. Cheating, unchecked, can cost students their futures.

I would like to leave you with the story of Walter, a former student of mine who came back to visit me when he was in high school. Walter will always be one of my favorite students. He was in fifth grade when I started working at his school. I only had two years with him before he moved up to middle and high school, but he made an impression on me. Walter was an old soul, my "little old man" in a fifth-grade body. He told stories with hand gestures and shook his head while he laughed at his own jokes. He was a very smart young man who excelled in math and science, and he never seemed to experience stress, no matter what the situation. For example, our school has "code" drills in which staff and students practice different emergency "lockdown" responses designed for various circumstances. Walter was with me in the resource room, talking about a project when the drill announcement came over the intercom. We pulled the shades, turned off the lights, locked the door, and sat in the middle of the dark, quiet classroom. After a few minutes, Walter said with a wide smile, "Well, I guess this is as good a place to die as any. ... Want to play poker?"

When he left elementary school and headed for middle school, Walter was a short, roundish young man with thick glasses and hair filled with many indecisive cowlicks. When he stepped into my room almost five years later, he was nearly six feet tall with a military-style crew cut, contacts, and a big smile on his face. The smile was almost the only way I could recognize him.

"Hey, Ms. Maupin! You shrank!"

After our greetings and my excitement on hearing all the details of how he was doing at school, learning what he was planning for college, and reminiscing about the projects he remembered from the resource room, he asked what I had been doing. I told him about this book and how my discovery that high-ability students were cheating had led to my further exploration about both the underlying causes and how to help. At that, Walter went quiet for a moment. Then he laughed.

"Did you catch a lot of students cheating?" he asked. I was surprised by the sudden laughter, but I explained that in most cases I had opened up the discussion about cheating and let students tell me about their experiences.

Then Walter rolled up his sleeve. He, or someone else, had doodled a tribal-like design on his arm near his left elbow with black markers. It was filled with swirls and spikes that circled around tiny words that I did not see until he pointed them out to me, tracing the lines as they wrapped around the dark design.

"Walter, is that a cheat sheet?"

"Yes, ma'am."

"How long have you been doing that?"

Walter considered. "Probably since about fourth grade?"

"How often do you use cheat sheets?"

"Like this? Not a lot anymore. We had a substitute in World History this week so I went back to a more primitive method. Mr. Mahoney doesn't know much technology, but he knows to look for a cheat sheet."

"Primitive method?"

Walter went on to explain how he often used his graphing calculator, his cell phone, or even the classroom computers and iPads to set up difficult-to-trace cheat sheets and to get access to the Internet whenever possible, as that usually alleviated the need for crib notes. What is more, he had stumbled upon a website that printed custom-designed temporary tattoos and discovered that he could print a limited number for a sample price. Walter would print up his notes in a way that made a small temporary tattoo and would apply them to his shin, the outside of his arm, or even the back of his hand prior to an exam. Teachers had never thought to look closely at a temporary tattoo, probably because they had no idea that students were capable of making their own. Walter had even begun to experiment with having custom shoelaces made that could have text printed directly onto them. He had already learned how to design water bottle labels that he had altered in Photoshop and printed to look almost identical to the original, sans clandestine notes.

"You must not be able to fit a lot of information on a temporary tattoo or printed on a shoelace," I said.

"Not really. Longer information is for a phone or programming into the graphing calculator. But the cheat sheets are more challenging."

And there it was. Another student bored with the regular challenge of school—even high school—who had resorted to highly creative albeit impermissible methods of stimulating his mind. Walter said he enjoyed parts of his high school experience: He felt calmer and more confident as a near-senior, he had more friends, and he looked forward to college. One thing that stood out to me, however, was the reason he gave for looking forward to higher education—he hoped it would be more challenging because high school, although it had been fun, felt far too easy for him.

I did not know what to say. I hoped that college would be more challenging for him so that he could experience true, authentic learning and a stimulating education. On the other hand, I was afraid that a truly difficult atmosphere would be overwhelming for him. Walter, a student for whom most things came extremely easily, had never developed the coping mechanisms to deal with failure, nor had he ever been able to associate hard work with success. He had chosen to focus on and enjoy the non-academic elements of school and dealt with the lack of daily challenge through supplying his own. His use of technology to support his problem solving was impressive and highly creative, but it still was being utilized towards a negative coping mechanism rather than true intellectual growth.

The Future of Cheating

As the sophistication of technology continues to grow, so does the capability of the students who use it. This combination of new technology and growing experience brings with it countless new possible cheating methods and behaviors with which teachers and parents will be unfamiliar. It is nearly impossible to stay ahead of every new cheating method as our students become more comfortable with their technological options. The Stuyvesant cheating incident, described in the Introduction to this book, was carried out entirely with text messaging. Today, students have access to wireless Bluetooth devices and miniscule earpieces that can be used to have a friend relay answers. Students can buy papers and download teacher textbooks, complete with answers, from online sites. Even newer technology that includes data feeds in sunglasses and watches are now coming to the market, as well as MP3 player pens and scanner pens—and with them comes a torrent of new ways for students to practice academic dishonesty. Cheating has become easier than ever before, yet for students like Walter, the novelty of continuous new mediums may spark the kind of personal challenge that traditional school has never accomplished. If teachers and parents do not support our bright children—all of our children—at their most basic needs to be challenged, authentic learners, then we are in for a cheating landslide.

The direction that the data take us in looking at how often our bright children cheat and how seldom they get caught in the act should cause us all to take notice. On the one hand, parents and teachers should be encouraged to know that being more intelligent does not make someone more inclined to cheat. Hold onto that comfort though, because on the other hand the same research suggests that high intelligence does not prevent cheating or even markedly decrease it and that the more creative our students are, the more likely they are to cheat *and* to justify their behavior.

All students cheat, if only just a little bit, but cheating is habit forming; the longer a student is able to practice and rationalize the use of his growing skill, the more ubiquitous it becomes. High-ability children may not be more likely to cheat because of their intelligence, but it can prevent them from being caught, which can prevent us from identifying their behaviors at a young age and helping them. Walter's story is one of warning. It tells us that children will not simply grow out of their cheating behaviors without support and attention to the underlying causes of their behaviors. Do not wait until behaviors are so prevalent that they become the primary coping mechanism. By high school, these negative habits may be highly practiced. Habits are not impossible to change, but the longer the coping mechanisms exist, the more difficult they are to isolate and eliminate.

Parents and teachers of talented youth need to work together to ensure that their students are being challenged on a daily basis so that they have opportunities, both inside and outside of the classroom, to positively struggle toward a goal and to cope with setbacks using their creativity and grit. Bright children deserve opportunities for a variety of educational groupings as well as multiple social groups that reflect their asynchronous development profiles. The adults in a bright child's life should understand their emotional overexcitabilities and sensitivities and offer them bright role models and mentors. Perfectionist tendencies, fear of failure, and fixed mindsets can be replaced with efforts toward growth, as well as a redefinition of what a grade means—not only in a curricular sense but also to the student's sense of identity.

As parents and teachers, we are the first line of defense for our bright children, but we can use their help in the battle. Talk with your students about cheating; do not be afraid to broach the subject or discuss what they have done or would be willing to do. If a student is caught engaging in academic dishonesty, parents and teachers can help prevent the behaviors in the future by identifying underlying causes and addressing them separately from the emotions, which can cloud the issue and lead to punishment without rehabilitation.

Above all, remember that at the heart of every brilliant cheater is a sense that they are missing something that they crave. Whether that desire represents a need to fit in, to maintain the illusion of perfection, to be challenged, to be saved from their boredom, or simply to be understood, the means are out there to support them. By helping our bright children with these most basic needs, we not only greatly decrease the likelihood of their relying on negative coping mechanisms such as cheating, but we also help ensure that they reclaim their gifts and use their potential to live creative, productive, and honest lives.

References

Abagnale, F. (2001). *The art of the steal: How to protect yourself and your business from fraud—America's #1 crime.* New York: Broadway Books.

Abagnale, F., & Redding, S. (1980). *Catch me if you can.* New York: Broadway Books.

Abilock, D. (2009). Guiding the gifted to honest work. *Knowledge Quest 37*(3), 12-15.

Abramson, L., Seligman, M., & Teasdale, J. (1978). Learned helplessness in humans: Critique and reformulation. *Journal of Abnormal Psychology, 87,* 49-74.

Adderholdt-Elliot, M., & Goldberg, J. (1999). *Perfectionism: What's bad about being too good? (rev. ed.).* Minneapolis, MN: Free Spirit.

Adderholt-Elliot, M. (1989). Perfectionism and underachievement. *Gifted Child Today, 12*(1), 19-21.

Allen, J., Chango, J., Szwedo, D., Schad, M., & Marston, E. (2011). Predictors of susceptibility to peer influence regarding substance use in adolescence. *Child Development, 83*(1), 337-350.

Alvino, J. (1985). *Parents' guide to raising a gifted child.* New York: Ballantine Books.

Amabile, T. (1988). A model of creativity and innovation in organizations. *Research in Organizational Behavior, 10,* 123-167.

Amabile, T. (1996). *Creativity in context: Update to the social psychology of creativity.* Boulder, CO: Westview Press.

Anderman, E. M. & Murdock, T. B. (2006). *Psychology of academic cheating.* Burlington, MA: Elsevier.

Anderman, E. M. (2007). The effects of personal, classroom, and school goal structures on academic cheating. In E.M. Anderman & T. B. Murdock (Eds.), *Psychological perspectives on academic cheating* (pp. 87-106). San Diego, CA: Elsevier.

Archambault, F., & Hallmark, B. (1992, April). *Regular classroom practice with gifted students: Findings from the National Research Center on the Gifted and talented.* Symposium conducted at the meeting of the American Educational Research Association, San Francisco, CA.

Ariely, D. (2012). *The (honest) truth about dishonesty: How we lie to everyone—especially ourselves.* New York: HarperCollins.

Assouline, S. G., Colangelo, N., Ihrig, D., Forstadt, L., Lipscomb, J., & Lupkowski-Shoplik, A. E. (2003). *The Iowa acceleration scale: Two validation studies.* Paper presented at the National Association for Gifted Children Convention, Indianapolis, IN.

Baker, J. (1996). Everday stressors of academically gifted adolescents. *Journal of Secondary Gifted Education, 7,* 356-368.

Bisping, T., Patron, H., & Roskelley, K. (2008). Modeling academic dishonesty: The role of student perceptions and misconduct. *Journal of Economic Education, 38,* 4-21.

Blatt, S. (1995). The destructiveness of perfectionism: Implications for the treatment of depression. *American Psychologist, 50*(12), 1003-1020.

Bloom, B. (1974). *Taxonomy of educational objectives.* New York: McKay.

Borland, J. (2003). The death of giftedness. *Rethinking Gifted Education.* New York: Teachers College Press.

Brandes, B. (1986). *Academic honesty: A special study of California students.* Sacramento, CA: Bureau of Publications, California State Department of Education.

Bridges, S. (1973). *Problems of the gifted child IQ-150.* New York: Crane, Russak, & Co.

Bronson, P., & Merryman, A. (2009). *Nurtureshock: New thinking about children.* New York: Hachette Book Group.

Bukiet, M. J. (2012, July 01). *Why smart kids cheat.* Retrieved from NY Daily News: http://www.nydailynews.com/opinion/smart-kids-cheat-article-1.1105034

Casteel, J. D., & Stahl, R. J. (1973). *The social science observation record (SSOR): Theoretical construct and pilot studies.* Gainesville, FL: Yonge Laboratory School.

Carson, S. H., Peterson, J. B., & Higgins, D. M. (2003). Decreased latent inhibition is associated with increased creative achievement in high-functioning individuals. *Journal of Personality and Social Psychology, 85(3),* 499-506.

Center for Academic Integrity. (2014). Retrieved from CAI research: http://www.academicintegrity.org/icai/integrity-3.php

Cizek, G. J. (2003). *Detecting and preventing classroom cheating.* Thousand Oaks, CA: Corwin Press.

Clark, B. (1979). *Growing up gifted.* Upper Saddle River, NJ: Pearson Education, Inc.

Colangelo, N., Assouline, S., & Gross, M. U. (2004). *A nation deceived: How schools hold back America's brightest students.* Iowa City, IA: University of Iowa, The Connie Belin and Jacqueline N. Blank International Center for Gifted Education and Talent Development.

Columbus Group. (1991, July). *Unpublished transcript of the meeting of the Columbus Group.* Columbus, OH.

Corbett, B. (1999). *The cheater's handbook.* New York: HarperCollins.

Covington, M., & Beery, R. (1979). *Self-worth and school learning.* New York: Holt.

Cropley, D. H., Cropley, A. J., Kaufman, J. C., & Runco, M. A. (2010). *The dark side of creativity.* New York: Cambridge University Press.

Dabrowski, K. (1964). *Positive disintegration.* Boston, MA: Little, Brown.

Dabrowski, K. (1967). *Personality-shaping through positive disintegration.* Boston, MA: Little, Brown.

Dabrowski, K. (1972). *Psychoneurosis is not an illness.* London, UK: Gryf.

Dacey, J. (1989). Discriminating characteristics of the families of highly creative adolescents. *Journal of Creative Behavior, 23,* 263-271.

Daniels, S., & Piechowski, M. (2009). *Living with intensity.* Scottsdale, AZ: Great Potential Press.

Davis, G. (2003). *Character education: Activities and exercises for developing positive attitudes and behavior (2nd ed.).* Unionville, NY: Royal Fireworks.

Davis, G., & Rimm, S. (2004). *Education of the gifted and talented.* Boston, MA: Pearson Education, Inc.

Davis, S. F., Drinan, P. E., & Gallant, T. B. (2009). *Cheating in School: What we know and what we can do.* Chichester, West Sussex: Wiley-Blackwell.

Delcourt, M., & Evans, K. (1994). *Qualitative extension of the learning outcomes study.* Storrs, CT: The National Research Center on the Gifted and Talented.

Delcourt, M., Cornell, D., & Goldberg, M. (2007). The effects of programming arrangements on the achievement and self-concept of gifted elementary school students. *Gifted Child Quarterly, 51*(4), 359-381.

Dellas, M., & Gaier, E. L. (1970). Identification of creativity: The individual. *Psychological Bulletin, 73,* 55-73.

Deslisle, J. (1992). *Guiding the social and emotional development of gifted youth.* New York: Longman.

Diamond, M. (1988). *Enriching heredity: The impact of the environment on the anatomy of the brain.* New York: Free Press.

Duckworth, A. L., Kirby, T., Tsukayama, E., Berstein, H., & Ericsson, K. (2010). Deliberate practice spells success: Why grittier competitors triumph at the National Spelling Bee. *Social Psychological and Personality Science, 2,* 174-181.

Dweck, C. S. (2006). *Mindset: The new psychology of success.* New York: Ballantine Books.

Dweck, C. S., Goetz, T. E., & Strauss, N. (1980). Sex differences in learned helplessness: IV. An experimental and naturalistic study of failure generalization and its mediators. *Journal of Personality and Psychology, 38,* 441-452.

Eby, J., & Smutny, J. (1990). *A thoughtful overview of gifted education.* New York: Longman.

Education, U. C. (1972). *Education of the gifted and talented.* Washington, DC: USCPO: 92nd Congress, 2nd Session.

Education, U. D. (1993). *National excellence: A case for developing America's talent.* Washington, DC: Government Printing Office (PIP 93-1202).

Edwards, M., & Butler, K. (1987). Hyperthermia of trickery. *Pediatric Infectious Disease Journal, 6,* 411-414.

Eysenck, H. (1997). Creativity and personality. In M. Runco (Ed.), *The creativity research handbook: Volume 1* (pp. 41-66). Cresskill, NJ: Hampton Press.

Faust, D., Hart, K., & Guilmette, T. (1988). Pediatric malingering: The capacity of children to fake believable deficits on neuropsychological testing. *Journal of Consulting and Clinical Psychology, 56,* 578-582.

Feldhusen, J., & Kroll, M. (1991). Boredom or challenge for the academically talented student . *Gifted Education International, 7,* 80-81.

Feldman, M. (2004). *Playing sick?: Untangling the web of Münchausen syndrome, Münchausen by proxy, malingering, and factitious disorder.* London, UK: Routledge.

Feldman, R. (1985). The promise and pain of growing up gifted. *Gifted/Creative/Talented, 1.*

Fetterman, D. (1988). *Excellence & equality: A qualitatively different perspective on gifted and talented education.* Albany, NY: State University of New York Press.

Fiedler, E. D. (1992). In search of reality: Unraveling the myths about tracking, ability grouping, and the gifted. *Roeper Review, 16,* 4-7.

Fine, M. (1977). Facilitating parent-child relationships for creativity. *Gifted Child Quarterly, 21,* 487-500.

Fonseca, C. (2011). *Emotional intensity in gifted students: Helping kids cope with explosive feelings.* Waco, TX: Prufrock Press.

Fonseca, C. (2014). *Quiet kids: help your introverted child succeed in an extroverted world.* Waco, TX: Prufrock Press.

Gallagher, J. (1975). *Teaching the gifted child.* Boston, MA: Allyn & Bacon.

Gallagher, J., Harradine, C., & Coleman, M. (1997). Challenge or boredom? Gifted students' views on their schooling. *Roeper Review, 19*(3), 132-136

Gascon, L., & Kaufman, J. (2010). Both sides of the coin? Personality, deviance, and creative behavior. In D. H. Cropley, A. J. Cropley, J. C. Kaufman, & Runco, M. A. (Eds.), *The dark side of creativity.* (pp. 235-254). New York, NY: Cambridge University Press.

Gavin, H. (1843). *On feigned and factitious diseases, chiefly of soldiers and seamen, on the means used to simulate or produce them, and on the best mode of discovering imposters.* London, UK: John Churchill.

Geddes, K. A. (2013, June 25). *Academic OneFile.* Retrieved from Gifted Child Today: http://go.galegroup.com/ps/i.do?id=GALE%-7CA251725185&v.2.1&u=22516&it=r&p=AONE&sw=w

Gentry, M., & Owen, S. (1999). An investigation of the effects of total school flexible cluster grouping on identification, achievement, and classroom practices. *Gifted Child Quarterly, 43,* 224-243.

George, D. (2011). *Young gifted and bored.* Bethel, CT: Crown House.

Giang, V., & Cortez, S. (2012, Dec. 27). *13 Former Criminals Who Turned Their Lives Around.* Retrieved from Business Insider: http://www.businessinsider.com/criminals-who-turned-their-lives-around-2012-12?op=1#!HDpUR

Gilligan, C. (1982). *In a different voice: Pscyhological theory and women's development.* Cambridge, MA: Harvard University Press.

Gilligan, C., Ward, J., & Taylor, J. (1988). *Mapping the moral domain.* Boston, MA: Harvard University Press.

Gilman, B. J. (2008). *Academic advocacy for gifted children: A parent's complete guide.* Scottsdale, AZ: Great Potential Press.

Gino, F., & Ariely, D. (2011). The dark side of creativity: Original thinkers can be more dishonest. *Journal of Personality and Social Psychology, 102*(3), pp-pp.

Glass, D., & Singer, J. (1972). *Urban stress: Experiments on noise and social stressors.* New York: Academic Press.

Glasser, H., & Easley, J. (1998). *Transforming the difficult child: The nurtured heart approach.* Tuscon, AZ: Nurtured Heart Publications.

Goertzel, V., Goertzel, M.G., Goertzel, T.G., & Hansen, A. (2004). *Cradles of Eminence: The childhoods of more than 700 famous men and women.* Scottsdale, AZ: Great Potential Press.

Gottman, J. (1994). *What predicts divorce?* Hillsdale, NJ: Lawrence Erlbaum Associates, Inc.

Greenspoon, T. (2002). *Freeing our families from perfectionism.* Minneapolis, MN: Free Spirit.

Gross, M. (2003). *Exceptionally gifted children* (2nd ed.). New York: Falmer Press.

Gunn, A., Richburg, R., & Smilkstein, R. (2007). *Igniting student potential: Teaching with the brain's natural learning process.* Thousand Oaks, CA: Corwin Press.

Gurian, A. (n.d.). *Gifted girls—Many gifted girls, few eminent women. Why?* Retrieved from The Child Study Center NYU Langone Medical Center: http://www.aboutourkids.org/articles/gifted_girls_many_gifted_girls_few_eminent_women_why

Hartshorne, H., May, M., & Shuttleworth, F. (1930). *Studies in the Organization of Character.* Oxford, UK: MacMillan.

Heinrichs, J. (2007). *Thank you for arguing.* New York: Three Rivers Press.

Hollingworth, L. (1939). What we know about the early selection and raising of leaders. *Teachers College Record, 40,* 575-592.

Hooper, J., & Teresi, D. (1986). *The three-pound universe.* Los Angeles: J. P. Tarcher.

Jackson, P. (1995). *Bright star: Black sky origins and manifestations of the depressed state in the lived experience of the gifted adolescent: A phenomenological study.* (Unpublished master's thesis). Vermont College of Norwich University, Norwich, VT.

Jackson, P., & Peterson, J. (2003). Depressive disorder in highly gifted adolescents. *The Journal of Secondary Gifted Education, 14,* 175-189.

James, K., Clark, K., & Cropanzano, R. (1999). Positive and negative creativity in groups, institutions, and organizations: A model and theoretical extension. *Creativity Research Journal, 12*(3), 211-226.

Jensen, E. (1996). *Completing the puzzle: The brain-based approach.* Del Mar, CA: Turning Point Publishing.

Kanter, R. (1988). When a thousand flowers bloom: Structural, collective, and social conditions for innovation in organizations. *Research in Organizational Behavior, 10,* 169-211.

Kenny, D. A., Archambault, F. X., & Hallmark, B. W. (1995). *The effects of group composition on gifted and non-gifted elementary students in cooperative learning groups (Research Monograph 95116).* Storrs, CT: The National Research Center on the Gifted and Talented, University of Connecticut.

Kerr, B. A. (2014). *Smart girls in the 21st century: Understanding talented girls and women.* Tucson, AZ: Great Potential Press.

Kerr, B. A. (1994). *Smart girls: A New Psychology of Girls, Women, and Giftedness, Revised edition.* Scottsdale, AZ: Great Potential Press.

Klein, A. (1996). Self-concept and gifted girls: A cross sectional study of intellectually gifted females in grades 3, 5, 8. *Roeper Review, 19*, 30-34.

Kline, B., & Short, E. (1991). Changes in emotional resilience: Gifted adolescent females. *Roeper Review, 13*, 118-121.

Knowlton, J., & Hamerlynck, L. (1967). Perception of deviant behavior: A study of cheating. *Journal of Educational Psychology, 58*(6), 379-885.

Kohlberg, L. (1964). Development of moral character and moral ideology. *In M. L. Hoffman & L. W. Hoffman (Eds.), Review of Child Development Research, Vol. I* (pp. 381-431). New York: Russel Sage Foundation.

Kotulak, R. (1996). *Inside the brain.* Kansas City, MO: Andrews & McMeel.

Kranowitz, C. (2006). *The out-of-sync child: Recognizing and coping with sensory processing disorder.* Location, LO: Perigree Trade.

Kulik, J. (2003). Grouping and tracking. In N. Colangelo & G. Davis (Eds.), *Handbook of gifted education* (3rd ed.) (pp. 268-281). Boston, MA: Allyn & Bacon.

Kulik, J. A., & Kulik, C. L. C. (1990). Ability grouping and gifted students. In N. Colangelo & G. Davis (Eds.), *Handbook of gifted education* (pp. 178-196). Boston, MA: Allyn & Bacon.

Langer, E., & Benevento, A. (1978). A self-induced dependence. *Journal of Personality and Social Psychology, 36*, 886-893.

Lazarus, R. (1993). From psychological stress to the emotions: A history of changing outlooks. *The Annual Review of Psychology, 44*, 1-21.

Lee, S. A., & Dow, G. T. (2011). Malevolent creativity: Does personality influence malicious divergent thinking?. *Creativity Research Journal, 23*(3), 73-82.

Libow, J. (2000). Child and adolescent illness falsifications. *Pediatrics, 105*(2), 336-342.

Lind, S. (2001). Overexcitability and the gifted. *The SENG newsletter, 1*, 3-6.

Marzano, R. (2003). *What works in schools* (p. 37). Alexandria, VA: Association for Supervision and Curriculum Development.

McCabe, D. (2001). Cheating: Why students do it and how we can help them stop. *American Educator, 25*(4), 38-43.

McGee, J. (2003, May). *High score education: Games, not school, are teaching kids to think.* Retrieved from Wired: http://www.wired.com/wired/archive/11.05/view.html

Mitnick, K. D., & Simon, W. L. (2002). *The art of deception: Controlling the human element of security.* Indianapolis, IN: Wiley.

Mitnick, K., & Simon, W. (2011). *Ghost in the wires.* New York: Little, Brown.

Moon, S. (2002). Counseling needs and strategies. In S. Neihart, S. Reis, N. Robinson, & S. Moon (Eds.), *The social and emotional development of gifted children: What do we know?* (pp. 213-222). Waco, TX: Prufrock Press.

NAGC. (2012-2013). *State of the nation in gifted education: Work yet to be done.* (Survey Report). Washington, DC.

Newton, A. (2012, August 9). *Why are all the smart kids cheating?* Retrieved from The Quick & The Ed: http://www.quickanded.com/2012/08/why-are-all-the-smart-kids-cheating.html

Nowak, T. J., & Handford, G. A. (2004). *Pathophysiology: Concepts and applications for health care professionals, Third Edition.* New York: McGraw-Hill.

Ohio State University. (2009, August 12). Epidemic of student cheating can be cured with changes in classroom goals. *Science Daily.* Retrieved from: www.sciencedaily.com/releases/2009/08/090810025249.htm

Orange, C. (1997). Gifted students and perfectionism. *Roeper Review, 20,* 39-41.

Page, E., & Keith, T. (1996). *The elephant in the classroom: Intellectual talent.* Location, LO: Johns Hopkins University Press.

Parker, M., & Colangelo, N. (1979). An assessment of values of gifted students and their parents. In N. Colangelo & R. Zaffrann (Eds.), *New voices in counseling the gifted.* Dubuque, IA: Kendall/Hunt.

Pepperell, J., & Rubel, D. (2009). The experience of gifted girls transitioning from elementary school to sixth and seventh grade: A grounded theory. *The Qualitative Report, 14,* 341-360.

Perrone, K., Jackson, V., Wright, S., Ksiazak, T., & Perrone, P. (2007). Perfectionism, achievement, life satisfaction, and attributions of success among gifted students. *Advanced Development, 11,* 106-123.

Peters, D. (2013). *Make Your Worrier a Warrior: A Guide to Conquering Your Child's Fears.* Tucson, AZ: Great Potential Press.

Pickett, K., & Corboy, T. (2013). *Skin picking disorders: Top twelve roadblocks to recovery.* Los Angeles: OCD Center of Los Angeles.

Piechowski, M. (1979). Developmental potential. In N. Colangelo & R. Zaffrann (Eds.), *New voices in counseling the gifted* (pp. 25-57). Dubuque, IA: Kendall/Hunt.

Plucker, J., & McIntire, J. (1996). Academic survivability in high potential, middle school students. *Gifted Child Quarterly, 40,* 7-14.

Reis, E. A. (1993). *Why not let high ability students start school in January? The curriculum compacting study.* Storrs, CT: National Research Center on the Gifted and Talented.

Reis, S., & Purcell, J. (1993). An analysis of content elimination and strategies used by teachers in the curriculum compacting study. *Journal of the Education of the Gifted, 16,* 147-170.

Reis, S., & Renzulli, J. (2014) The Schoolwide Enrichment Model: A how-to-guide for talent development, Third Edition. Waco, TX: Prufrock Press.

Renzulli, J., & Park, S. (2000). Gifted dropouts: The who and the why. *Gifted Child Quarterly, 44,* 261-271.

Richert, E., Alvino, J., & McDonnel, R. (1982). *National report on identification: Assessment and recommendatinos for comprehensive identification of gifted and talented youth.* Sewell, NJ: Educational Information and Resource Center.

Rimm, S. (2002). What's wrong with being perfect? *Sylvia Rimm on Raising Kids Newsletter, 12*(4), 1-41.

Rimm, S. (2005). *Growing up too fast: The Rimm report on the secret world of America's middle schoolers.* Emmaus, PA: Rodale.

Rimm, S. (2008). *Why bright kids get poor grades and what you can do about it.* Scottsdale, AZ: Great Potential Press.

Rimm, S., & Rimm-Kaufman, S. (2001). *How Jane won: 55 successful women share how they grew from ordinary girls to extraordinary women.* New York: Crown.

Rimm, S., & Rimm-Kaufman, S. R. (1999). *See Jane Win: The Rimm report on how 1,000 girls became successful women.* New York: Crown.

Robinson, A. (2009). Myth 10: Examining the ostrich: Gifted services do not cure a sick regular program. *Gifted Child Quarterly, 53*(4), 259-261.

Roedell, W. (1986). Socioemotional vulnerabilities of young gifted children. In J. Whitmore (Ed.), *Intellectual giftedness in young children* (pp. 17-30). New York: The Haworth Press.

Rogers, K. (1991). *The relationship of grouping practices to the education of the gifted and talented learner.* Storrs, CT: The National Research Center on the Gifted and Talented.

Rogers, K. (2002). *Re-forming gifted education: How parents and teachers can match the program to the child.* Scottsdale, AZ: Great Potential Press.

Rogers, R. (1988). *Clinical assessment of malingering and deception.* New York: The Guilford Press.

Rowe, M. B. (1972). *Wait-time and rewards as instructional variables: Their influence in language, logic, and fate control.* Paper presented at the National Association for Research in Science Teaching, Chicago, IL.

Rowe, M. B. (Spring 1987). Wait times: Slowing down may be a way of speeding up. *Journal of Teacher Education, 11,* 38-43.

Ruf, D. (1998). *Enviornmental, familial, and personal factors that affect the self-actualization of highly gifted adults: Case studies.* (Unpublished dissertation). University of Minnesota, Minneapolis, MN.

Ruf, D. (2005). *Losing our minds: Gifted children left behind.* Scottsdale, AZ: Great Potential Press.

Schab, F. (1991). Schooling without learning: Thirty years of cheating in high school. *Adolescence, 26*(104), 839-847.

Schrimsher, R., Northrup, L., & Alverson, S. (2009). A survey of Samford University students regarding plagiarism and academic misconduct. *Plagiary, 3*(2), 1-17.

Schroeder, C. (2004). *Perfectionism and learned helplessness: Their influence of achievement motivation in average and high achieving adolescents.* (Unpublished thesis). Bethel College, Mishawaka, IN.

Schuler, P. (1997). *Characteristics and perceptions of perfectionism in gifted adolescents in a rural school environment.* (Unpublished doctoral dissertation). University of Storrs, Storrs, CT.

Schuler, P. (1999). *Voices of perfectionism: Perfectionistic gifted adolescents in a rural middle school.* Storrs, CT: Natinoal Research Center on the Gifted and Talented.

Schuler, P. (2002). Perfectionism in gifted children and adolescents. In M. Neihart, S. Reis, N. Robinson, & S. Moon (Eds), *Social and emotional development of gifted children: What do we know?* (pp. 71-79). Washington, DC: National Association for Gifted Children.

Seligman, M. (1975). *Helplessness: On depression, development, and death.* San Francisco: W. H. Freeman.

Seligman, M., & Peterson, C. (2004). *Character strengths and virtues: A handbook and classification.* New York: American Psychological Association/ Oxford University Press.

Shaughnessy, M. (2002). A reflective conversation with Robert Sternberg about giftedness, gifted education, and intelligence. *Gifted Education International, 16,* 201-207.

Silverman, L. (1991). Helping gifted girls reach their potential. *Roeper Review, 13*(3), 122-123.

Silverman, L. (1993). Social development, leadership and gender. In L. Silverman, *Counseling the gifted and talented* (pp. 291-327). Denver, CO: Love.

Silverman, L. K. (1994). The moral sensitivity of gifted children and the evolution of society. *Roeper Review, 17*(2), 110-115.

Slavin, R. (1987). Ability grouping: A best-evidence synthesis. *Review of Educatinoal Research, 57,* 293-336.

Slavin, R. (1990). Achievement effects of ability grouping in secondary schools: A best-evidence synthesis. *Review of Educational Research, 60,* 471-499.

Smutny, J. (1999). Gifted girls. *Understanding Our Gifted, 11*(2), 9-13.

Solorzano, L. (1983, August). Now, gifted children get some breaks. *U.S. News & World Report, 8,* 32.

Sowa, C., McIntire, J., May, K., & Bland, L. (1994). Social and emotional adjustment themes across gifted children. *Roeper Review, 17*(2), 95-98.

Sprenger, M. (1999). *Learning & memory: The brain in action.* Alexandria, VA: Association for Supervision and Curriculum Development.

Stahl, R. J. (1990). *Using "think-time" behaviors to promote students' infor-mation processing, learning, and on-task participation: An instructional module.* Tempe, AZ: Arizona State University.

Stern, L. (1991). Disavowing the self in female adolescence. In C. Gilligan, A. Rogers, & D. Tolman (Eds.), *Women, girls and psychotherapy: Reframing resistance* (pp. 105-117). New York: Harrington Park Press.

Swiatek, M., & Dorr, R. (1998). Revision of the social coping questionnaire: Replication and extension of previous findings. *Journal of Secondary Gifted Education, 10,* 252-259.

Talwar, V., & Lee, K. (2002). Development of lying to conceal a transgression: Children's control of expressive behavior during verbal deception. *International Journal of Behavioral Development, 26,* 436-444.

Terman, L. (1959). *The gifted group at mid-life: Thirty-five years follow-up of the superior child.* Palo Alto, CA: Stanford University Press.

Tolan, S. (1985). Stuck in another dimension: The exceptionaly gifted child in school. *Gifted Child Today, 41,* 22-26.

Tolan, S. (1989). Special problems of young highly gifted children. *Understanding our Gifted, 1*(5), 7-10.

Tomlinson, C. A. (2001). *How to differentiate instruction in mixed-ability classrooms (2nd Ed.).* Alexandria, VA: Association for Supervision and Curriculum Development.

Tough, P. (2012). *How children succeed.* New York: Houghton Mifflin Harcourt.

Tucker, B., & Hafenstein, N. (1997). Psychological intensities in young gifted children. *Gifted Child Quarterly, 21,* 66-75.

University Of Toronto. (2003, October 1). Biological basis for creativity linked to mental illness. *Science Daily.* (2003). Retrieved from: http://www.sciencedaily.com/releases/2003/10/031001061055.htm

Vaughn, V. (1990). *Meta-analysis of pull out programs in gifted education.* Paper presented at the annual convention of the National Association for Gifted Children, Little Rock, AR.

Von Oech, R. (2008). *A whack on the side of the head: How you can be more creative.* New York: Business Plus.

Ward, M. (1982). The "ostrich syndrome": Do gifted programs cure sick regular programs? *Gifted Child Quarterly, 26,* 34-36.

Webb, J., Gore, J., Amend, E., & DeVries, A. R. (2007). *A parent's guide to gifted children.* Scottsdale, AZ: Great Potential Press.

Weissberg, P., & Springer, K. (1961). Environmental factors in creative function. *Archives of General Psychology, 5,* 64-74.

Westberg, K., Dobyns, S., & Salvin, T. (1992). Regular classroom practices observation results. In J.S. Renzulli (Chair), *Regular classroom practices with gifted students: Findings from the National Research CEnter on the Gifted and Talented.* Symposium conducted at the meeting of the American Educational Research Association, San Francisco.

Wicklund, R. (1974). *Freedom and reactance.* Potomac, MD: Lawrence Erlbaum.

Willingham, D. T. (2009). *Why don't students like school? A cognitive scientist answers questions about how the mind works and what it means for the classroom.* San Francisco: Jossey-Bass.

Willis, D. A. (2009) *Inspiring middle school minds: Gifted, creative, and challenging.* Scottsdale, AZ: Great Potential Press.

Winebrenner, S. (2001). *Teaching gifted kids in the regular classroom: Strategies and techniques every teacher can use to meet the academic needs of the gifted and talented.* Minneapolis, MN: Free Spirit.

Wortman, C. B., & Brehm, J. (1975). Responses to uncontrollable outcomes: An integration of reactance theory and the learned helplessness model. In L. Berkowitz (Ed.), *Advances in experimental social psychology, (Vol.8).* New York: Academic Press.

Endnotes

Introduction

1   Center for Academic Integrity, 2014
2   Anderman, 2007
3   Anderman, 2007
4   Davis, Drinan, & Gallant, 2009
5   Bukiet, 2012; Newton, 2012
6   McCabe, 2001
7   Brandes, 1986
8   Hollingworth, 1939
9   Hartshorne, May, & Shuttleworth, 1930
10 Schab, 1991
11 Plucker & McIntire, 1996
12 Cizek, 2003
13 Cizek, 2003
14 Silverman, 1994
15 Some parents and teachers use the term "liar" rather than "deceiver," but liar is probably the wrong term. To call someone a liar is an incendiary term that stirs up controversy and negativity; additionally, it is an inappropriate term because 'liar' fails to approach the complexity and masterfulness of what bright students can achieve beneath the radar. What these students do is something harder to name, though by the nature of its dishonesty, of course, it is sometimes called a lie.

Chapter One

16 Rowe, 1987
17 Casteel & Stahl, 1973; Rowe, 1972; Stahl, 1990
18 McCabe, 2001
19 Knowlton & Hamerlynck, 1967
20 Fonseca, 2011
21 Rimm, 2008

22   Rimm, 2008
23   Dweck, 2006
24   Rimm, 2008
25   McCabe, 2001
26   Cizek, 2003
27   U.S. Department of Education's report, 1993
28   Webb, Gore, Amend, & DeVries, 2007
29   Marland, 1972; Reis et al., 1993; Rogers, 2002
30   Curriculum compacting is a resource to eliminate unnecessary work for high-ability students. In this process, teachers identify objectives that students must be able to show in order to demonstrate mastery of a concept or lesson. Students are then pretested on those objectives to determine what can be eliminated from their curriculum. By "compacting" material, students are then able to work on enrichment or accelerated options. Curriculum compacting is a flexible, ongoing strategy for providing students enrichment work.
31   Ruf, 2005
32   Webb, Gore, Amend, & DeVries, 2007
33   Dweck, 2006; Kohlberg, 1964
34   Clark, 1979

Chapter Two
35   Parent Institute, 2013
36   Davis & Rimm, 2004
37   Gallagher, Harradine, & Coleman, 1997
38   Reis, et al., 1993; Rogers 2002
39   Marland 1972; Rimm 1997; Rogers 2002
40   Diamond, 1988
41   Hooper & Teresi, 1986
42   Willingham, 2009
43   Stephen King, *On Writing*, 2001
44   Who's Who Surveys, 1996
45   Cizek, 2003
46   Cizek, 2003
47   Cizek, 2003
48   Rimm, 2008
49   Fonseca, 2014
50   Pirate's Gold Logic Game Solution:
     In short, if each pirate acts in accordance with the rules, each pirate wants to survive above all. After that, the next priority is the maximum amount of gold. Finally each pirate would rather throw another overboard if the results would otherwise be equal. To find the solution, you must accept that all pirates know this of their shipmates and are logically thinking through their decisions,

keeping in mind seniority, as it breaks any tie. To this end, the most rational solution is to begin by working backward.

Gunner & Cabin Boy

The Cabin Boy will never get to make a suggestion because, if it comes down to the Gunner and the Cabin boy, the one with seniority has the vote and he will chuck the Cabin Boy overboard. Therefore, if the Captain, First Mate, and Boatswain are thrown overboard, the Gunner would propose (and win) this:

- *Gunner* – 100
- *Cabin Boy* – 0

Boatswain

The Boatswain knows that if he gets to make a suggestion in the case of the Captain's and the First Mate's demise, he would have to offer the Cabin Boy anything better than nothing in order to win his vote. He cannot offer anything to the Gunner, since the Gunner would rather throw him overboard and get all 100 coins. Therefore, his winning offer would be this:

- *Boatswain* – 99
- *Gunner* – 0
- *Cabin Boy* – 1

First Mate

If the Captain is gone, the First Mate only has to offer the Gunner more than he would get if the Boatswain's proposal won. Even though the Gunner will get all 100 if everyone else is thrown overboard, it would never get that far, since the Boatswain can get the support of the Cabin Boy. Therefore, all the First Mate has to do to win is offer the Gunner one more coin than he would get if the First Mate were thrown overboard. His offer would be this:

- *First Mate* – 99
- *Boatswain* – 0
- *Gunner* – 1
- *Cabin Boy* – 0

Captain

Of course, the Captain can figure all this out, so all he has to do is offer the Cabin Boy and Boatswain one more coin to win the vote, since they have nothing to win from the First Mate's plan succeeding.

- *Captain* – 98
- *First Mate* – 0
- *Boatswain* – 1
- *Gunner* – 0
- *Cabin Boy* – 1

51 Archambault & Hallmark, 1992; Westberg, Dobyns, & Salvin, 1992
52 National Association for Gifted Children, 2012-2013

53   The National Research Center on the Gifted and Talented (NRC/GT) is located at the University of Connecticut in Storrs, CT. It is funded under the Jacob K. Javits Gifted and Talented Students Education Act, Institute of Education Sciences, United States Department of Education. For research-based resources, on-line resources, links, and more information on their program and services, visit www.gifted.uconn.edu/nrcgt/.
54   Rogers, 2002
55   Winebrenner, 2001
56   Fiedler, Lange, & Winebrenner, 1992, p. 3
57   Fonseca, 2011
58   Alvino, 1985
59   Rimm, 2008
60   Marzano, 2003; Hattie 1992

Chapter Three
61   Cizek, 2003
62   Ruf, 1998; Tolan, 1985, 1989
63   Gross, 2003
64   Ariely, 2012
65   Daniels & Piechowski, 2009
66   Ariely, 2012
67   Kenny, Archambault, & Hallmark, 1995
68   Alvino, 1985
69   Terman, 1959; Kerr, 1994; Moon 2002, Reis 2002, Rimm 2002
70   Rimm et al 1999; Swiatek & Dorr, 1998
71   Alvino, 1985
72   Gilligan et al, 1988; Stern, 1991; Schwartz, 2005
73   Kerr, 1994; Silverman, 1993
74   Pepperell & Rubel, 2009
75   Eby & Smutny, 1990, Kerr, 1994
76   Ward, 1982; Robinson, 2009
77   Delcourt, Cornell, & Goldberg, 2007
78   Ruf, 2005
79   Ruf, 2005
80   Slavin, 1987, 1990
81   Gentry & Owen, 1999
82   Vaughn, 1990
83   Page & Keith, 1996; Kulik & Kulik, 1990
84   Rogers, 1991; Kulik & Kulik, 1990
85   Sternberg, via Shaughnessy, 2002
86   Delcourt & Evans, 1994; Rogers, 1991; Slavin, 1987
87   Reis & Renzulli, 2014

88   Ruf, 2005, p. 259

89   Borland, 2003

90   Colangelo, Assouline, & Gross, 2004

91   Colangelo, Assouline, & Gross, 2004; Assouline, Colangelo & Forstadt, 2003

92   Kerr, 1994; Moon, 2002; Reis 2002; Rimm, 2002

93   *Academic Advocacy for Gifted Children* by Gilman is a valuable resource for parents.

94   An excellent place for parents to start is to visit the National Association for Gifted Children (www.nagc.org) for their resources directory, conference information, and to get in contact with their network of other parents and teachers of high-ability children. Other wonderful online resources include www.hoagiesgifted.org, www.davidsongifted.org, and Johns Hopkins Center for Talented Youth "Talent Search," for grades 2-8, which includes summer programs, online courses, and other services and resources for advanced learners: cty.jhu.edu/talent/

95   Kerr, 1994

96   Terman, 1959

97   Cizek, 2003

98   Ariely, 2012

99   Gino & Ariely, 2011

Chapter Four

100   Schab, 1991

101   Fonseca, 2011

102   Schuler, 1999

103   Orange, 1997

104   Schuler, 2002

105   Daniels & Piechowski, 2009

106   Adderholt-Elliot, 1989

107   Blatt, 1995

108   Rimm, 2008

109   Asynchronous development is more fully explained in Chapter 6. Many high-ability learners have abilities that match different age groups simultaneously. For example, a child may be chronologically six, but have different reading, writing, vocabulary, maturity, and motor skill levels. Thus, depending on the activity, a bright child may seem to be any number of ages besides their chronological one.

110   Dweck, 2006

111   Dan Peters award-winning book, *Make Your Worrier a Warrior*, offers many practical guidelines for overcoming catastrophizing.

112   Daniels & Piechowski, 2009

113   Fonseca, 2011

114   Pickett & Corboy, 2013
115   Rimm, 2008
116   Adderholt-Elliot, 1989
117   Dweck, 2006
118   Adderholt-Elliott, 1987; Dweck, 2006
119   Dweck, 2006, p. 9
120   Dweck, 2001, p. 236
121   Greenspon, 2002, p. 207
122   Dweck, 2006
123   Alvino, 1985
124   Rimm, 2008
125   Rimm, 2008
126   Tough, 2012
127   Dweck, 2006; Von Oech, 2008
128   Von Oech, 2008
129   George, 2011
130   Feldman, 1985
131   Schuler, 1997; 2000
132   Cizek, 2003
133   Von Oech, 2008
134   Perrone et al., 2007
135   Tough, 2012
136   Duckworth, Kirby, Tsukayama, Berstein, & Ericsson, 2010
137   Seligman & Peterson, 2004

Chapter Five
138   Rogers, 1988
139   Gavin, 1843
140   Feldman, 2004; Ruf, 2005
141   Rimm, 2008
142   Covington & Beery, 1976
143   Cizek, 2003
144   Webb, Gore, Amend, & DeVries, 2007
145   Rimm, 2005
146   Rimm et al, 1999; Swiatek & Dorr 1998
147   Rimm, 2005
148   Alvino, 1985
149   Pepperell & Rubel, 2009, p. 336
150   Davis & Rimm, 2004
151   Eby & Smutny, 1990
152   Kerr, 1994
153   Kerr, 1994, Terman, 1959

154 Gilligan, 1982
155 Silverman, 1991
156 Kerr, 2014
157 Swiatek & Dorr, 1998
158 Silverman, 1993
159 Talwar & Lee, 2002
160 Bronson & Merryman, 2009
161 Talwar & Lee, 2002
162 Feldman, 2004
163 Libow, 2000
164 Nowak & Handford, 2004
165 Faust, Hart, & Guilmette, 1988
166 Gunn, Richburg, & Smilkstein, 2007
167 Alvino, 1985
168 Richert, 1982
169 Pepperell & Rubel, 2009
170 Dabrowski, 1967

Chapter Six
171 Fonseca, 2011
172 The Columbus Group, 1991
173 Tolan, 1989
174 Amend, DeVries, Gore, Webb; 2007
175 Silverman, 1994
176 Piechowski, 1992
177 Roedell, 1986
178 Lind, 2001; Tucker & Hafenstein, 1997
179 Kranowitz, 2006
180 Kranowitz, 2006
181 Webb, Gore, Amend, & DeVries, 2007; p. 193
182 Fonseca, 2011
183 Daniels & Piechowski, 2009

Chapter Seven
184 Fonseca, 2011
185 Rimm, 2008
186 Daniels & Piechowski, 2009
187 Fine, 1977
188 Rimm, 2008
189 Bridges, 1973
190 Fine, 1977
191 Fonseca, 2011

192 Webb, Gore, Amend, & DeVries, 2007

193 Daniels & Piechowski, 2009

194 Schroeder, 2004

195 Langer & Benevento, 1978

196 Glass & Singer, 1972; Wortman & Brehm, 1975; Wicklund, 1974

197 Seligman, 1975; Abramson et al. 1978; Dweck, Goetz, & Strauss, 1980

198 Tough, 2012

199 Rimm, 2008

200 Alvino, 1985

201 Borland, as quoted in Alvino, 1985

202 Tough, 2012

203 Alvino, 1985

204 Geddes, 2013

205 Ruf, 2005

206 Allen, Chango, Szwedo, Schad, & Marston, 2011

207 Heinrichs, 2007

208 Heinrichs, 2007

209 Gottman, 1994

210 Rimm, 2008

Chapter Eight

211 Victor didn't start using the word "mark" until after I suggested it to him as a synonym for target. Incidentally, the origins of the word mark have been attributed to the old carnival workers, or "carnies," who would surreptitiously place a chalk mark on the back of an individual who was easily fooled in order to let other carnies know that there was a gullible individual coming their way.

212 Hollingworth, 1939

213 Mitnick, 2011

214 Abagnale & Redding, 1980

215 Mitnick, 2011

216 Abagnale, 2001

217 Webb, Gore, Amend, & DeVries, 2007

218 Alvino, 1985

219 Goertzel, Goertzel, Goertzel, and Hansen (2004).

220 Abagnale, 2001

221 Mitnick & Simon, 2002

222 Note: This can be used to a teacher's advantage! Next time you are looking for an incentive for a bright student, promise (and deliver) information that other students in the class do not have. A look inside a room in the school that other students have never seen is a perfect example. Offer a peek inside a storage closet, a guided tour of the school basement, or even a look inside a cabinet you keep closed all year to appeal to their deep curiosity.

223 Abagnale, 1980
224 Lee & Dow, 2011
225 Dellas & Gaier, 1970; Dacey, 1989; Eysenck, 1997
226 Carson, Peterson, & Higgins, 2003
227 Clark & James, 1999
228 Amabile, 1988, 1996; Kanter, 1988
229 Cropley, et.al, 2010
230 Rimm, 2008
231 Gascon & Kaufman, 2010
232 Abagnale, 2001
233 Gino & Ariely, 2011
234 Davis & Rimm, 2004
235 Davis & Rimm, 2004
236 Rimm, 2008
237 McGee, 2003
238 Glasser & Easley, 1998
239 Willingham, 2009
240 Willingham, 2009
241 "Hire the Hacker" term was first used by Kevin Mitnick, (Mitnick & Simon, 2002).
242 Giang & Cortez, 2012
243 Abagnale, 2001
244 Abagnale, 2001
245 Davis, 2003
246 Ruf, 2005
247 Willingham, 2009
248 Willingham, 2009
249 Von Oech, 2008
250 Jensen, 1996
251 Willis, 2009.
252 Sprenger, 1999
253 Von Oech, 2008
254 Von Oech, 2008

Index

About the Author

Kate Maupin has worked with gifted children around the world for over 11 years. After being involved in many enrichment programs in her youth, she began as a volunteer curriculum aide for Department of Defense Dependent Schools in Germany. Recognizing "the good, the bad, and the ugly" of gifted education programming, she was inspired to become involved in advocacy work and research that would provide better enrichment resources for bright youth. She received her B.S. in Elementary Honors Education from the University of Maine and her M.A. in Educational Psychology with a focus on the education of the gifted and talented at the University of Connecticut, where she was honored to study and work at the National Research Center on the Gifted and Talented. She subsequently worked with gifted children throughout New England and in China. Currently, she is an enrichment specialist and teacher for a school district in Connecticut, where she lives with her husband, son, and far too many pets.